# Contemporary Irish Cinema

 Irish Studies

Sanford Sternlicht, *Series Editor*

# Contemporary Irish Cinema

From *The Quiet Man* to *Dancing at Lughnasa*

*Edited by*
James MacKillop

Syracuse University Press

First Edition 1999
99  00  01  02  03  04  05      7  6  5  4  3  2  1

Permission by Harlan Kennedy to reprint "Shamrocks and Shillelaghs: Idyll and Ideology in Irish Cinema" is gratefully acknowledged. Copyright © 1994, 1999.

The paper used in this publication meets the minimum requirements of American National Standard for Information Sciences—Permanence of Paper for Printed Library Materials, ANSI Z39.48-1984. ♾

**Library of Congress Cataloging-in-Publication Data**
Contemporary Irish cinema : from The Quiet Man to Dancing at Lughnasa
    / edited by James MacKillop.—1st ed.
        p.    cm.—(Irish studies)
    Filmography: p.
    Includes bibliographical references and index.
    ISBN 0-8156-2798-X (cloth : alk. paper).—ISBN 0-8156-0568-4
(paper : alk. paper)
    1. Motion pictures—Ireland.    I. MacKillop, James.    II. Series:
Irish studies (Syracuse, N.Y.)
PN1993.5.I85C66 1999
791.43'09417—dc21        98-52456

# Contents

# Preface

I like a good picture, myself. I fancy a good western, I must admit that.
John Ford, now I'd cross Ireland to see a John Ford. He's my man.

> —Fr. Phil O'Hara, in Richard Power, *The Hungry Grass*
> (1969)

Smaller in population than São Paolo, lesser economically—even in these days of the Celtic Tiger—than metropolitan Detroit, Ireland seems an unlikely locale to have developed a film industry, let alone a film culture. Yet the Land of Saints and Scholars now also fosters cineastes. And as with scholarship and sainthood, making films requires more than mass populations and bounteous financial resources. Unique experiences in language, famine, internecine warfare, decolonization, religion and anticlericalism have forged a distinct voice in several literary genres. The Irish long ago achieved mastery in prose fiction, stage dramas, and poetry, producing four Nobel Prize laureates in literature. As a people with much to say, often saying it well, the Irish could not be kept from the most resonant medium of this last century, the movies.

Whereas filmmakers elsewhere would shun being described as "literary," as if that necessarily implied less cinematic films, Irish filmmakers have rooted their films firmly in the nation's literature. The most celebrated of Irish stage plays, Synge's *Playboy of the Western World*, has been filmed twice (1962, 1975). Works by James Joyce have appeared on film a half-dozen times, twice with distinction, Finnula's Flanagan's *James Joyce's Women* (1983) and John Huston's *The Dead* (1987). Ireland's leading contemporary filmmaker, Neil Jordan, was first known as a short-story writer. Jim Sheridan (*My Left Foot, In the Name of the Father, The Boxer*, etc.) was a cofounder of Dublin's Project Arts Centre, the small experimental stage that also served as an incubator for the like of Gabriel Byrne, Daniel Day-Lewis, and Liam Neeson. Playwright Stewart Parker shifted readily from live theater to the television miniseries. Sam Hanna Bell's *December Bride* and William Trevor's *Fools of Fortune* were admired novels long before they were filmed. Although its director does not cite it, the worldview of Samuel Beckett informs Cathal Black's Pigs (1984). And even the consistently reviled *Quiet Man* (1952) can be traced to Listowel writer Maurice Walsh, with antecedents in Dion Boucicault, Edith Somerville, and Martin Ross.

Made an English-speaking nation by force, Ireland shares the language of a half billion of the world's people, many of them the island's own sons and daughters scattered in diaspora. This advantage, not shared by, say, Hungary or Greece, diminishes Ireland's isolation from world currents. It has encouraged foreign filmmakers to employ Ireland's resources, as in the Italian-made political drama, *Sacco and Vanzetti* (1971) or the British futurist adventure, *Zardoz* (1974), accumulating a body of work not explored here. At the same time, films made in Ireland, *The Commitments* (1991) or *Michael Collins* (1996), can find ready access to cineplexes in Asheville or Adelaide and not be ghettoized in art houses as are most works from great film cultures like France, Italy, or Japan.

Britain and America are usually offstage presences in Irish-made films. Thus in *My Left Foot* (1989) Christy Brown's funeral cortege wends past familiar Dublin landmarks, College Green and the Four Courts, in a sequence it could not follow in life, but it gives a reassuring signal to viewers in London and Los Angeles. Dawson Street's photogenic Mansion House has doubled as a filmic luxury hotel, a visual assertion plausible only for foreign viewers, but rarely appears as itself or as Dubliners know it.

Simultaneously, emerging Irish filmmakers are free of parochialism and provincialism. Documentarist John T. Davis moves effortlessly from a misty Belfast street corner to bone-dry Route 66. Pat O'Connor goes to Yorkshire for *A Month in the Country* (1987), Toronto and New York for *January Man* (1989), and returns to Ireland for *Circle of Friends* (1995). Neil Jordan's *Interview with the Vampire: The Vampire Chronicles* (1994), from American horror mistress Anne Rice, takes on an international glossiness but gives the character played by Stephen Rea an unmistakable Irish accent.

Little space is given here to the hotly contentious, inexhaustible question of what makes an Irish film "Irish." Readers interested in this question should consult the headnote to Anthony Kirby's filmography and are free to second-guess which titles should be switched from the "Irish" to "Irish-Related Categories."

Valuable suggestions for this collection were made by Walda Metcalf, Mari Kathleen Fielder, Mary Helen Thuente, Richard Bizot, Marilyn

Lonergan, Margaret Hall, Leonard Frey, Lori Rogers, Marina Burke, Susan Bernardo, Ian Crump, Marianne Eismann, and Helen Emmitt.

Special thanks to Harlan Kennedy for his generous permission to reprint "Shamrocks and Shillelaghs: Idyll and Ideology in Irish Cinema." Copyright 1994, 1999 by Harlan Kennedy.

Syracuse, New York                                    James MacKillop
May 1998

# Contributors

**Margot Gayle Backus** is assistant professor of English at St. John Fisher College in Rochester, New York. She has published articles on aspects of Irish studies in the *Canadian Review of Comparative Literature* and *Tulsa Studies in Women's Literature*. Her book, *The Gothic Family Romance: Compulsory Heterosexuality and the Anglo-Irish Settler Colonial Order*, is forthcoming from Duke University Press.

**Douglas Brode** has published more than twenty volumes of film criticism, including studies of Steven Spielberg, Denzel Washington, Dustin Hoffman, Robert DeNiro, Jack Nicholson, and Woody Allen, which have been widely translated. He is longtime newspaper critic, whose complete reviews would fill several more volumes. The feature film of his script for *Midnight Blue*, with Dean Stockwell, Harry Dean Stanton, and Anabella Scofield, appeared in 1996.

**Jennifer C Cornell** teaches English at Oregon State University. Her collection of short stories, *Departures*, published by the University of Pittsburgh Press, and known in Britain and Ireland as *All There Is*, published by Brandon Press, won the 1994 Drue Heinz Literature Prize. She is the author of several articles on the representation of Northern Ireland in British television drama, and a recipient of a 1998 Creative Writing Fellowship from the National Endowment for the Arts.

**Pamela Dolan** received a master of theological studies degree from the Divinity School at Harvard University. She is currently at New York University, pursuing her interests in medieval culture, the literary construction of motherhood, and the ethics of sacrifice.

**John Hill** is senior lecturer in media studies at the University of Ulster and chair of the Northern Ireland Film Council. He is the author of *Sex, Class and Realism: British Cinema 1956–63* (1986), coauthor of *Cinema and*

*Ireland* (1988), coeditor of *Border Crossing: Film in Ireland, Britain and Europe* (1994) and *Big Picture, Small Screen: The Relations Between Film and Television* (1996).

**Harlan Kennedy** is an internationally known American film critic resident in London. He is perhaps best known as a regular contributor to *Film Comment,* where he has published studies of Roman Polanski, Marco Bellochio, Mike Leigh, Derek Jarman, Scottish cinema, and British war films. A frequent guest of television talk shows, he has also served as a judge for the Cannes Film Festival.

**Kerstin Ketteman** holds a master's degree in English from the University of Oslo. Her special areas of interest include Irish film and literature, magical realism, popular culture, and nineteenth- and twentieth-century American fiction. Previous publications include articles on writing pedagogy and learning in the "electronic classroom." She currently teaches at the University of Rhode Island.

**Anthony Kirby,** a member of the O'Higgins family, grew up and was educated in Counties Mayo and Dublin. Emigrating to Canada in 1966, he completed a bachelor's degree in English & Media Studies at Concordia University in 1978. He has contributed to such periodicals as *The Irish Times, Irish Echo,* and *The Irish Literary Supplement.* At present he is completing a novel based on the life of an uncle who served in World War I.

**Jim Loter** holds a master's degree in film studies from the University of Iowa. He currently resides in Iowa City where he is systems analyst for the University of Iowa Libraries. His current research focuses on theories of communication and new technologies.

**James MacKillop** is the author of six volumes, including *The Dictionary of Celtic Mythology* for Oxford University Press, *Fionn mac Cumhaill* and *Irish Literature: A Reader,* with Maureen O'Rourke Murphy, for Syracuse University Press. A longtime film and theater critic, he published the pioneering article "Ireland and the Movies" in 1984. He is also past president of the American Conference for Irish Studies.

**Kathleen McCracken** is a Canadian-born critic and poet, with degrees from York University and the University of Toronto, now on the faculty of the University of Ulster at Jordanstown. She has published studies of Paul Muldoon, Seamus Heaney, Paul Durcan, Michael Davitt, Stewart Parker, and Irish cinema. Her volumes of poetry include *Blue Light, Bay and College, The Constancy of Objects, Into Celebration*, and *Reflections*.

**Brian McIlroy's** book-length study *Ireland* (1988), volume 4 in Flicks Books World Cinema series, helped launch the current critical interest in Irish cinema. A member of the Theatre and Film Department at the University of British Columbia, McIlroy has published on Canadian, British, and Swedish cinema. He has also published studies of such contemporary writers as Michael Longley, John Banville, and Brian Moore.

**Martin McLoone** is senior lecturer in media studies and head of the School of Media and Performing Arts at the University of Ulster. Born in Derry and educated in Dublin, he was formerly education officer for the Irish Film Institute, where he was instrumental in establishing many of Ireland's first initiatives in film and media education. His publications include *Culture, Identity, and Broadcasting in Ireland* (1991), which he edited; *Border Crossing: Film in Ireland, Britain, and Europe* (1994), which he coedited; *Big Picture, Small Screen: The Relations Between Film and Television* (1996), which he coedited; and *Broadcasting in a Divided Community: Seventy Years of the BBC in Northern Ireland* (1996), which he edited.

**Moylan C. Mills** is professor and head of the Department of Integrative Arts at the Pennsylvania State University. He has written extensively on film, literature, and theater, most recently on Brazilian films for *Studies in Latin American Popular Culture* and on German films and novels for *Literature/Film Quarterly*. His essay on music dramas was recently published in *The Art World and Its Audience*. He has received the Lindback Award for excellence in teaching.

**Maria Pramaggiore** is assistant professor of film studies in the English Department at North Carolina State University in Raleigh. She holds a doctorate from the Institute for Liberal Studies at Emory University and master's degree in Economics from Lancaster University (UK). She is coeditor of *Representing Bisexuality: Subjects and Cultures of Fluid Desire* (NYU, 1996), with Donald E. Hall.

**Sanford Sternlicht** is a widely published critic and poet, known for studies of Jean Rhys, Stevie Smith, Stephen Spender, Siegfried Sassoon, James Herriot, Padraic Colum, and others. His editions of Colum's poetry, fiction, and drama are often credited with reviving interest in that previously neglected author. An actor and longtime theater director, he is currently editing for publication a series of new Abbey Theatre dramas with Christopher Fitz-Simon.

**Kathleen Gallagher Winarski** holds a doctorate from University College, Dublin, with a dissertation on the poetry of John Montague; a master's degree from Boston College; and a bachelor's degree from Emmanuel College.

# Contemporary Irish Cinema

# 1
# Shamrocks and Shillelaghs
Idyll and Ideology in Irish Cinema

## Harlan Kennedy

"Ireland for the Irish!" The cry has echoed across the land for 800 years, and for most of this century it has reechoed on the cinema screen. But just whom, in the country's ceaseless struggle for political and spiritual selfhood, *does* Ireland belong to? And which Ireland are we talking about? North/South? Present/past? Real/mythical?

Ask the average moviegoer to free-associate about Ireland and the tape of memory/archetype would yield a semicoherent printout: leprechauns, terrorists, Maureen O'Hara, mackerel skies, shamrocks, Darby O'Gill, John Ford, Black and Tans, curly-smoked thatched cottages. This Ireland is not so much a country as some auctioneer's dream from the Great Iconographic Unconscious—a pixillated, trouble-wracked land not only politically and culturally but also in its artistic identity. It remains so, despite the fact that honest-to-God Irish filmmakers have begun to be heard from in recent times, and the schematic has been enlarged to encompass Stephen Rea, Gabriel Byrne, Brenda Fricker, *The Commitments* and *The Snapper,* and various tortured/exultant faces of Daniel Day-Lewis.

Is Ireland a land at all, in the sense of a self-determining country and culture, or is it a product of everyone else's perceptions? And if "Ireland" is misty, what can we make out when we attempt to sight Irish cinema? Neil (*The Crying Game*) Jordan, Jim (*My Left Foot, The Field, In the Name of the Father*) Sheridan, Pat (*Cal, Fools of Fortune*) O'Connor . . . and who else? Hollywood has embraced the foregoing artists, even waved an Oscar on six at their most successful, breakout films. But on the whole Irish cinema remains, with heartbreaking economic inevitability, a cottage industry, it heroes and heroines unsung.

Yet movies about Ireland—wherever and by whomever made— are one of cinema's richest seams. It secretes the emerald-green roman-

1

ticism of *The Quiet Man* and *Ryan's Daughter,* the agitprop expressionism of *The Informer* and *Odd Man Out,* the dying-fall beauties of John
Huston's *The Dead.* "Irish cinema" accommodates the almost Irish
(Sean O'Feeney that was), the distantly Irish (Ron Howard), the fanci-
fully Irish (Huston), the propagandistically Irish (Ken Loach), and all
those filmmakers who have wrestled from outside Ireland with the
dozen different Irelands of movie tradition.

The wildly capricious resonance of "Ireland for the Irish" has it
roots in political history. Centuries of resented British occupation
ended notionally in 1921 with a partition treaty dividing Éire from Ulster. Ireland's Protestant-dominated northeastern corner then bowed
alone to the British Parliament while largely Catholic Éire (four-fifths
of the landmass) sat back to enjoy self-government and renounce further territorial claims. Or so went the theory. In point of fact, Éire's less
enchanted citizens, the Irish Republic Army, continued and continue
to hack at Britain's remaining handhold on the island; Britain maintains 20,000 troops in Ulster; that province's own heavies, the Ulster
Defence Regiment (legal) and Ulster Freedom Fighters (illegal), try to
match the IRA in violence; bombings, shootings, torchings make the
international news.

Is this a political feud or a religious one? A fight about territory
and temporal advantage, or a playoff between the ancestral sanctity of
Catholicism—ah! the keening music of eternity in the voices of Mon-
signor Cecil Kellaway and Father Barry Fitzgerald—and the ancestral
opportunism of British Protestantism, born out of Henry VIII's short
marital attention span?

No one can be surprised, then, if each subgenre of cinema about
Ireland has its own built-in weather system of paradoxes. Romantic
movies from *The Quiet Man* to *Far and Away* hint at a never-never
Golden Age, a time of simple pastoral integrity. Church-blessed com-
munity spirit, heroic faith in the Irish Struggle. Yet these films' views of
"Irishness"—in the picturebook villages and faery folklore, in the
gnarled    quaintness    of    characters    played    by    Fitzgerald/John
Mills/Cyril Cusack—can seem no less patronizing and oppressive
than the collar-and-lead colonialism long exercised by Britain. Stepan
O'Fetchit, step forth.

At the other extreme, modern-dress movies like Tony Luraschi's
*The Outsider,* Mike Hodges's *A Prayer for the Dying,* and Ken Loach's
*Hidden Agenda* purport to present a real, contemporary Ireland while
effectively reducing it to a traffic snarl-up of faceless ideologues wield-
ing guns, balaclavas, and gritty one-liners.

Colonialism is not just a matter of alien army-boots stomping across the natives' front yards. There is annexation by art and thought, foreign rule by the presumption of other people's fiction and faction. The best Irish film of modern times, Neil Jordan's *The Crying Game*, found something to say about the country by leaving it in the second reel. Jordan took his Irish hero (Stephen Rea) to London, where both the crudely magnified "certainties" of the Irish Struggle and the garishly incongruous romanticism of the Irish landscape (IRA hideout as Celtic Sherwood Forest) dissolved and re-formed in a caustic city of nondenominational discontent and psychosexual quest.

Jordan's film suggests that Ireland became a two-headed myth so strong—a land twinning picturebook atavism with newsreel shockwaves—that only by fleeing both can one survive to look back anew. Even then, success isn't assured, or disengaged objectivity guaranteed. The two—headed beast-seductive anima Miranda Richardson, brute animus Adrian Dunbar—pursues the hero all the way to Spitalfields for a grisly showdown. In the same way, the Irish struggle spills over from Belfast into mainland British lives, putting a bomb under all our comfortable prejudices and arm's-length perspectives.

Yet however adversarial they seem, the Ireland of the Gibraltar killings, of the Enniskillen massacre, of *Hidden Agenda* is profoundly, if perversely, symbiotic with the Ireland of John Ford and Ron Howard. If idyll and ideology are opposites, they are magnetic, coexistent ones. Ford himself knew this intuitively. *The Quiet Man* and *The Informer* are flipsides of the same record. *The Informer* (1935) has an antihero, Victor McLaglen's Gypo Nolan, whose dismissal from the IRA leads, through a combination of socioeconomic desperation and dimwittedness, to his informing on a best friend wanted for political murder. Set in 1921 before partition, the movie creates a metaphor for political turmoil out of the fog rolling through Ford's studio-wrought Dublin; the clear-aired rural Ireland of *The Quiet Man* is present by its absence. The informer's tortured negatives—no color, no sky, no love story, no pastoral images, no family life—could be used to print all the positives found in the later film.

*The Quiet Man* (1952), in turn, is an idyll defined and made piquant by the opposites that threaten it. The "Troubles" crowd sardonically round the film's edges. We're told that the odd chap in jodhpurs, beret, and Hitler Youth–style getup belongs to the IRA; John Wayne's elfin pal Barry Fitzgerald serenades a "nice soft night" by saying, "I think I'll go and join me friends and talk a little treason"; and Victor McLaglen's land-hungry squire clearly suggests a member of the Anglo-

Irish "Ascendancy" (McLaglen himself was English-born) eternally at odds with the natives.

Though *The Quiet Man* also has the standard stage-Irish trimmings—thatched cottages, tippling locals, feisty red-haired heroine (Maureen O'Hara)—Ford is not uncritical of them. Part of his film's argument is that this "Oirish" vision derives from an outsider American's viewpoint—not just the title character's but, by implication, Ford's own as director. "Only an American would have thought of emerald green!" coos the Protestant vicar's wife sarcastically on sighting Wayne's newly painted woodwork. And when O'Hara comes upon Wayne planting flowers, she spoofs his impractical romanticism: "Roses? Fine farmer you are. Not a cabbage or a potato . . ."

A darker, more confrontational tradition in outlanders' Irish cinema spun off from Ford's self-consciously Expressionist *The Informer,* Carol Reed's *Odd Man Out* (1947), Basil Dearden's *The Gentle Gunman* (1952, with John Mills as a tormented IRA defector), and Tay Garnett's *A Terrible Beauty,* aka *The Night Fighters* (1960, with Robert Mitchum as ditto). This subgenre pays lip service to the angular verismo of newsreel "truth" while creating a cinema arguably more artificial than the slow-rolling pastoralism of *The Quiet Man* or *Ryan's Daughter,* or even of remoter costume pieces like *Barry Lyndon* and *Far and Away.*

*Odd Man Out,* which in cinema about Ireland has become a classic almost as impregnable as *The Informer,* focuses still further the conundrums of myth vs. reality. We could ask what is the difference between an American (Ford in *The Quiet Man*) coming to rural Ireland to turn the country into a bucolic pipe dream, and an Englishman (Carol Reed in *Odd Man Out*) coming to Belfast to turn it into a doomsday film noir? Both impose predesigned visions on a country. The difference is that Reed presents his vision as reality—with an Expressionist skew for extra emotional "truth"—while Ford has an alter ego hero through whom he admits that foreigners bring their own colored lenses, their own sentimental lies, to the unfamiliar land.

David Lean's *Ryan's Daughter* (1970) may be the cinema's richest summation of this confused traffic. The project began with a politically programmatic screenplay by Robert Bolt, a story about an English army officer (Christopher Jones) romancing an Irish girl (Sarah Miles, Mrs. Bolt) married to a gentle schoolmaster (Robert Mitchum). In this Hibernian *Romeo and Juliet,* the Capulets and Montagues become the Brits and the Irish, and the romance is overshadowed by a thunderous plot about arms shipments and pre–Easter Rising discontent. At the same time, Bolt's village priest (Trevor Howard) is a battered spiritual referee, God's aging whistleblower in a Catholic community where every human action can have an equal and unpredictable divine reaction.

But the perverse élan of the Lean-Bolt partnership lies in the extent to which the parties pull in different directions. Once behind the camera, Lean swamps both politics and religion with epic pastoralism. Who now remembers anything about Anglo-Irish historical tensions or church-and-people ruminations? In memory's eye the film is three hours of fervent Celtic skies, foaming seascapes, lyric ribbons of sand, Brueghelesque villages, and vernal woodlands burgeoning with sperm and spring.

*Ryan's Daughter* also marks a turning point in the history of movies about Ireland. Before it, a sort of frontier existed between the Political Movie (*The Informer, Odd Man Out,* et al.) and the Bucolic Movie (*The Quiet Man, Darby O'Gill and the Little People, Young Cassidy, Finian's Rainbow* . . .). After it, as if prompted by its loony enactment of every operatic excess Irish film fiction could aspire to, the best "Irish" movies were those in which pastoral and political motifs were sophisticatedly intertwined, and Ireland became a place in which the ominous is at one with the idyllic. "Terrible Beauty" now describes Ireland's uniqueness as a battle zone. Hills and hedgerows, dunes and seashores, sun-lanced forests are the camouflage of everyday terror. And in *Barry Lyndon* (1975), Stanley Kubrick's seemingly Troubles-free Thackeray epic, an allegory of modern political anguish is embedded in an early-nineteenth-century road movie.

The best modern movies about Ireland all approach their subject obliquely, emblematically. In Jordan's *Angel* (U.S.: *Danny Boy,* 1982), the tale of a nightclub musician (Stephen Rea) hunting the killer of the band's manager zigzags across an Ireland alive with nondenominational menace as well as with the labeled agitators of the Conflict. In the same director's *The Miracle* (1991), two youngsters act out a divided love story that plays riffs on the motherland/motherhood (beguiling "older woman" Beverly D'Angelo eventually revealed as the boy's long-lost ma) and on Ireland as a place of muscular vagabond folklore (the girl takes up with a circus strongman). And Gillies MacKinnon's *The Playboys* (1992) is a Hardyesque comedy-romance in which Irish village girl Robin Wright must choose between the lithe, imaginative values of a folkloric Ould Ireland (traveling player Aidan Quinn) and the bullnecked authority of the oppressive Anglo-Irish status quo (Albert Finney, Irish-accented but trailing clouds of orotund theatric Britishness).

While fable edges out lecture in today's best movies about Ireland, the worst are unmasked by their determined clinging to the old adversarial pattern: dark-toned docu(melo)drama steeped in political Sturm und Drang vs. escapist essays in timeless pastoralism. Into the first basket we can drop Loach's *Hidden Agenda* (1990), whose agitprop crudities reduce Ireland to a standoff between tweedy Brits plotting in smoke-filled rooms and virile Micks singing treason in smoke-filled pubs. Into the other basket goes Peter Chelsom's *Hear My Song* (1991), wherein Ireland is a land of unTroubled comic opera quaintness chockablock with funny old castles, funny old cows, and funny old tenor singers.

Even Neil Jordan did his bit for Funny Old Ireland with *High Spirits* (1988). A busload of Americans descend on Lord Peter O'Toole and his open-for-visitors haunted castle, bringing stereotyped Yankee crassness to Irish bibulous guile. The movie reeks of let's-find-an-international-market-for-this-Celtic-twaddle, not least in the wholesale importing of U.S. stars Beverly D'Angelo, Daryl Hannah, and the ineffable Steve Guttenberg. But then this casting trend has become epidemic. See Forest Whitaker in *The Crying Game*, Wright and Quinn in *The Playboys*, Mary Elizabeth Mastrantonio in *Fools of Fortune* (at least she's Mrs. Pat O'Connor), Tom Berenger in *The Field*, Mickey Rourke and his Method Irish accent in *A Prayer for the Dying*, Brad Dourif and Frances McDormand in *Hidden Agenda*. It's partly a bid to turn "Ireland for the Irish" into "Ireland for the world," to amplify the land's box office charisma.

The corralling of American stars hints at something else, too: that "Irish-American" is a more natural kinship than "Anglo-American"; and that Ireland is a cultural-spiritual halfway house between the U.K. and the U.S. The American seeking his roots in the Emerald Isle has become a leitmotif going on a cliché, both in real life (R. Reagan revisiting the soil that had nurtured a future star, president, and blarney expert) and in the movies. Irish-American "homecomings" provide the narrative kernel of a dozen Irish films. That same kernel, transplanted to Hollywood, grew into the most famous pop epic in history.

*Gone with the Wind* is about an Irish family in the American South, one whose daughters may have caught the Southern accent but whose father (Thomas Mitchell) preserves a peat-thick Hibernian brogue. This family enacts a four-hour Irish mystery play incorporating every ancestral trope of Irish fiction, from the possession and dispossession of land, to the sentimental power of homecoming, to the terror of

﹋famine, to the melodramatic passion of Scarlett's relationship to the ﹋earth and what it brings forth. If "Irish cinema" ever had to select its ﹋own logo, it would surely be the image of Scarlett clutching that turnip ﹋as the roiling Celtic sunset rhymes with the roiling furrows of the ﹋earth.

Besides the O'Haras of Tara, "Irish-American" has other lustrous points of intersection with Hollywood cinema: Orson Welles's Wandering Irishman ("Me name's Moichael O'Hara") in *The Lady from Shanghai;* Clark Gable failing to be Irish—or box-office—in *Parnell;* Spencer Tracy failing not to be Irish in every film he ever made; James Cagney showing a touch of the blarney is helpful when you take over organized, or disorganized, crime in American cinema; and John Huston crowning his late career with the only movie ever to do fit honor to James Joyce, *The Dead.*

The common "Irishness" in these farflung ex-Pats, real or fanciful, is a kind of expansive or explosive primitivism. It can be an old man seeing through wistful veils of elegy into the primal energy of creation and disintegration (Huston/Joyce). It can be a family fighting for survival with fists and native wit (*GWTW,* Raoul Walsh's *Gentleman Jim*). Or it can be the pugnacity of men like Cagney and Tracy, wearing the rolled-up sleeves and rolled-down frowns of a race born on the wrong side of the Irish Sea.

Indeed, "Irish" as a movie flavor could be defined as anything that is not English. The classic Englishman in world cinema is a product of (over)-breeding: a paradigm of repressed virtue (from Ronald Colman to Dirk Bogarde), or of suave, perfidious vice (from Basil Rathbone to Alan Rickman). The Irishman is broader in voice and gesture, more tousled and spontaneous in thought and manners, deeper in his tap roots to precivilization, closer in touch with the mystical-poetic-atavistic. Even Catholicism, with its 2,000-year-old Bible-blessed pedigree, speaks loud for ancestral integrity, far louder than a Church of England born 1,500 years later in a blaze of secular expediency.

These might seem cliches of national description if Irish filmmakers themselves—at least, those who have won exposure abroad—did not endorse them. Jim Sheridan's *My Left Foot* (1989) and *The Field* (1991) present their Irish heroes virtually as elemental forces. Daniel Day-Lewis's Christy Brown is an artist at once cursed and blessed by living in a primitive, pre-articulate state. The sign language of painting or the body language of gesture and tantrums substitute for the (debased?) vocabulary of literate speech. And Richard Harris's Lear-like village elder in *The Field* is a force of nature growling out runic prophecies under a cloud of white hair.

These national differences are not merely cosmetic. They underwrite the very conflict between Ireland and England. This is not just a feud between Catholics and Protestants or colonials and colonizers. It's a face-off between a land priding itself on a tradition of large and passionate communion with man and nature—Ireland as the world's Bard, its emblem the harp, its artists such cosmic minstrels of the gab as Shaw, Yeats, and Joyce—and a land that nurtures the narrower, more opportunist "virtues" of political expediency, imperial control, cultural satrapy.

part of film history

England and Ireland, one could argue, even "lie" differently. The first Irish film to enter history's hall of fame was Robert Flaherty's *Man of Aran* (1934). For years this epic documentary about fisherfolk, its images hewn from rock and wave, was presumed to be the Real Thing. Later we learned that the Irish-extracted but Michigan-born Flaherty, to perfect his essay in <u>primitivism</u>, had coaxed the islanders back into long-forgotten practices, or into practices they had never practiced in the first place.

It was a lie—but what a lie! It was a lie for romantic hyperbole: "If it was never like this, it should have been." Irish lies are smiling. English lies are pondered, poker-faced, strategic. For *Man of Aran,* or "Life on the Rock," read *Death of the Rock,* or "Men of Gibraltar." Here screen culture, if it did not create the lie, famously arbitrated over it. *Death on the Rock* (1988) was a Granada TV documentary exploring the killing by British soldiers of three supposedly armed IRA terrorist suspects in Gibraltar in March 1988. The Irish victims, severally shot at point-blank range in broad daylight, were suspected of having planted a car bomb planned to explode during a military parade. That they carried no weapons and that no bomb was actually found (other than miles away and days later in a garage in Malaga, Spain) left British politicians flanneling to excuse what looked like an outright act of state terrorism. (It also looked like confirmation that Britain had a shoot-to-kill policy, as rumored, vis-à-vis Northern Ireland.) *Death on the Rock* was promptly banned, then—in the face of outcry—unbanned. The British government, wrongfooted, tried to regain balance by ordering an inquiry into the show's dodgy methods and faulty conclusions (so alleged). But the published inquiry vindicated the program and, by doing so, effectively damned the Gibraltar action.

Before and after *Death on the Rock,* other TV programs on Ireland—fiction and nonfiction—have caused the British government to rush for the OFF switch on telly screens. The policy of secrecy tells us not just about the English way of lying but about the whole drift of Anglo-Irish politics and the way it is directed from Parliament at Westminster. And not just in regard to Anglo-Irish politics, but Anglo-Irish cinema. Secrecy creates, by craft or convenient chance, a climate in which movies attempting to confront the Troubles head-on, like Loach's *Hidden Agenda,* butt into a brick wall of unyielding silence. And that collision can make the movie, not the government, look ridiculous.

*Hidden Agenda* is an irresistible force outwitted by an immovable object. Loach's portrait of a labyrinthine Ireland in which every British cover-up covers up another cover-up ended up as an exercise in investigative hysteria. The movie, had its running time been hours or days, might have bored a convincing hole through the layers of conspiracy. Instead it spent ninety minutes and ended with a broken drill and pile of paranoid exclamation marks.

Even at the more populist, pinbrained end of modern cinema—*Patriot Games* (1992)—the gag on effective debate ripples across the world to encourage the growth of batty stereotypes as representing the truth about a nation's struggles and ideals. Sean Bean's IRA villain is a psycho from Shamrockland; clapped out British Royalty, the last best hope for Western democracy (!); and the hero, an Americanized Irishman—Harrison Ford's Jack Ryan—for whom the Atlantic is 3,000 miles separating civilization (U.S.A.) from anarchy (IRA).

Perhaps the picture—this picture, every picture, the "whole" picture—will be put right by Kevin Costner's mooted movie about IRA founder Michael Collins. Then again, perhaps the picture will just be modishly reversed. Collins was an advocate of violent resistance who, like the Gibraltar victims seventy years later, ended with a British bullet in the back of his head. But if Costner's track record is anything to go by (who else could turn Jim Garrison into Gary Cooper?), Michael Collins may end up as a plain man's warrior-saint munching on a *Reader's Digest* version of Anglo-Irish politics.

The obliquity of fable still seems the most telling and penetrating mode of discourse in modern Irish cinema. This is "lying" as poetry, and poetry is art's best, guerrilla answer to the prose majeure of last-ditch colonial politics being played out by Britain in Ireland. *The Crying Game*—we begin and end with it—proposes a cinema about Ireland that rhymes a nation's Troubles with the troubles of all of us; that diffuses state politics into sexual and emotional politics; that explores identity and frontier not just in the map of nations but in the human psyche; that plants metaphors like landmines; and that discovers that Everything Is Not What It Seems.

The only modern cinema that can do justice to Ireland is one that acknowledges the tragedies of its past and the agonies of its present while insisting that humanity can coexist with history, myth with reality, poetry with prose. And that the fluidity of personal destiny can be both example and weapon against the obdurate imperative of political destiny.

# 2

# Poetic Documentary

The Films of John T. Davis

## Kathleen McCracken

> The world about us would be desolate except for the world within us. There
> is the same interchange between these two worlds that there is between one
> art and another, migratory passings to and fro, quickenings, Promethean
> liberations and discoveries.
>
> —Wallace Stevens
> *The Necessary Angel*

When the Canadian theorist Marshall McLuhan began to publish his
groundbreaking analyses of mass communication in the early sixties,
his emphasis on the ways electric media, and the cinema in particular,
had freed the arts from the traditionally descriptive/narrative plane of
the written word contributed an important dimension to our understanding of the close connection between film and print. McLuhan's
catchphrase "the medium is the message" is perhaps nowhere better illustrated than in the similar structural configurations characteristic of
film and poetry. His case for this fundamental affinity, based on a common tendency to juxtapose, or "bunch," complex groups of items and
events[1] at the expense of logical sequence and lineal connection is
rooted in the precepts of the modernist project, and extends Arnold
Hauser's postulation that the new mosaic concept of time that entered
into all forms of art in the twentieth century was in large part a response to the technical methods of film.[2]

Although both theses have been challenged on the grounds that,
because cinema and literature are essentially "print" media, structural
parallels are inevitable and therefore make traces of definite influence
all but impossible to detect,[3] the broad implications they have for contemporary interart relations remain seminal. For if looking at film from
a literary perspective gives but a partial view of the cinema, it also suggests an approach especially suited to the independent film, which is

in many respects closer in form and subject matter to modern poetry than to popular cinema.

Elsewhere I have discussed the tendency amongst independent Irish filmmakers to adopt strategies generally ascribed to poetry.[4] To explore further the significance of this exchange in a specifically Irish context, I will now focus on a director whose work consistently exemplifies the vitality Wallace Stevens claims can be gained from interart exchange. "Quickenings," "discoveries," crossings from "the world about us" to "the world within us" are terms that offer roads in to the films of Belfast director John T. Davis.

Since he began making movies with an 8 mm camera in the early seventies, Davis's work has been characterized by an eclectic blend of styles and techniques. Variously referred to as "lyrical," "impressionistic," and "romantic," each of Davis's films, from *Shellshock Rock* (1979) to the later *Hobo* (1992), are in fact television documentaries. Not the genre in which one would expect to find the makings of a visual poem (though it may be that television, as the populist medium, is an ideal means of returning poetry to the people.) Conventionally, a documentary has a twofold purpose: to educate its audience and to persuade them that the point of view it enforces is socially correct. It achieves this by presenting "the facts" in a nonfictional, noninvolved manner. A controlled overvoice directs the viewer through a series of realist images that stand as a record of actual events, and which, because of their objectivity, purport to tell "the truth." Davis's films depart from this traditional format at almost every turn: there are no authoritative voice-overs, there is no endorsement of a fixed point of view. One might even go so far as to say that there is no attempt to educate in the orthodox sense, so unencumbered is the viewer by documentary's usual battery of facts and formulations. What we are given instead is a collage of visual impressions, meditations from various angles on a single subject which, when brought together, expose the director's vision. This paradoxical "objective subjectivity" is the primary source of Davis's oppositional, or poetic, style. For if documentary in its purest form aims to eliminate all traces of subjectivity, Davis, without passing judgment on any of his subjects, allows both the material and the methods of shooting and editing to challenge quotidian expectations regarding perception, expression, and the notion of absolute truth. This, however, does not mean that they are counterdocumentary. Davis's adherence to the genre has resulted in a restructuring of prevailing methods and the development of an approach to filmmaking that aspires toward a particular condition of language, the language of poetry.

The idea that a director could use the camera to write a philosophy or worldview with the same degree of subtlety and flexibility that a novelist or poet expresses thoughts on paper was first given full explication in Alexandre Astruc's 1948 article, "The Birth of a New Avant-Garde: *la caméra-stlyo*."[5] Although the theory would not be practically realized until over a decade later, in the cinema of the New Wave, it was also formulated by Orson Welles, who claimed "film is something dead, a band of celluloid like the blank sheet on which you write a poem. A film is what you write on the screen."[6]

If Welles's statement is untenable in terms of Hollywood productions, where directing and scriptwriting are generally separate activities,[7] it becomes relevant in the context of unscripted documentary, where the director is, in effect, the writer, and therefore free to organize material as he or she sees fit. This feature, which is as much a product of attitude as style, manifests in the treatment of time, and therefore narrative structure, and of reality, which in documentary is both subject and material. His or her approach to these key cinematic concepts is in turn shaped by the conflation of two normally discrete, though not entirely unrelated genres. Poetic realism and cinema verité are here wedded to create a looser, more impressionistic format that may be called "poetic documentary."

While Davis himself places Bogdanovich's hymn to small-town America *The Last Picture Show* (1971) first among the films that he believes have most influenced him, his own work pays more direct homage to American Direct Cinema and French cinema verité, and to the image-centered, multiperspectivist films of Antonioni, Bresson, or Straub. In clarifying his synthesis of styles, Davis cites the American filmmaker Don Pennebaker: "I take my images from reality, but the films are an imaginary dream of what really happened." As he goes on to explain, "what you're seeing has happened, but the fact that it's abstracted by the actual process of making the film makes it different. You're not bending or changing reality, but you change things about to make sense of what you perceive has happened . . . you're making it (reality) more concise and you're fitting it into the film mode.[8] Although Davis holds with one of the principal tenets of Direct Cinema, allowing the subject to emerge, as it were, "organically" out of the filming process, his willingness to impose some sort of order on the material in subsequent editing is the source of both his departure from and, in terms of depth and coherence, his advance over purist verité. Indeed, the process as Davis describes it is not unlike that of composing a poem, in which the writer "disorders" reality to make it correspond to his or her impression of a particular experience.

Documentary? Yes, but with a difference. Davis's films are unabashedly personal and, like those of many directors whose visions and obsessions are visible in their work, they contain certain recurrent images and motifs which, taken together, yield a fairly coherent worldview. These preoccupations, ranging from punk rock to country-and-western music, from the cultural diversity of the United States to the cultural insularity of Northern Ireland, are never permitted to overburden as essentially interrogative, unbiased presentation of the facts. Consequently, the films are not designed to reflect any preconceived theme; what they do reveal is a commitment to and empathy with their subject matter that precludes the need for heavy-handed statement. There is a fine balance between the lyrical "I-centered" elements and social realities, which in turn directs the audience's emotional and intellectual response. Again, the analogy with the lyric poem, which is an integration of private and objective experience, presents itself.

In the films, this concord is maintained by the dual approach Davis takes to visual and aural reality. On a basic, indexical level, the film presents the world as it is: the highways and byways of Belfast and Nashville, the voices and opinions of street preachers, cowboys, prison guards. This predominant method of depiction is shot through with a symbolical exploration of the ironies and complexities beneath the surface, a darker, and sometimes lighter, side that is conveyed through landscape, season, facial expression. The mixture of reality with symbol and allusion, which has grown steadily more prevalent and more refined, builds up multiple perspectives, layered narratives, and a literary texture that is absent from pure documentary. And this comprehensive treatment of subject matter finds its technical counterpart in expert visual and aural editing.

Davis's treatment of time is, again, a compound of documentary and avant-garde techniques. Whereas documentary usually incorporates some degree of narrative structure, it rarely approaches the oblique format of experimental cinema, and is careful to avoid any resemblance to the fictionalized chronology of the feature film. Davis is open to both models and has, on occasion, adopted their conventions. If we look closely, we find that his poetic style is as much a function of narrative, or organizational pattern, as it is of his choice of and attitude toward subject. John McKenna's reference to *Shellshock Rock* as "an almost Joycean treatment of the punk rock scene" is a not inaccurate description of the narrative method Davis has reworked in each of his films.[9] In a manner reminiscent of Godard's notebook films, faces, places, voices, and music are placed alongside one another to build up a narrative that is associative, digressive and, in the case of *Route 66* (1986) and *Dust of the Bible* (1989), semifictional. In the absence of commentator, characters, or plot in the conventional sense, we are confronted by visual and aural signs that, while they draw our attention to the filmmaking process, forcing us to acknowledge the film as an artifact with its own reality, also implicate us in the "drama" of decoding their significance within those parameters. Davis's films differ most radically from conventional documentary in composition and editing. In their concentrated juxtapositioning of word and image, and by allowing the variety of meaning inherent in reality to emerge unaltered from the images themselves, they approximate most closely the modernist poem.

To show how the techniques I have been discussing are implemented, I will consider two of Davis's films, *Route 66* and *Dust on the Bible*. The first film Davis made was an 8 mm conceptual piece about human relationships full, according to one commentator, of "avant-garde bravado."[10] His other early films were commissioned works taken on by independent Holywood Films, which he and partner Alwyn James operated out of Davis's home in Holywood, County Down. One of these, a forty-minute promo for the Portrush-based "Project Evangelism," prefigures the studies of Protestant Fundamentalism he would make in *Power in the Blood* and *Dust on the Bible*. Davis's first fully fledged film was made in 1978–79, when he decided to record Belfast's then-flourishing punk rock scene. Like each of his subsequent works, this was to be a "heart" film—one he not just wanted but needed to make. Along with the two subsequent films *Protex Hurrah* and *Self-Conscious Over You*, which completed the musical trilogy, *Shellshock Rock* bears the hallmarks of what would become a distinctive style: live performances and to-camera interviews intercut with striking linking sequences (sweeping pans, aerial shots, and low shots of Belfast by day and night); apposite incidental music (Hank Williams's "I'll Be a Bachelor Till I Die," The Cascades' original recording of "Rhythm of the Rain"); an atmospheric use of grainy black-and-white, slow motion, and lighting; a fast-paced rhythm synchronous with the music and the energy of the punk movement. After being banned from the 1979 Cork Film Festival on the grounds that it was not up to technical standard, then going on to win the Silver Award in the Art and Music category of the New York Film and Television Festival later the same year, Davis took *Shellshock Rock* to New York in search of American distribution. It was here that the idea for a film about America's once-great highway, Route 66, began to take shape.

Billed as "a personal film," "an impressionistic portrait" and "a musical journey," *Route 66* documents, in the first instance, the history and present condition of a road which for more than two decades was the nation's major thoroughfare. The facts are all there: built in the thirties, Route 66 became the passageway west for the over a half million Americans who fled the Dust Bowl of the thirties; spanning 2,200 miles and eight states, it formed a direct link between Chicago and Los Angeles and opened up new lines of continental communication; before it was bypassed in the fifties by more efficient super highways, Route 66 had been celebrated in song and literature, on television and in the cinema as the symbol of freedom, prosperity, and the future. But the opening sequence (an up-tempo montage composed of shots of each of the states bisected by the highway—the film in fast forward—framed by the sweeping maneuvers of a red convertible and synchronized with the Rolling Stones' version of "Route 66") makes plain that these facts are not about to be presented in any ordinary informational fashion. Standard narrative configuration is here displaced by a stream of visual and aural images connected by their emergence out of and return to the highway. The film gives a composite picture made up of "soliloquies" spoken by the "characters" who live and travel along Route 66. And this collage is punctuated by live music and radio bands that reveal the character of each state, as well as black-and-white archival footage of the building of the road intercut with the voice of Studs Terkel reading from Steinbeck's *The Grapes of Wrath*. The "poetry" resides as much in the subject matter, which is both elegy and indictment, as in the way images and sequences build out of one another to effect a narrative of ironic or contiguous juxtaposition (the mid-day downpour that gives way to a frenzied radio evangelist's "out of the Belly of the Whale" broadcast; the first words spoken in the film—"Everything immortal must first pass away"—as they introduce extended shots of the disused highway, one catching a "Road Closed" sign), or stand alone, detailed meditations on the history and aseity of objects (paint peeling from a wooden Indian; a musicbox playing in a deserted curio shop; derelict gas bars; a graveyard of cars). Rooms and landscapes straight out of paintings by Hopper or Wyeth are placed against the manufactured images of pop art (postcards, advertisements, graffiti, neon), while the music and the lyrics create another strain in this paean to the spirit of America. The effect is of a jagged, unsettling, but constantly energized rhythm that evokes the laments and celebrations of the Beat generation and its successors. For despite its disavowal of explicatory comment, *Route 66* is deeply involved with words, both as source and analogue. The introduction of an oblique, semifictional narrative around which actual footage is arranged in a mosaic pattern demonstrates a desire to work with film in much the same way as the poet works with words.

Davis has described *Route 66* as "my own view of America," and as such it is governed by the director's selective and highly subjective eye. Although this could work to the film's disadvantage, it in fact effects the reverse, giving direction to a lengthy and potentially diffuse trek and providing the audience with a point of reference. Lyrical intensity finds focus in the film's narrative center, an anonymous figure driving a red 1968 Chevrolet Impala convertible. The wanderer's frequent passes through the film act as a visual refrain, drawing attention to other recurrent images, including green and white road signs indicating Highway 66, cracked asphalt, abandoned motels. The car, though, is the film's strongest image, epitomizing the American ideal of freedom and escape, and we are invited to identify with the driver's peripheral, nonjudgmental and, most importantly, disappointed point of view.

If for Davis *Route 66* represented "a dream realized" in that it allowed him to confront American culture head-on, to enter, as it were, the "myth-ditty" of a generation, it also obliged him to consider how dreams and myths are broken, to explore conflicts between reality and imagination. "I wanted," Davis has said, "to make a film comparing my lifelong images of America with the reality of life there." [11] This dichotomy lies at the root of the film and, in a manner that is extended and refined in *Power in the Blood* and *Dust on the Bible*, determines the organization of *Route 66* round stylistic and thematic contrasts. For example, divisions and connections between the actual and the imaginary, between Northern Ireland and the southern United States, between the city and the country are reinforced by alterations in pace, lighting, and sound track. Davis's objective of exposing the "underbelly" of the United States is realized on a purely documentary level via an all too realistic record of the poverty, despair, prejudice, and cruelty that lie at the heart of the American Dream, while in metaphoric terms the highway is metonymic of the state of the nation: "America is grinding and cracking at the seams. Just as Route 66 is. And so '66' is symptomatic of what is happening to America." [12] What confirms *Route 66* as a "poetic documentary" is the way these two approaches to reality—the antisocial and the symbolic—are fluidly integrated to produce a film that manages with skill and integrity to express ideas by means of a literary and a visual vocabulary. In a broader sense, it is a film that epitomizes the outward-looking character of Irish art in the eighties, a period when, as Fintan O'Toole has aptly put it, "works of art could be at the same time both realistic and surreal, both documentary and fantastic."[13]

Shortly after completing *Route 66*, Davis made the following statement: "Encompassed in *66* is some kind of obsession with God, to do with spirituality."[14] His next two films, *Power in the Blood* and *Dust on the Bible*, are journeys into that obsession, yet the impression they give is not one of self-indulgence, but of a deepening consolidation of method, material, and vision. Both take as their subject Protestant Fundamentalism in the North of Ireland. *Power in the Blood* follows the mission of born-again preacher Vernon Oxford from Franklin, Tennessee, to Belfast, making a direct connection between Ulster and America. Although the film maintains many of the stylistic idiosyncrasies that characterize Davis's films, it is a more straightforward documentary than either *Route 66* or *Dust on the Bible*, and in this respect may be likened to his more recent films, *Heart on the Line* (1990) and *Hobo*.

*Dust on the Bible*, however, is a visual poem in the truest sense. Its conflation of reading from the Book of Revelation and a narrative structure that brings to mind *Pilgrim's Progress* with country-and-western music and revivalist hymns, extreme long shots of apocalyptic suns, and a crossfade sequence of frenzied Lambeg drums, all contained within the framework of the seasons changing the Ulster landscape creates a collage rich in literary and cultural allusion.

*Dust on the Bible* is introspective, lyrical. Yet it is also dramatic, for it contains both a character and plot line, albeit loosely defined, which personalize the documentary elements. The journey-cum-quest motif is again central, and here the connecting thread is the presence of a young man driving a car from one revivalist meeting to the next. The derivation from *Route 66* is problematic, and has given at least one commentator cause to hope that in the future Davis will be able to "exorcise himself of the Jesus-drove-a-59–Chevy-down-the-road-to-Ballymena preoccupation."[15] There are, however, obvious differences between the figures, the most important being that, whereas in *Route 66* we are prevented from seeing the driver's appearance or responses, our attention being directed instead toward the car, here we are encouraged to identify quite closely with this wanderer-protagonist. Tight close-ups of his gaunt, serious face—his eyes in the rearview mirror, his lips nervously pursing a cigarette, his hands on the wheel—are visual signs of his skepticism and inhibition. He is, we may infer, a modern North of Ireland Everyman whose burden of guilt has been instilled by the Fundamentalist songs, sermons, and slogans he encounters at every turn. His search in meditative isolation for knowledge, forgiveness, belief is dissimilar to that of the driver in *Route 66* in the same way as the "voice" or "persona" in one of a sequence of poems may be essentially unlike that in the next. His liminal position vis-à-vis the documented "action"—the baptisms, the sermons, the street rallies—leaves him silent until, in the final sequence, he breaks into song: "Lord, I've tried everything but you." While the fluid camerawork prompts us to look from his viewpoint, his presence *in* the film, combined with the camera's involved but noncommittal relation to what is observed, distances our response. At once drawn out and held at bay, we as viewers experience the same double bind in relation to the text as does Davis's pilgrim toward his social and religious environment.

The organization of the film around this man's journeying focuses and, in effect, creates the narrative. His story consists of a series of encounters that implicate other interconnected patterns as the film progresses. In this respect, the structure of *Dust on the Bible*, like that of *Route 66*, is poetic, relying on the spectator's ability to discover meaning in a gradual accumulation of visual and aural images. As Davis has stated, "I present images, comment and music as powerfully as possible and leave it up to viewers to draw their own conclusions."[16] This rich ambiguity is complemented by a range of techniques that approximate poetry's figurative use of language. The willingness of the camera to linger over details (the tattoo on a preacher's left hand, the way he lays the Bible on the palm of his right, the stilled hands of a sleeping drunk), to focus on a single image for a protracted length of time (wind turning the pages of an open Bible; the silhouette of a dead bird on a barbed wire fence; the spiked, tortured outline of thorn and gorse), to study a person or object from several angles (Belfast's street preachers, Belfast after snow, Belfast during a hard rain) all contribute to the film's polyvalent imagery.

As in each of Davis's films, the composition, lighting, and camerawork produce scenes and sequences that are in themselves visually impressive, but that also carry symbolic and ironic connotations: a time lapse of racing storm clouds, tilled land and a country church, parenthetical shots of a windsurfer catching the breeze on the same lough where a baptismal service is being performed. Comparably meticulous editing places the chorus of the title song—"Dust on the Bible, Dust on the Holy Word"—over scenes of a province that refuses to let the dust

settle, causing the refrain to niggle at the conscience of the uncon-
verted. Its direct message speaks for a religion that demands an indis-
soluble fit between belief and language. Appropriately, the most
pervasive and also the most powerful images in *Dust on the Bible* are
the signs proclaiming the Fundamentalists' doomsday message: "The
Wages Of Sin Is Death." "Seek Ye The Lord While He May Be Found."
"Prepare To Meet Thy God." Posted on hoardings and houses, trees
and rocks, worn like battle gear by the preachers themselves, they en-
gross and alienate the viewer. Spatializing language, they function as
verbal and visual texts, obliging us to make connections. For about all
of this the film remains impartial, allowing the words and images to
circumscribe their own narrow horizons within the larger circumfer-
ence of big skies and open fields.

The strength of these visual images is intensified by an aural imagery that complements and interprets what we see. The blues-based
strains of Philip Donnelly's guitar parallel Davis's depiction of the
North's bleak but inspiring psychological and physical terrain, while
the unlikely blend of country music and gospel hymns establishes an
atmosphere that, like the songs and the situations, is disturbing yet uplifting. Music and song function as poems, offering indirect commentary on the realities that have occasioned them. But it is the
concentration of visual and aural images—for example, the palimpsest
of music, bare trees, preachers' admonishments, and the testimonials
of the saved that makes up one of the initial sequences (echoing the
laying on of hands that opens *Power in the Blood*)—that points up the
film's closest affinity with poetry's multilevel structuration.

Perhaps the most striking, and certainly the most consciously literary aspect of *Dust on the Bible* is the even-tempered, off-camera voice of
poet Damian Gorman reading intermittently from the Book of Revelation. Tonally opposed to the harsh voices of the preachers, the verses
paradoxically endorse and undercut Evangelical dogma. Positioned as
counterparts to the visual images, the readings form an oblique commentary that is critical to the film's depiction of the cyclical movement
of the days and seasons, of man's falling away from and return to God.
They also suggest that discrepancies may exist between the practice of
the preachers and the words of the Bible. For instance, as one man
orates vehemently on a Belfast street, the voice-over reads from Revelation 5: "And I saw a strong angel proclaiming with a loud voice, Who
is worthy to open the book, and to loose the seals thereof? And no man
in heaven, nor in earth, was able to open the book, neither to look
thereon." The close of *Dust on the Bible* is similarly ambiguous. As the

young man drives through a night of torrential rain, the voice speaks. "And let him that is athirst come. And whosoever will, let him take the water of life freely" (Rev. 22:17). Whether the rain is destructive or redemptive is ambiguous. This resistance to closure is crucial to Davis' vision and style, for it enables a productive play of meaning not only within the film text, but also between cinematic and literary, specifically poetic, methods.

In a recent assessment of Victor Sloan's photography, a body of work which, in its approach to visual documentation, invites comparison with Davis's, the critic Brian McAvera comments on how, since 1970, Northern Irish art has become "much less innocent": "the nature of political realities here—'whatever you say, say nuthin'—has ensured a coded response. The strategy is one of a series of maneuvers through which the artists explore obliquely the problems of the province."[17] Davis's "poetic documentaries" are, I would venture, conditioned by this need to make a "coded response." Although no film takes "the Troubles" as its principal subject, each is concerned to probe and, in some degree, lay open familiar territory. Placed in a broader sociopolitical context, the "liberations and discoveries" Davis achieves by merging verbal and visual "languages" can be understood as contributing to an emerging agenda for the arts in the North which, evidenced by the work of visual artists like Victor Sloan and Willie Doherty or poets like Paul Muldoon and Ciaran Carson, draws out resonances between text and image as one way of encoding a complex personal response to the Ulster situation. To return to Wallace Stevens, this is an art that encourages that most necessary connection between the world about us and the world within.

# 3

# History Without Borders

Neil Jordan's *Michael Collins*

## Brian McIlroy

> Oddly, the movie is like a prism that reflects every development of the recent situation.
>
> —Neil Jordan[1]

> "The years covered by the film are not the past. In the eyes of the IRA they are unresolved. That is why the film is potentially so inflammatory. It will summon up the ghosts."
>
> —Simon Partridge[2]

In the year that Neil Jordan was shooting his film *Michael Collins,* Robert Rosenstone published two books on the problematic but stimulating relationship between film and history.[3] Rosenstone, a historian, raises some of the key issues that have not been fully addressed by the incredible amount of criticism and commentary that Jordan's film has excited.[4] A reading of Rosenstone helps to extricate us from the reductive, defensive, disingenuous, and accusatory approaches to which *Michael Collins* has been subjected. Irish cultural criticism can, at times, appear to be prejudiced politics by other means, and this tendency makes it all the more important to seek out better frames of reference than those cultural criticism has thus far generated.

Rosenstone's contribution to the debate on "historical film" is to make it clear that films cannot be held captive to books, since the former are primarily visual and oral documents. Films have their own rules and codes of representation, and any criticism must take these into account. Little is to be gained by too closely comparing a film to received written history, yet it seems equally limiting to isolate history from film representations and to view them as separate activities.[5] What Rosenstone valorizes instead is a film that revisions our conception of history. In his writings, he shows us that films can do important

22

historical work, providing insight into both the past and the c figuration of that past.

Rosenstone's strengths are in the area of American history and film, having acted as a historical adviser for Warren Beatty's *Reds* (1981). He believes that costume dramas, a category to which *Michael Collins* arguably belongs, are less important than independent and experimental films which interact forcefully, and self-reflexively, with notions of historical truth. For Rosenstone, films do present a historical truth, one reading of the past that must be assessed *alongside*, not against, accounts using other media. That truth may alter, omit, invent, condense, and exaggerate more than professional historians would prefer, but films are nonetheless thinking and historical works. To be sure, historians do not fabricate evidence, but they must place emphasis to make an argument, and it is over these emphases that historians and filmmakers debate.

As I have mentioned above, Rosenstone would not place great historical store by Jordan's film, yet as Guy Westwell has suggested, strong reasons exist to believe that the conventional historical film can provide us with "progressive models" to revision history.[6] I see *Michael Collins* as one such progressive model, a film that explicitly looks backward but implicitly looks to the present and future. Before one can argue this position to its fullest extent, one must first measure *Michael Collins* against the Hollywood model of classical cinema. David Bordwell, informed by Russian formalist writings, has written at length on the specific characteristics of this kind of cinema which we now take for granted to the point of near blindness to its operations.[7]

As Bordwell outlines it, Hollywood cinema is both structurally and stylistically recognizable. We expect three acts or sections: an established scene, a violation or disturbance of that scene, and an eventual reassertion of order. We expect causal links; time compression; a plot and subplot; a deadline to be met; a likable, psychologically defined individual as the main interest; secondary characters who are unidimensional; characters defined by their objectives; and presentation over description. Stylistically, we expect establishing shots; shot/reverse-shot formations; matching cuts; background music; locations chosen to suit the psychology of the characters or the dynamics of the action; a camera viewpoint with an omnipotent or privileged perspective; and smooth or invisible editing. More generally, we expect a heterosexual romance; meaning to be communicated through content not structure; clarity of lighting, sound, and framing; a happy ending or definitive closure; and anemic politics. From an economic and marketing perspective, Hollywood cinema is also recognizable. For a mainstream studio budgeted feature, over $20 million is normal; big-name stars are required, and supporting roles are also often played by well-known actors and actresses.

Jordan's $30 million film accords with most of the above, but with some major and minor departures that are worthy of comment. One could not argue that the politics of the film is in any way anemic; if anything, the film is about politics. Within the confines of this classical Hollywood film, it is difficult to deal effectively with historical and biographical material when action and dramatic pacing must be constantly sought out. Yet, it is to Jordan's credit that he is both true to the historical record in places—Michael Collins did, for example, have a romantic relationship with Kitty Kiernan, and Harry Boland and he did seek her affections—and yet also finds space in places to grapple with controversial historical interpretation: the role, for example, of Eamon de Valera in Collins's death. This, then, is no ordinary biographical film, or "biopic" as the genre is known. It looks only at the 1916–22 period, with the guerrilla-leader-turned-politician Collins as its center. In this respect, Jordan interestingly departs from the usual Hollywood approach, which would have looked to early childhood events to explain subsequent actions—for example, the murder of Frankie McGuire's father in Alan Pakula's *The Devil's Own* (1997) is recounted visually to "explain" the son's IRA membership and violence, thereby personalizing the politics to its detriment.[8] By eschewing this approach, Jordan forces us to deal with the politics head on. In fact, the weakness of the heterosexual romance, in terms of extended screen time, also helps to direct the audience's attention to the political issues involved. Another departure from the Hollywood norm is the cut near the end of the film to actual 1920s black and white footage of Michael Collins's funeral cortege, attended by hundreds of thousands of Irish people. This aesthetic decision adds weight and gravitas to the authenticity of the historical record that Jordan is seeking to explore. Finally, the way in which the assassinations are choreographed alerts us to the makeshift, awkward nature of murder. The style used for the killings is circumspect, not in a Sam Peckinpah or Quentin Tarrantino mode of representation, where blood and gore are either aestheticized or parodied, but much more in the vein of Martin Scorsese's *Mean Streets* (1973) in which the act of shooting people is shown to be painful and frequently haphazard. Having said that, I want to note that the cross-cutting technique utilized between the assassinations of the English secret service agents and Collins and Kiernan in the Gresham Hotel is a fairly standard device, employed in films such as Francis Ford Coppola's *The Godfather* (1972). Scorsese's *Mean Streets* may also be an influence on Jordan in terms of the uneasy relationship between Roman Catholicism and violence.

In looking backward to the War of Independence and the Civil War, Jordan's film approximates the ideals of a "National Imaginary," a D. W. Griffith *Birth of a Nation* (1915), minus the race issue. This ambition helps to explain the Irish Film Censor's unusual commentary on the film as a "landmark" in Irish cinema, and the parade of political figures to the film's opening in Ireland. Since the two main political parties of the Republic of Ireland, Fine Gael and Fianna Fail, have their origins in the actions and beliefs of Michael Collins and Eamon de Valera, respectively, it is not surprising that the film would elicit questions about the state's progress and development from its turbulent beginnings.

What Jordan illustrates is the barbarity of this struggle for nationhood, even if the necessity for it is unquestioned.[9] The escalation of the violence from killing Irishmen who work for the British administration, to killing English secret service agents, to the killing of former comrades is presented as a seductive drug motivated by the prospect of control and power. This interpretation works best in any analysis of Jordan's de Valera (Alan Rickman) who seems to be the arch manipulator, with a greater, though more deceitful, strategic sense than that possessed by Collins. De Valera sent Collins to negotiate the peace treaty knowing that hard-line Republicans would not be able to accept any compromise. In that sense, de Valera gave himself options, and he chose civil war rather than exert his undoubted abilities of persuasion to seek accommodation. Although Jordan implies that de Valera was "in the mix" with the plans to ambush Collins, a problematic interpretation to many historians, it is not the most provocative aspect of the film, nor is it a new accusation.[10]

If the film serves to release the ambivalence felt in the Republic of Ireland about its violent genesis, it most likely succeeds. It effectively speaks to the notion that the new state grew out of violence to be, for the most part, a peaceful country. The film then carries this transformative notion as a metaphor for the current situation in Northern Ireland. It is a problematic carry forward because the differences are as confusing as the similarities. The reason for Collins to attend the peace talks in London was ostensibly because he could by force of personality convince both British and Irish people of the seriousness of the issues at stake, and he could best deliver the hard-liners. In much the same way, Provisional Sinn Fein and the IRA in Northern Ireland need Gerry

Adams and Martin McGuinness to attend peace talks to find a way to disengage from a very long war that cannot be won militarily. But, as with Collins's experience, negotiations carry risks once a compromise is reached. News of splits within the IRA membership over the prospect of a compromise has already been grounds for comment in 1997. The rhetoric of Jordan's film is utilized in part to explain to a wide audience in Ireland, Britain, and the United States of America that the men and women of violence, as represented politically by Adams and McGuinness, will need to be accepted into negotiations and, further, *helped* to overcome the splits that will undoubtedly emerge after a treaty settlement has been arranged.

On a more specific level, the film reverberates with Northern issues—the casting of Liam Neeson as Michael Collins is fascinating. Neeson is from Ballymena in Northern Ireland, a town represented by the ultraunionist Ian Paisley. Neeson was thus a Roman Catholic who grew up within a very Protestant culture. This casting decision, although many years in the works, does link the minority Catholic population of the North with a form of liberation from Britain. On the other side of the coin, we have Ned Broy, played by Stephen Rea, an Ulster Protestant who is on record as having no sympathies for the unionist position. It seems no accident that Rea plays the role of a government employee who is persuaded by the Republican arguments of Michael Collins, since it appears that Rea has taken that political route in his own life.[11] This subtext literally explodes on one occasion—when a Belfast police detective (Ian McElhinney) arrives in Dublin to bring some "Belfast efficiency" to the Southern Irish police force, and is immediately blown up in his car. This scene has been much commented upon—the anachronistic use of car bombs (a feature of the IRA's 1970s campaign, not that of Collins's volunteers during the War of Independence) is cited first, leading on to the comment that it is a not-so-subtle veiled attack on Protestantism and unionism.[12] Even the use of an armored car at the Croke Park massacre, another historical "mistake," is suggestive of the army and police vehicles that traversed Northern Ireland in the 1970s and 1980s.

Furthermore, the black-and-white newsreel footage of the introduction of the Black and Tans, who are billed as having fought at the Battle of the Somme in 1916, is another potent Northern metaphor. These unruly figures are akin to the violent "B" Specials (part-time policemen) who were active in Northern Ireland in the 1920s and in the late 1960s suppressing nationalist aspirations and civil rights for Catholics. The petrol bombing of the Black and Tans at one point in the film brings this connection strongly to the surface, an action common-place at the beginning of the recent Troubles; in addition, the reference to the Battle of the Somme is significant, since it is the Ulster Protestant and Unionist sacrificial event of note in 1916 as distinct from the Easter Rising.

Moreover, the specter of the North hovers ominously during the catalogue of assassinations in the film, conjuring up the many hundreds of English soldiers and Northern Irish police who have been killed in the present conflict. The often hyperventilating young volunteers who do the killing put a human face on dark deeds, a choice that can be contrasted with the cold efficiency of murders in classic gangster films and contrasted even with contemporary accounts of the Ulster crisis, such as Alan Clarke's *Elephant* (1989).[13] Jordan also raises the controversial connection between the Roman Catholic Church and the armed struggle. One of the assassins prays in church before he kills his fellow Irishman, even uttering a blessing to the condemned man before he shoots. Another policemen is shot leaving a church, and one is very conscious of the religious icon atop the hill from where the antitreaty forces ambush and kill Collins. The Protestant Unionist perception that the Roman Catholic Church is too often ambivalent in its relation to IRA insurgency is, in a sense, confirmed by the film.

The concentration on Collins forces Jordan to omit a great deal. One can only do so much in two hours of screen time. From a Southern perspective, the War of Independence is fought for the most part as a Dublin-centered affair, ignoring the many rural "flying columns" (mobile guerrilla units) that typified the era, as found portrayed in one of the first indigenous Irish features, Tom Cooper's *The Dawn* (1936). Jordan is also pressed to convey the social and collective nature of Sinn Fein's spectacular victory in the elections of 1918. The omission of the treaty negotiations in London, undramatic as they would be visually, prevents the viewer from seeing Collins the politician in action, leaving us only with a few speeches in town squares and in the Dáil (the Irish parliament).[14] The absence of these negotiations allows Jordan to bypass the embarrassing affair Collins supposedly had in London with Hazel Lavery and to omit the arguments about accommodating partition and on what terms. From a Northern perspective, the omission of the negotiations extends to the general structuring absence in the film of the unionist case. Why one million Irish people did not want a united, republican Ireland remains unasked and unanswered. If Gerry Adams is a modern Michael Collins, then perhaps it is a politically moral act for Jordan not to have to include Collins's famous line that he had signed his death warrant when he appended his name to the treaty with the British.

What historical, social, and cultural work does Jordan's film ultimately do? For the Republic of Ireland, it sets to rest the violent past; it puts Collins and de Valera together as two separate roads that Ireland could have chosen between but for the ambush and death of Michael Collins in 1922. For Jordan to use the comment of de Valera's, reportedly uttered at the fiftieth anniversary of the 1916 Rising, that Collins would prove to be the most important figure in twentieth century Irish history at the expense of the "Long fellow," is to suggest that even de Valera, who had enormous influence throughout the Republic of Ireland from the 1930s to the 1970s, was conscious of the major contribution of a man who changed from a guerrilla fighter to a man of treaty and compromise. It was, after all, a path de Valera followed in the late 1920s. More narrowly, de Valera's comment, and the film generally, helps to bind Fine Gael, Fianna Fail, and Sinn Fein as equal elements of the political mosaic of the Republic of Ireland. If a bias exists in the film, it is toward the Dublin-centered Free Staters, who formed Fine Gael, and whose party now represents a mainly urban and educated bourgeoisie, not unlike Neil Jordan himself. This educated elite have accepted that the unionists of the North must consent peacefully to any future united Ireland, and if they do not, they should not be forced into one. As Neil Jordan has said, albeit uneasily, "There are many ways of being Irish, and I suppose that Protestant Unionist is one of them."[15]

For Northern Ireland, however, the film, despite Jordan's often conflicting commentary on this matter in interviews, is a warning to Provisional Sinn Fein, the IRA, and nationalist and republican voters. The national question remains unresolved and may continue to be so, but a treaty will have to result from negotiations, if peace is to be had. Violence and assassination may be good enough to get to the conference table, but it does not provide the political courage to honor a compromise. To the unionist population, Jordan's film reaffirms the anti-imperialist myth: that republicans need deal only with Britain and not with the Ulster Protestant and the Unionist voter, who are judged as weak and "deluded lackeys."[16] For the Unionist audience of Northern Ireland, then, Jordan's *Michael Collins* crosses the border and visualizes them out of history.

# 4

# "The Past Is Always There in the Present"

*Fools of Fortune* and the Heritage Film

## John Hill

Although not a new phenomenon, a fascination with the past has been a predominant characteristic of British cinema since the 1980s. British films have looked back to various eras, including World War II and the 1950s, but it has been the first two decades of the century that have attracted most attention as films such as *Chariots of Fire* (1981), *Heat and Dust* (1982), *A Passage to India* (1984), *Another Country* (1984), *A Room with a View* (1985), *A Handful of Dust* (1987), *Maurice* (1987), *Where Angels Fear to Tread* (1991), *Howard's End* (1991), and *Carrington* (1995) all testify. Taken together, these films have been seen to demonstrate a more general British obsession with "national heritage," and the films themselves have often been labeled as "heritage films."

As Charles Barr has argued, the British cinema has traditionally sought to draw upon England's "rich historical and cultural heritage" as a source of prestige drama, and it is this tradition which British filmmaking in the 1980s revived.[1] For Andrew Higson, such films may be regarded as constituting a genre that "reinvents and reproduces, and, in some cases simply invents, a national heritage for the screen."[2] The historical heritage that such films construct, however, tends to be a particular version of the national past: one that is associated with the upper or upper-middle classes, the country and the south of England, or ex-colonies. Similarly, the cultural heritage upon which the films rely is that of the British literary and theatrical tradition, and many of the films are adaptations, employing "quality" actors more commonly associated with the stage. As a result, one of the key characteristics of the heritage film is its aesthetic of "display": a concern to "show off" the landscapes and properties as well as the dress and performance qualities of the actors.

Inevitably, discussion of heritage films has focused on the relation-ship between the past and present that is implied in them and that has generally been taken to be nostalgic. The heritage film, in this respect, is often read as a response to the economic and political failures, social tensions and troubled sense of national identity that have been a fea-ture of British society since the 1970s. The films, therefore, may be seen to be retreating into a past where such problems do not exist or at least have the merit of being resolvable. This seems to be the case even when social tensions are in evidence as the significance of these is characteris-tically undercut by the films' fascination with, and nostalgia for, the vi-sual splendor of a bygone age. In terms of their approach to the past, therefore, heritage films tend to substitute an interest in surface appear-ance for the provision of genuine historical insight or understanding.

Among the British heritage films of the 1980s, there are at least two that are concerned with Ireland: *The Dawning* (1988) and *Fools of For-tune* (1990). Set in the past and focusing on the privileged lifestyles as-sociated with the Anglo-Irish Ascendancy and the "Big House," these were generally regarded by critics as being unexceptional examples of heritage filmmaking. Although filmed in Ireland by an Irish director from an Irish novel, *Fools of Fortune* was still regarded by the critics as "classically British film-making" and "Illustrated Brit Lit."[3] However, what I wish to explore in this essay is whether these assessments are so clear-cut and whether the Irish subject matter of the films does, in fact, make any difference.

There are two initial issues that might be raised in this regard. The first concerns the nature of the past that is represented. A part of the appeal of the heritage film is often its presentation of a social world that is apparently more settled and stable than that of the present. However, Ireland in the 1920s, especially during the War of Indepen-dence, is much less readily available as an object of nostalgia than the comparable period in England. The past, in this respect, is so obviously characterized by violence and social tension that it is clearly difficult to project it as any kind of golden age.

It is, of course, the case that heritage films (such as those set in India) do often chart the beginnings of the end of Empire, and thus the demise of the settled social order that British rule supposedly pro-vided. However, the past that they represent does tend, nonetheless, to be seen as sealed off from the present. As Higson suggests, history is rendered "as spectacle, as separate from the viewer in the present, as something over and done with, complete, achieved."[4] In the case of Ireland, however, this separation from the past is much more problematic given the continuation of the Troubles into a much later era and, thus, the unresolved character of the conflicts with which they deal. Thus, although Higson suggests the heritage film holds the spectator at a distance and refuses "the possibility of a dialogue or confrontation with the present," it is much more difficult, in the case of the Irish films, for the audience to avoid reading the presentation of the past in contemporary terms.[5] Thus, at least one critic felt able to claim of *Fools of Fortune* that its study of the effects of violence was, in fact, "more relevant than ever."[6]

The past that *Fools of Fortune* and *The Dawning* evoke, therefore, is not so much one from which violence is absent as one in which the main characters are unaware of, or are protected from, its existence. Thus, both films set up lapsarian narratives in which characters experience the disruption of their youthful idylls. In the case of *The Dawning*, the adolescent Nancy (Rebecca Pidgeon) is forced, through her encounter with the IRA fugitive Angus Barry (Anthony Hopkins), to see beyond her own sheltered existence and confront the realities of the war around her. As Barry puts it in the novel on which the film is based: "The first fact of life you have to grasp . . . is that life isn't full of sweetness and light and gentlemen standing up when ladies come into the room. On the contrary, it's full of violence, injustice and pain."[7] In the same way, *Fools of Fortune* charts the collapse of Willie's childhood idyll in the face of Black and Tan violence against his family. Thus, the film begins with the contrast between the young Willie (Sean T. Mc-Clory) at play, shot in imitation of a home movie, and his elder self (Iain Glen), recollecting his past and crying out in despair.

However, what differentiates *Fools of Fortune* from *The Dawning*, and complicates its portrait of the Big House, is its interweaving of different timescales and occasional blurring of the boundaries between different periods. The film spans over twenty years and repeatedly jumps back and forward in time (as well as between "objective" and "subjective" perceptions of events) in ways that are often quite confusing and that make it difficult to construct a temporally coherent "story" out of the film's "plot." Thus, as the reviews reveal, at least some critics were misled as to when Willie left for the west of Ireland (in some cases, mistakenly assuming this to have occurred before, rather than after, Willie's killing of Rudkin [Neil Dudgeon]).[8] Inevitably, this loss of a clear temporal order within the film undermines any sense of the past's "separateness" and reinforces the strong connections between the past and subsequent eras that the film is concerned to make. As a result, the film is unable to offer the past as a nostalgically desirable refuge from present conflicts as the present is so clearly infused with the past's influence. As Father Kilgarriff (Tom Hickey) explains to Willie, in lines eloquent of the film as a whole, "We can't understand the present without knowing something about the past. The past is always there in the present."

This confusion of temporal boundaries may also be linked to another deviation the film makes from the norms of the heritage film. In contrast to popular Hollywood filmmaking, heritage cinema is characteristically associated with tastefulness and restraint, and the offer of reassurance rather than shock. Indeed, director Pat O'Connor's earlier heritage film, *A Month in the Country* (1987), set in England in the aftermath of the First World War, was criticized by one critic precisely because of its "too self-consciously English" reliance upon "understatement and good taste."[9] *Fools of Fortune*, however, is much less restrained and much more inclined to veer toward melodrama. Thus, whereas William Trevor's original novel is characteristically taciturn and oblique, often relying on retrospective revelation, the film tends to be explicit and direct. It shows the burning of the Big House and subsequent killings which are only partly, and somewhat confusingly, described—from Willie's point of view—in the novel. Willie's repeated stabbing of Rudkin, which is barely described at all in Trevor's original, is also shown with a degree of gothic intensity. This sense of melodramatic excess is added to by the emotional pitch at which much of the action is played and the foreshortened and exaggerated sense of dramatic consequence which results, in part, from the film's excision of material from the novel, such as Willie's schooldays. This sense becomes particularly evident in the chain of events leading from the burning of the Big House at Kilneagh to the suicide of Willie's mother's (Julie Christie), the failed romance and decline into mental instability of Josephine (Niamh Cusack) and the hysteria and retreat into silence of Imelda (Catherine McFadden). These events, in turn, conform to the characteristic emphasis of film melodrama on female masochism and suffering. Thus, whereas Higson links the heritage film to an underplaying of emotion and avoidance of dramatic contrivance, this could hardly be said to be the case in *Fools of Fortune*.[10]

This gravitation toward melodrama may also be linked to the film's evolving perception of the past. Peter Brook has encouraged a view of melodrama as not simply a set of dramatic conventions but also as a mode of imagination: a mode that seeks to go beyond surface appearance and give voice to latent moral meanings ("the moral occult," in his terms).[11] The melodramatic excesses in evidence in *Fools of*

*Fortune* thus suggest an attempt to go beyond the fetishistic surfaces and depthlessness of the heritage film in order to uncover a deeper pattern involving the destructive hold of the past over subsequent generations and the resulting repetition of history. The characters of the film, in this regard, become the "fools of fortune" of the film's title: victims of a deadly "heritage" of violence, hatred, and revenge. As such, the film locks into a well-established tradition of representing Ireland and Irish history in terms of fatalism and this necessarily disrupts some of the appeal that the past conventionally holds for the heritage film (an effect achieved at a local level by the repeated cross-cutting between the young and old Willie).[12]

But if *Fools of Fortune* renders the nostalgia of the heritage film more awkward than usual, it does not escape it entirely, with the result that the film's attitude toward the past is still highly ambiguous. To some extent, this ambiguity is the result of a central tension within the heritage film as a whole. Although heritage films may be nostalgic for the past, they are generally unable to ignore the social divisions or injustices that were a feature of the periods in which they are set. However, as has been noted, while the plots of such films may contain elements of social criticism, these are characteristically undercut by the fascination of the films with the visually spectacular trappings of the past: the buildings, the landscapes, the props, and the dress. *Fools of Fortune* also inherits this problem. So, although it condemns the debilitating and destructive hold that the past possesses over the present it is nonetheless locked into a mode of representation that is characteristically nostalgic for the past and thus associates the film with the very problem it is attempting to overcome. Therefore, although the "message" of the film—the need to forget the past—distinguishes it from other heritage films, the film's use of heritage film conventions nonetheless prevents it from providing the forward-looking vision to which it aspires. There are a number of themes that illustrate this central tension.

For the film, as with the novel, the central means through which the past is perpetuated is language and the stories that language permits. As Celeste Loughman suggests of the original novel, the retelling of history not only preserves the past but also forces others to relive it.[13] Thus, Father Kilgarriff lectures Willie on the past and his family history, Willie's mother defies his calls to forget the past and keeps reminding him of his father's killer Rudkin, while Marianne (Elizabeth Mastrantonio) insists upon telling her daughter Imelda about her family's dark past. In this respect, one solution that the film seems to

offer as an escape from the past, and that also has links with melodrama (and the expression of the "moral occult"), is silence. In this respect, the relatively minor character, Declan O'Dwyer (Seamus Forde)
assumes a significant thematic function: he may not speak but he functions satisfactorily as a clerk and intermediary nonetheless. From this
point of view, the retreat of Imelda into silence may be seen to represent a break with the past and even—as in a film such as *Ascendancy*
(1983) where Connie (Julie Covington), the daughter of a Belfast ship-
yard owner, also ends up silent—a form of protest against the legacy of
violence.[14] However, if silence interrupts the continual retelling (and
hence reliving) of the past, it is also achieved at a high price: the descent of Imelda into madness. As her mother scathingly retorts to
Willie, "she's not a saint, she's insane." In this respect, Imelda's silence
is less an active resistance to the past than further evidence of its continuing destructiveness, the traumatic consequence of the historical
legacy imposed upon her.

As a result, the meanings suggested by the film's final scene are
highly ambivalent. In this scene, Willie and Marianne appear to be af-
forded a much earlier release from the past than in the novel, where it
takes another forty years for them to come together. The smile on "the
Blessed Imelda's" face as she watches beatifically over her newly re-
united parents also suggests a degree of optimism on the part of the
film. However, the break with the past that this scene attempts is only
partially successful. The enactment of the couple's reunion is not only
linked to Imelda's madness (the culmination of the cycle of violence)
but also, through its identification with Imelda's visions, involves a
further retreat into the past: both a recreation of the past as it was (the
house at Kilneagh) and a reimagining of a past as it might have been
(the couple at play in the garden). The repetition of Willie's look
straight to camera also suggests a circularity to the film's movement
and a failure to add a forward momentum. So although Imelda's visions may have become more benign than her earlier ones, they are
still locked into a yearning for the past and occur at precisely the moment when her parents are attempting to put the past behind them.

Imelda's retreat into silence may also be linked to her father's
withdrawal from his normal world following his murder of Rudkin.
Although in some respects a form of penitence, it is also a part of his
healing process, an apparent way forward from the dreadful violence
of the past (as is suggested by the movement away from images of
drunken despair toward those of repair—the thatching of the roof—
and cultivation—the tending of the garden). In the novel, Willie be-

comes an exile, adopting an itinerant lifestyle that takes him from South America to Italy. In the film, however, he remains within Ireland but travels to a remote island community on the western seaboard (Inis Oirr in County Galway). This is a significant change and brings a number of different associations into play. Although it does contain an element of the "otherness" that non-English landscapes may provide for the heritage film, the imagery of the island is nonetheless distinct from that of other heritage films and possesses a specifically Irish dimension. As has often been noted, the west and its association with bleakness and austerity has held a particular appeal for cultural nationalism for which it has provided a model of a distinctive and "authentic" Irish identity. As Gibbons has argued, it was also this vision of the west that Robert Flaherty's *Man of Aran* (1934) so successfully embodied and that guaranteed it a sympathetic response in de Valera's Ireland of the 1930s.[15] The scenes set in the Aran Islands in *Fools of Fortune* also occur in the 1930s, and it is hard not to associate them with similar scenes in *Man of Aran* (especially such scenes as the landing of the fish). The imagery that the film employs, in this respect, is therefore hardly "innocent" and carries with it a set of connotations that inevitably cut across the film's apparent intentions. So, although Willie's life in the west is, in dramatic terms, associated with a break with the legacy of the past, the imagery through which the drama is shown is, nonetheless, caught up in a backward-looking vision of its own: precisely that of a "primitive" Irish society that the forces of modernity have left untouched.

It is a vision, moreover, that is associated with a particular conception of Irish identity. As such it is of interest both for how it connects to the discourses of national identity (albeit English identity) that are often at the heart of the heritage film and to the problems within the past that the film identifies as propelling its series of disastrous events. As has already been suggested, the past invoked by *Fools of Fortune* is partly resistant to nostalgia because it has to be seen as flawed and unstable. Although it is the external threat of the Black and Tans that destroys the security enjoyed by the Quintons at the film's beginning, the family's downfall is also seen to have its roots in the family's own internal instability. This instability is linked, in particular, with their confusion of identities and allegiances. As William Trevor has observed, the Quintons "were people who were traitors to their class, and traitors to their background."[16] So, although they are the Anglo-Irish occupants of the Big House, they identify themselves as Irish; although they are Protestants, they count themselves the "friends" of the Catholics around them and permit the ex-priest Father Kilgarriff to live with them and educate young Willie. They also identify with the cause of Irish Home Rule and lend their support to the IRA. "I'm much obliged to both of you," says the mysterious IRA man (Ian McElhinney) as he bids farewell to Mr. and Mrs. Quinton. It is this visit to the house at Kilneagh by the IRA man, identified as Michael Collins in the original novel, which assumes a particular dramatic importance and triggers the film's fatal pattern. As he leaves the house he is watched by the informer Doyle (Sean McGinley) and is subsequently killed in a Black and Tan ambush; Doyle's body is then left hanging on the Quinton's land (where it is discovered by Josephine); the Black and Tans take their revenge by burning Kilneagh and, watched by Willie, killing Quinton (Michael Kitchen).

The significance of the Quintons' behavior is complicated. At a surface level, the film may be read as offering sympathy to characters whose liberal sentiments and sense of justice encourage them to attempt to transcend the prejudices of their age and cut across conventional social barriers. It is in this spirit that Gregory A. Schirmer links William Trevor's work with that of E. M. Forster, a favored source for the heritage film, and, in particular, his dictum "only connect."[17] But it is the tragedy of Trevor's stories that such attempts at connection invariably fail, and Schirmer also invokes Eliot's lines "I can connect/nothing with nothing."[18] There is a comparison here with *The Dawning* and the work of Jennifer Johnston more generally. As Christine St. Peter suggests, Johnston's stories revolve around characters "who take risks to reach across class/age/sexual/religious divisions" and create new "cross-caste relations."[19] In the case of *The Dawning*, it is Nancy, the adolescent girl, who is prepared to strike up a relationship with the much older IRA man on the run, Angus Barry. However, such alliances are condemned to be only temporary and are characteristically thwarted, as in the case of *The Dawning*, by the intrusion of external circumstance. As St. Peter suggests, "a sense of despair about finding 'solutions' to the Irish Troubles" is usually the result.[20]

In the same way, the Quintons' desire to cut across traditional social divisions in *Fools of Fortune* also proves unsuccessful and, given the film's melodramatic structure of fatalism, is also linked with a certain despair about the possibility of "cross-caste" relations. Indeed, it may be possible to go further and argue that it is not just the case that the film cannot envisage the success of such alliances but that, through its employment of a fatalistic structure, the film appears to suggest that it is the very confusion of identities and allegiances that the Quintons represent that is primarily responsible for setting the cycle of destruction in motion. In this respect, the film may be seen to be hankering for the very fixity of identities that it might otherwise be regarded as seeking to overcome. This hankering may be detected in the film's portrait of both gender and national identities.

It has already been indicated that a key factor in triggering the film's fatalistic plot is the apparent "treachery" of the Quinton family. It is also noticeable, however, that it is the Quinton women who are the most obvious "traitors." Three different generations of English women have come to live at Kilneagh and all have, in effect, "crossed over." The first of these was Willie's great grandmother, Anna Quinton, who was disowned by her parents, according to Father Kilgarriff, because "during the Famine she begged everyone to do something about the terrible situation." The second English woman was Willie's mother, Evie, who supports the Irish cause even more energetically than Willie's father. She tells the IRA man who visits their house that "we want to do anything we can to be of help to you" and is prepared to let him drill in the grounds and store arms (even though her husband is not). Marianne arrives much later, after Irish independence has been achieved, but nonetheless rejects advice to go back to England and develops a strong sense of the injustices visited upon Ireland by the English. From one point of view, these women may be regarded as sympathetic characters who attempt to break out of their inherited identities and reach out to others. From another perspective, however, these women may also be seen to have been the source of the Quintons' downfall precisely because their "love" of Ireland has also involved a kind of "treachery." As ambiguous figures, they may be related to the female characters in other heritage films that chart the decline of Empire (such as A Passage to India and Heat and Dust) where women function as the "weak link" of colonialism, cutting across traditional social divisions and undermining the masculine ability to rule successfully. In this respect, the liberal sympathy extended to the women and their behavior is tempered by a more brooding sense of its consequence.

Seamus Deane has observed how rare it is to find a novel about the Big House in which a "sinister element is absent" and identifies how, within a peculiarly Irish variant of Gothic fiction, the Big House is "transformed into a haunted mansion, beset by the ghosts of a guilty past."[21] Significantly, Kilneagh also has its ghost: in this case that of Anna Quinton, which, according to Father Kilgarriff, appeared shortly after her death. Her ghost is not seen but the film does repeatedly draw our attention to her portraits, which may be seen to keep alive her spirit within the Quinton household. It is therefore significant that Father Kilgarriff's opening speech to Willie about the importance of the past should be introduced via a tracking shot across a sideboard on which Anna Quinton's picture is seen standing. A larger portrait is seen subsequently (when Father Kilgarriff explains her history), and then again when it is engulfed by flames during the burning of Kilneagh. The import of this last shot is, however, ambivalent. On the one hand, it may be taken to signify the failure, in the face of violence, of the "love and mercy" which Father Kilgarriff suggests to Willie that Anna Quinton represents. On the other hand, within the structure of melodramatic fatalism that the film employs it is also a somewhat melancholy reminder of the destabilizing role that the Quinton women have played historically and the "fatal flaw" that this may be taken to represent (a "flaw" itself compounded, in the case of Evie and Marianne, by an "unnatural" readiness to condone male violence). So although the portrait of Anna Quinton is a part of Imelda's vision at the end, it is perhaps symptomatic of the film's conservatism toward women that the youngest female Quinton has now fallen silent and lacks the "voice" that her predecessors had possessed.

There is a similar conservatism in the film's treatment of national identity. For all its gloom, the original novel does at least offer a way forward to Willie which involves an outward journey and an internationalizing influence. In a sense, it offers a reimagining of Irish identity within an international frame. However, in the film Willie's journey involves a return from England to Ireland. In making this change, the film, as I have already suggested, provides a backward-looking vision of "authentic" Irishness that is at odds with the apparently forward-looking character of Willie's psychic development. But it also offers an image of a sort of "pure" Irishness, uncomplicated by external influence, that reinstates an ideologically weighted and relatively narrow conception of Irish identity, linked to the country, Catholicism, and the Irish language (and, given the noticeable absence of women, traditional forms of masculinity). In a sense, Willie resolves the identity crisis of the Quintons by immersing himself in a clear-cut Irish identity that dispenses with the very in-betweenness of the previously attempted "cross-caste" relations.

In conclusion, therefore, it can be seen that the central tension of *Fools of Fortune* is linked to its desire to temper the nostalgia that is generally a feature of the heritage film and to uncover the roots of contemporary conflicts in the past. However, despite its hostility to the past's influence, the film cannot break out of a backward-looking mode. This is partly the consequence of the conventions of the heritage film which, despite the film's manifest content, exert a pull toward the past. It is also the result of the film's particular inflection of the heritage film, which sets up a melodramatic structure of fatalism that undermines its ostensive concern to imagine a break with the legacy of the past. This inflection is particularly evident in the film's ultimately conservative vision of national and gender identities. Unable to envisage the successful construction of new identities, and the crossing of social boundaries that these would entail, the film ends up falling back on the relatively fixed notions of identity that, at one level, the film might otherwise be seen to be striving to overcome.

# 5

## *December Bride*
A Landscape Peopled Differently

### Martin McLoone

In the opening shot of Thaddeus O'Sullivan's *December Bride* (1990), the heroine, Sarah (Saskia Reeves), gazes out over the landscape to the sea beyond. She stands to the left, balanced on the right of the frame by a gnarled and unruly tree, its bare branches suggesting the winter cold of the film's title. It is a stylized, carefully composed shot, resembling a still photograph or a painting, more than a cinematic composition. This is an aesthetic style that recurs throughout the film and has the effect of drawing the audience's gaze toward the natural setting, almost to the detriment of the merely human actors whose drama is played out against its breathtaking beauty. Indeed, in composition after composition throughout the film, the human characters are rendered as "figures in a landscape," dwarfed by hills, seascapes and elemental skies. Even their dwellings—sturdy farmhouses and cottages dotted around the hills and the shoreline—are often shot from on high, pushing them into the landscape as if to emphasize the tenuous hold that culture seems to have over nature.

The opposition between culture and nature seems to lie at the center of the film's concerns. Thus, after the opening shot described above, there is an almost disturbing jump-cut to a close-up of Sarah, framed inside a gloomy interior, with the landscape visible through the doorway behind her. This claustrophobic framing, shot in a naturalistic style that creates a somber, unembellished atmosphere, is characteristic of the way in which the film's interiors are shot throughout. The slow, measured compositions of the exterior locations, combined with the tight compositions of the interiors, create a film that veers from the spectacular to the bleak and is suffused with a sense of barely disguised intensity and passion.

For O'Sullivan himself, the locations for the exteriors were crucial. The landscape around Strangford Lough in Northern Ireland, the set-

40

ting for the original novel by Sam Hanna Bell, provided "low undulating hills, which you can't find anywhere else in Ireland."[1] This may, or may not, be the case but the real significance of *December Bride* is not that it is set in a different kind of Irish landscape but that it is set in a landscape that is peopled and shot differently. This is a point that the director acknowledges elsewhere when he observes that had the film been shot in a more obviously recognizable Irish rural community, like Kerry, the form of the film would have been very different. "In *December Bride,* the humor is very dry, very Presbyterian, but in Kerry you would get a vast amount of irony which sometimes will antagonize you and other times make you laugh."[2]

The point here, of course, is that the representation of Irish Catholic communities is already caught up in a circuit of convention and tradition that raises certain expectations in the audience and that puts a particular onus on the director to respond to in some way. The strength of O'Sullivan's film is that it creates another community altogether and locates it within a recognizably Irish setting already deeply significant through this circuit of convention and tradition. The opening sequences, for example, show Sarah and her mother, Martha, leaving their cottage to go to work as servants in the Echlin household. The iconography of rural life that these sequences reveal is very traditional, and the framing of the thatched cottage within a bountiful nature carries connotations of a romantic rural community most closely associated with Catholic, nationalist Ireland. The fact that the community inhabiting this landscape is a Presbyterian, Unionist one, is an important break with this dominant tradition. The film, then, gives cinematic expression to a community largely absent from traditional representations of Ireland and in doing so, raises many interesting questions about these traditions themselves. In addition, *December Bride* also displays, in an unusual and complex manner, themes and concerns that are characteristic of the best of recent Irish cinema, and the manner in which O'Sullivan choses to frame and shoot the landscape becomes an important element in these themes.

The seemingly obvious opposition within the film, that between culture and nature, provides a useful way into discussing these themes and of assessing the importance of the film to a very contemporary debate about culture and identity in Ireland. To explore this, though, it is necessary to recast this opposition somewhat, for at its core, the film is concerned more with the relationship between "community" and "the landscape," a much more complex relationship than the romantic opposition indicated by culture and nature.

## Reimagining the Community

The narrative of the film is concerned with the relationship that Sarah forms with the Echlin brothers, Hamilton and Frank (Donal McCann and Ciaran Hinds) after their patriarchal father is drowned in a boating accident. The relationship is scandalous to the tight-knit and God-fearing Presbyterian community that surrounds the Echlin farm, and when Sarah gives birth to a son, she not only refuses to marry one of the brothers, she also refuses even to name which one of them is the father. The community's outrage is felt and expressed most directly by the Presbyterian minister, Mr. Sorleyson (Patrick Malahide), and a key dramatic tension in the film is that between Sorleyson and the strong-willed Sarah. What is clear from this confrontation is that Sarah's rejection of the church is both rational and uncompromising. Her actions are motivated by a desire to construct another pathway for herself beyond that which Sorleyson, her own mother Martha, and the community at large expect her to follow. She attempts, in other words, to reimagine and reinvent the family unit and through this, to construct "community" beyond the hypocritical norms of her Presbyterian environment. Her inspiration for this project was the Echlin patriarch, Andrew (Geoffrey Golden).

In a number of important early scenes, Andrew's influence on Sarah is made clear. For a start, it is obvious that, despite his church attendance, Andrew is a strongly independent thinker, making his own mind up about what aspects of his Presbyterian community he is prepared to accept. He belongs to this community only on his own terms, a point which Sarah comes to realize when she quizzes him about his rejection of the Orange drums and the Twelfth of July celebrations. Her own resolve is strengthened when Andrew invites Sarah and Martha to share the Echlin family pew in the church, despite the improprieties and minor scandal that this entails. At this point, as well, Sarah realizes the considerable material benefit that accrues from her relationship to the Echlin family—the social advancement from mere servant to family member is one that she will not give up easily, and it reinforces for her the fact that the "community" also maintains a rigid class structure. However, the final turning point for Sarah is the manner of Andrew's death. As he, Sarah, and the two sons cling to the overturned boat in the surging storm seas of the lough, Andrew calculatedly sacrifices himself so that the three younger people can survive.

For Sorleyson, the fact that Andrew was "taken" and the others were saved is confirmation of God's plan and divine wisdom. Sarah's first confrontation with the minister is to reject emphatically this passive religiosity. Andrew chose to sacrifice himself, bending nature and destiny to his own purpose for the greater good of his family. It is this example of a strong and determined free will, this rationality, that will guide Sarah in the construction of her own alternative community. In the end, Sarah controls her own fate and dictates the terms under which she will give up her sexuality and her domestic labor to the Echlin brothers. This inevitably means that her reimagined family/community will be a utopian one, operating outside the strictures of religion and the community at large and bringing down, especially upon herself, the disapproval, the envy, and eventually the wrath of her neighbors.

The outcast nature of Sarah's utopian community inevitably creates tensions within. In the early years of her reimagined community, these revolve around the confused desires of the younger brother, Frank. It is he who first starts a sexual relationship with Sarah and later, when he realizes that he must share her with his older brother, Hamilton, his attitude to her becomes increasingly ambivalent. Much more so than the easygoing Hamilton, Frank realizes that the relatively independent patriarchy of his father has been replaced by the tradition-challenging matriarchy of Sarah. This realization isolates him even more so from the wider community and it is this isolation more than mere sexual jealousy, which leaves Frank morose and discontent. The effect on Frank is important for understanding the true nature of Sarah's rebellion. It is essentially a woman's revolt against a male-ordered world and one in which a male definition of religion holds sway. Frank is part of Sarah's new order, but the sacrifice he must make, in terms of the conventions and expectations of the community outside, proves difficult.

In an important scene that initiates the events that will lead to his tragedy, Frank stands outside the farmhouse listening to the sound of distant Orange drums echoing from the hills. Hamilton joins him and listens for a second before remarking casually that it will soon be the Twelfth again. Frank responds with the word that sums up the cause of his surly malaise. "Community," he mumbles. As a way of rejoining the wider community, he attends the Twelfth of July celebrations and, despite the obvious disapproval and hostility of his neighbors, attempts to establish a more conventional relationship with a young local woman. The result is a savage beating from her family which leaves him crippled, and resigned to Sarah's community, for life.

However, despite Frank's surliness, the film makes it very clear that Sarah's version of community does provide a freedom and a joy that is clearly lacking in the wider Presbyterian neighborhood. In the early first flush of the threesome's unconventional relationship, it is clear that all three are happy and fulfilled in a way that offends, challenges, and disturbs the locals, again revealed to the audience largely through the effect on Sorleyson. He hears the laughing sounds of abandonment echoing off the hills around the Echlin place while he is fishing out on the lough, and if he is disturbed by Hamilton's laconic disregard for religious custom, he is profoundly unhinged by Sarah's more straightforward challenge to his religion and his religious authority. This occasions a crisis of faith in himself and increases his own sexual frustration to a point where he indecently touches Sarah during his last attempt to persuade her to conform. Sarah's effect on the minister seems to confirm the subversive potential of her attack on the oppressive religion around her. It is almost as if her example has a liberating potential for even the most committed churchgoers, if only they too could be less passive and less resigned and were prepared to take charge of their own destinies.

Sarah's rebellion, then, is a rational response to the circumstances that oppress her, both as a woman and as a servant. She has invented her own community and taken charge of her own life, defeating the oppressive forces of religion, community, and class into which she was born. However, like Andrew before her, there comes a time when she too must make a sacrifice to save the younger generation. Eighteen years later, her own grown-up daughter, also called Martha, is approaching marriage herself but her future within the wider community depends on Sarah sacrificing her principles and belatedly getting married. "He let go," young Martha reminds her mother, referring to the sacrifice that initially inspired her rebellion. Sarah eventually accepts that this is so, but there is no sense of defeat in the way in which O'Sullivan chooses to shoot Sarah's "December wedding."

In the church, Sarah is flanked by Hamilton and Frank, and as the three of them look back defiantly at the camera, it is impossible for the audience to know which brother Sarah is actually marrying. Indeed, the look of triumph on Sarah's face recalls the similarly defiant sacrifice of Barbara Stanwyck at the end of King Vidor's *Stella Dallas* (1937). For both women, the sacrifices that they must make to secure their daughters' future is the final culminating triumph of a lifetime struggle against conformity. For if Sarah, like Andrew before her, must make a sacrifice for the sake of the young, then she will do so in a coldly rational manner, again organizing her own destiny, bending fate and nature to her own purpose. The triumph of "normal" society here, as in *Stella Dallas,* is a decidedly ambivalent one. In rewriting the ending of Sam Hanna Bell's original novel and shooting it in such a defiantly ambivalent manner, O'Sullivan maintains the thrust of Sarah's rebellion right to the end. (In the original novel, the ceremony is performed by Sorleyson's son; Sarah's son, young Andrew, is the best man, and since Frank is dead, Sarah marries Hamilton. The younger generation, thus, reestablish the community's oppressive norm over their revolutionary elders, even if old Sorleyson still feels that Sarah is unrepentant. Thus, although the author is, himself, aware of the ambiguity in Sarah's final capitulation, nonetheless, Bell's original novel suggests a much more resigned and defeated Sarah than O'Sullivan's version does.)

**Landscape and the Picturesque**

This human narrative is played out, of course, against a landscape magnificently framed and shot by O'Sullivan and his cinematographer, Bruno de Keyzer. As the director himself said, "I don't like to see a background become just a backdrop. If you chose a background carefully and photograph it properly, it's got something very important to say."[3] The landscape in *December Bride* does indeed say something very important, not just about the community that peoples and molds it, but also about the traditions of representation, especially cinematic representation, to which it refers. It is in this regard that the film taps into a set of complex debates about culture and identity in contemporary Ireland and offers a radical break with dominant cinematic representations of Ireland and the Irish. It is in this regard, as well, that *December Bride* most closely echoes the concerns of the best of recent Irish cinema.

The representation of landscape in Ireland has been the subject of much contemporary cultural debate. For example, Luke Gibbons has attempted to locate cinematic representations of Ireland within a historical context where Irish landscape was used to promote a particularly European romantic sensibility. At its most simple this sensibility was promoted by a European intelligentsia in flight from the urban, industrial world of the eighteenth and nineteenth centuries and especially from its darker aspects of poverty and blight. Ireland, and other peripheral parts of Europe like Scotland, Wales, and the Lake District in England, became favored destinations for this first breed of romantic tourists, and their representations of the landscape were to prove extremely influential. Thus Ireland "came to embody all the attributes of a vanished pre-industrial era." To achieve this, the romantic gaze elided all references to work, especially the productive labor of the Irish themselves.[4]

Of course, this romantic gaze was essentially an outsider's perspective, and even if the gaze became, as we shall see, "internalized" by the Irish themselves, especially in pursuit of nationalist objectives, it nonetheless remained essentially an outsider's point of view. There is, however, an added complication in this romantic gaze. Eamonn Slater has traced a duality in the romantic view of landscape that is important for understanding the subtleties of this outsider's perspective. Following Edmund Burke's original philosophy of aesthetics, Slater traces the way in which, historically, descriptions of landscape in Ireland drew a distinction between the "beautiful" and the "sublime." "Beauty was smooth, rounded, and it induced feelings of peace and well-being. Sublime on the other hand was rugged, awful and produced feelings of horror and fright."[5] The consequence of this duality is that the landscape painter, or the accounts of the landscape to be found in the writings of the "romantic tourists" of the nineteenth century, recomposed the landscape to fit a preordained convention of the "picturesque," in which the beautiful and the sublime were both contained within the one frame. The harmonious beauty of the landscape, often involving idealized peasants engaged in tranquil work, was contrasted with the elemental and awe-inspiring beauty of nature in the wild. The effect of this contrast, for both Gibbons and Slater, is that the sublime, with its intimations of the "divine," reminded the viewer of the transient nature of life and the impermanence of human culture. The appearance of old ruins in many of these representations was a symbolic rendering of the sublime's awesome power. As Gibbons argues, these ruins "conveyed a sense of an irretrievable past, their relapse into a state of nature underlining the transience of human achievement."[6] This transience is crucial, since the romantic sensibility is predicated on a rejection of the rational, scientific mind and its arrogant presumption that it can control and shape nature to its own end. Thus the manual, productive labor of the rural economy is elided; in Slater's phrase, the landscape is "delabored"[7] (and where humans appear in the picturesque, they are rendered as harmonious parts of the beautiful; at one with nature rather than at odds.)

Within this explanatory framework, Gibbons has reassessed the cinematic tradition of representing the Irish landscape and has located the influence of both antiquity and the nineteenth century in the "hard" and "soft" primitiveness of films like Robert Flaherty's *Man of Aran* (1934), John Ford's *The Quiet Man* (1952) and David Lean's *Ryan's*

*Daughter* (1970). Gibbons is sensitive to the subtle variations in Irish romanticism, and especially to an "ability of certain strains of Irish romanticism to conduct a process of self-interrogation, to raise doubts at key moments about their own veracity," a process that he identifies most obviously in *The Quiet Man*. His appropriation of Panofsky's distinction between "hard" and "soft" primitivism is to explain how the romantic gaze can be turned on the harsher aspects of rural life just as easily as it can on the more beautiful. What is significant about the traditional approach, whether the "hard" and "soft" primitivism of Panofsky's distinction, or the "beautiful" and the "sublime" of Edmund Burke, continues to be, as Gibbons argues, "the absence or elimination of the principle source of rural poverty and degradation: the experience of work and exploitation, the social reality of labor in the face not only of material scarcity but also of profound political and economic divisions."[8]

Turning again to the cinematography of *December Bride*, we can consider with interest how the outsider's gaze of O'Sullivan and de Keyzer fits within this explanatory framework. The opening shot of Sarah framed by the dead tree can now be reassessed. In one regard, this can be read as a fairly typical rendering of the sublime—the defoliated tree intimating the immutable power of nature to whose will even Sarah must bend. This reading is reinforced when the audience later realizes that the figure is the older Sarah, contemplating the decision that she must make to secure young Martha's future within the very community that she herself so completely rejected. However, in this reading of the shot, the rewritten ending of the film becomes crucial. The triumphant looks on the faces of the three rebels considerably qualifies the power of the sublime—right to the end, Sarah's reimagined community struggles against elemental nature, attempting to impose a rational framework on the otherwise mysterious workings of the "divine." The marriage scene at the end of the film is linked thematically to the drowning of Andrew and both of these to the studied intensity of this opening shot. Another interesting point emerges here.

In his review of the film, Mark Kermode regrets the fact that the drowning sequence is so obviously shot on a set, "which makes a jarring contrast with the otherwise exceptional lighting and photography. It is the one moment when the televisual shortcomings of *December Bride* are unfortunately apparent."[9] Leaving aside for the moment the unexplored nature of these "televisual shortcomings," we note Kermode's observation recalls similar comments that Luke Gibbons has made about the intensely cinematic style of John Ford. Noting that even in his most panoramic films, like *The Searchers* (1956), Ford was apt to shoot scenes in an obviously false set, Gibbons argues that similarly, in *The Quiet Man*, key scenes are shot in stylized studio setups. This is most obvious in the graveyard scene when nature responds with wind and rain to the passionate embrace of the two lovers—the wild, uncontrolled power of the sublime is rendered in the most obviously fake backdrop. "In the depiction of landscape, the 'social' . . . is given the full benefit of outdoor locations . . . while the 'natural,' paradoxically, is relegated to a twilight zone of props and studio sets."[10]

It might be argued that something similar happens in the drowning scene in *December Bride*, and it mirrors the deeper significance of Andrew's sacrifice. When nature is seemingly at its most sublime, at its most awesome, it is shot in a most obviously contrived manner. As in the painterly, studied composition of the opening shot, the sublime exhibits the designs of culture, in a manner that mirrors Andrew's and Sarah's attempt to impose their own designs on fate and destiny. In a similar way, Sarah, with the collusion to some extent of Hamilton, reconstructs Andrew's funeral to resist the imposition of Sorleyson's interpretation of "divine will." As Mark Kermode aptly notes, if Sarah's final wedding scene is shot more like a funeral than a wedding, the implication is that she, again with the collusion, this time, of both Hamilton and Frank, recodes this from her capitulation to an inevitable "divine will" to her own triumph over its seemingly immutable course.

It is important, too, to consider in more detail how the film characteristically shoots the outdoor locations, for here as well, we can identify a style that goes some way toward responding to the dominant romantic gaze. In an early sequence, Sarah has brought a jug of water to Andrew and stops to talk to him for a few moments. The scene is shot on the shoreline, the camera alternating its position from in front of and behind the couple, framing them against the doorway of the boathouse behind or through the doorway to the seascape in front. Their conversation is interrupted by an irritated Frank, who yells, "We're working here!" This is, indeed, the characteristic stylistic device of the film. There is hardly an outdoor scene that is not concerned to show the inhabitants of this beautifully shot landscape engaged in the daily grind of productive labor—gathering and drying kelp from the shore (as in this scene), harvesting and building haystacks, gathering potatoes, feeding the farm animals, plowing and sowing, or performing a host of fixing and mending chores. The rural economy is clearly part of this landscape—or, more accurately, this landscape has been molded by the productive labor of the rural economy. The exploitation and class tensions of this economy are clearly signposted—in Sarah's and Martha's social advancement, intimated in their promotion to the Echlin family pew, and especially in the materialistic motives behind Sarah's rebellion. As she says to her mother, in rejecting pleas to rejoin the church and its community, "All your lives you slaved for rich folk. Well, I'll not do it!"

*December Bride* is, therefore, concerned to reinsert into its representation of Irish landscape precisely those elements that the romantic gaze characteristically elides. As such, it already makes an important response to the traditions of representation that have for so long dominated cinematic Ireland. But there are other interesting complexities to the film that are worth teasing out and this brings us back to the notion that this is a landscape peopled differently.

## The Native and the Colonial Gaze

On occasions throughout the film, O'Sullivan interjects a series of painterly compositions similar in style to the opening shot. In these a character is framed in a somber sunset against the darkening skyline and hills. In a traditional romantic composition, these breathtaking shots would indicate the awesome power of the sublime, but here they are severely qualified by the fact the human character is beating furiously on a Lambeg drum, which echoes off the hills around him. These shots are open to a number of interpretations. The drumming, both seen and heard, can be read as the defiant sounds of human culture, imposing itself on the sublime, asserting the stubborn presence of humanity in a romantic composition that traditionally has elided its presence, both visually and aurally. It can also be read as the recalcitrant sounds of Ulster Protestants, imposing their presence and beating out a reminder of their historical triumph over this land, over these hills, over the wilderness of nature. From the point of view of Catholic, nationalist Ireland, of course, these drums represent the strident militancy of sectarian politics—an image that contrasts the sublime with the ridiculous, the beautiful with the socially threatening.

It is tempting, however, to see these shots as an ironic play with the traditions of representation that have dominated the image of rural Ireland for many years and that have been central to a nationalist sensibility since the Literary Revival and beyond. Luke Gibbons has pointed out that it was the "hard" primitivist variant of the romantic gaze that attracted cultural nationalists to the west of Ireland, and their attachment to the "sublime," as much as to the "beautiful," allowed them "to recreate the harsher aspects of rural life in the image of an ascetic, elemental Christianity."[11] A key dialectic, then, in Irish cultural nationalism, as in the romantic sensibility generally, was that between urban industrial society and the harsh or harmonious aspects of the rural. In Irish terms, the rejection of England was a rejection of industrial modernity and with it, the industrial culture of Protestant Belfast. The insertion of Orange drums and a devout Presbyterian community into the Irish landscape is a reminder that the industrial workers of Belfast are only part of the Protestant story and that the romantic nationalism of Catholic Ireland is only part of the story of Irish landscape.

It is equally tempting to see in *December Bride* another ironic reference to the canon of Irish romantic imagery, this time in the form of the cinema's most famous and most enduring representation, *The Quiet Man*. This can be seen in the sequence in which Frank attempts to reestablish his contacts with the wider community at the Twelfth of July celebrations. The scenes are shot outdoors on the shores of the lough, their flat, sandy beaches and low, undulating sand dunes recalling the horse race locations in Ford's film. This time, though, Ford's gallery of Irish stereotypes is replaced by bowler-hatted Orangemen, sober farmers, and a strident orator. The communal farce of the horse race is replaced by the earnest marching and the banners of the Orange parade.

The allusion to *The Quiet Man* goes further than this, however. Just as the horse race in the Ford film contains a bizarre courtship ritual, so too do the communal celebrations of the Presbyterians in *December Bride*. In *The Quiet Man*, the young women of Innisfree put up their bonnets on poles at the finishing line, the winner of the horse race having the choice of whose bonnet to collect and whose favors to pursue. In *December Bride*, the young women put up their shawls which are then laid on the ground equidistant from the young men seeking their favors. At a given signal, the men charge for the these shawls from opposite sides, the winner being the one who emerges from the ensuing scrum with the shawl held aloft. In *The Quiet Man*, Mary Kate has to be cajoled into putting up her bonnet and similarly, in *December Bride*, Molly, the young woman who has taken Frank's fancy, has also to be coaxed into putting up her shawl.

The sequences diverge from this point on, of course. In the Ford film, the bonnet sequence, typical of the general atmosphere of play and comic deceit that dominates the film, is an elaborate ruse that has been designed by the community to bring the lovers together. In O'Sullivan's film, Frank's success in the shawl ritual eventually leads to his crippling injuries and his final withdrawal from the community. But the similarities, both in setting and in narrative progression, are striking enough to alert the audience (especially the audience familiar with *The Quiet Man*) to the fact that a wholly different people have wandered into a recognizably Irish film. The aesthetic, political, and ideological implications are profound. To this extent as well, despite Mark Kermode's worries about the "televisual" genesis of *December Bride*, it is one of the most intensely *cinematic* of recent Irish films—not just because of its careful and studied cinematography, but because its complex themes are presented visually as well as narratively and because its wonderful cinematography is itself engaged in a debate precisely about the cinema's traditional representation of Ireland and the Irish.

There is nothing, however, particularly unusual in this strategy of peopling the familiar landscape of Ireland differently, or of attempting, through the cinema, to explore the sense of Irish identity promulgated by dominant cinema. This has been an effective strategy of a number of Irish filmmakers in recent years. Joe Comerford, for example, has peopled the west-of-Ireland landscape with a host of outsiders—aimless drifters, cynical politicos, the wretched and the dispossessed, and, in *Reefer and the Model* (1988), a studiously perverse symbol of Mother Ireland in the pregnant, ex-drug addict, ex-prostitute character of The Model herself. And Comerford too, like Bob Quinn, Pat Murphy, and a number of other filmmakers over recent years, has attempted to explore the aesthetic and ideological implications for contemporary Ireland of cultural nationalism and its legacy, especially as it impinges on cinematic representations of Irish landscape. What is unusual is that *December Bride* takes this exploration of Irish romanticism into the North and into the community most implacably opposed to its cultural legacy. This then begs the question—who is speaking in the world of *December Bride?* If the drums represent the presence of humanity in the wildness of nature, whose voice are we invited to hear?

In his discussion of Irish landscape and the picturesque tradition, Eamon Slater identifies two romantic "gazes," those of the colonializing landlord and of the tourist, both outsiders' perspectives. As we have seen, the ideological result of the picturesque is the exclusion from culture of the native people who actually live in the landscape. In opposition to these outsiders' gazes, Slater posits the notion of the "oral interpretation of (gazing on) the landscape, which is essentially a collective or native gaze." [12] This native gaze can be achieved only if the natives who actually live and work productively on the land are allowed to be seen and are allowed to speak. Indeed, by adopting the romantic sensibility, cultural nationalism—largely a product of the Irish urban intelligentsia anyway—adopted an outsider's gaze and effectively silenced and rendered invisible the actual working inhabitants of rural Ireland, and this was one of its shortcomings.

In *December Bride,* by rearticulating the visual and narrative frames of Irish landscape and by relocating the people and the productive work they are engaged in, back onto the land, O'Sullivan comes close to establishing this native gaze. The irony is that this native gaze is, in terms of nationalist Ireland, the gaze of the original colonists, the planters who dispossessed the native Irish and whose victorious conquest is beaten out so defiantly each Twelfth of July. The harsher political realities of this paradox are alluded to in the film, through Sarah's bitterly sectarian animosity to her Catholic neighbor, Bridie Dineen. There appears to be some secret female antagonism between these two women, one that the laconic Hamilton in particular cannot fathom. For Sarah, it is undoubtedly sectarian in origin, and the one aspect of her Presbyterian community that she finds hard to reject is its anti-Catholicism. This sectarian subtext is not pursued in the film and it hangs, like a cloud, over Sarah's utopian community.

When challenged about the sectarian aspect of Sarah's character, O'Sullivan noted that

> I didn't want it to be about that, I wanted to be in it, but not about it. I read these books about the Twenties, Thirties and Forties in Presbyterian communities in the north of Ireland, and they all lived together very well, provided there were certain demarcation lines. Interestingly, women were more prejudiced than the men. The men understood one another, having worked together in the fields, but the women didn't circulate in this way, so they seldom met Catholic women. When they did, they gawked at one another as if they were unreal. The truth was there, but I didn't want it to dominate the film.[13]

The film's setting in the past is, perhaps, crucial in this context. There is always the possibility that by setting the film in a lovingly recreated past, and imagining a false past that never existed, the harsher aspects of the contemporary are avoided. Even if the sectarian politics are left unexplored, nonetheless, the fact that this aspect of the past is there is important. *December Bride* is not about recreating a nostalgic view of the past, rather it is concerned to explore how, *in the past,* another future, warts and all, was dared to be imagined. In the context of Northern Ireland and its contemporary politics, the question of who speaks in and for this landscape is a matter of intense controversy. *December*

*Bride* does not relapse into a false past to offer an easy solution to the question, but its complex reworking of some of the familiar cultural signs of this debate is peculiarly apt and challenging in the contemporary context.

## Conclusion

The strength of *December Bride* lies not in the way in which it asserts or promotes an ideological or political resolution. Its strength lies in the way in which it explores and probes the dominant modes of representing rural Ireland and the extremely complex ways in which it challenges and unhinges many of the assumptions that lie behind these. Like the tentative but daring nature of Sarah's reimagined community, *December Bride* pushes beyond convention and custom and attempts to reimagine the cultural map of Ireland and the Irish differently. In peopling a recognizably Irish landscape with a Northern Protestant community, ultimately the film challenges sedimented assumptions about both.

# 6

# Revising Resistance

*In the Name of the Father*
As Postcolonial Paternal Melodrama

## Margot Gayle Backus

> You cannot live on love and on love alone,
> so you sail 'cross the ocean, away 'cross the foam
> to where you're a Paddy, a Biddy or a Mick,
> good for nothing but stacking a brick . . .
> where the summer is fine, but the winter's a fridge
> wrapped up in old cardboard under Charing Cross bridge.
> And I'll never go home now because of the shame
> of the misfit's reflection in a shop window pane.
>
> —Christy Moore
> "Missing You"[1]

## The Figure of the Irish Immigrant in the United Kingdom

In contemporary Irish discussions of emigration, whether in newspaper articles and editorials, in scholarship, or in contemporary songs or everyday discussions, the most prevalent, emotionally charged figure for Irish emigration is the image of a homeless male manual laborer sleeping rough on the streets of London and dreaming of the day when he can save enough from his paltry wages to return to Ireland. The bereft figure of the displaced Irish worker, forced to seek marginal employment within the robust metropolitan economy that his own nation's systematic depletion underwrote, parallels two earlier staples of Irish melodrama identified by Declan Kiberd: "the orphaned youth and the discredited priest."[2] Like the fates of these earlier figures, that

I am grateful to John Roche for his invaluable feedback in response to multiple drafts of this essay. I am also indebted to Purnima Bose, Sharon Delmendo, Linda Dittmar, Barbara Harlow, Susan Harris, and Linda Mocejunas for their help with this project at various stages.

of the Irish emigrant in England emblematizes the dispossessed condition of a colonially displaced culture "deprived of both God and of the consolations of a received code."[3] At the same time, more than the spoiled priest or the orphan, the image of the homeless (male) emigrant bears explicit, literal witness to the ongoing crisis that processes of colonization and economic and cultural imperialism have precipitated in Ireland.

In Jim Sheridan's *In the Name of the Father,* and in Hanif Kureishi's *Sammy and Rosie Get Laid,* which I will discuss in this essay's second half, intrapsychic and material transformations of male postcolonial immigrants in Great Britain enact a particular conception of space. Simultaneously public and private, these transformations are brought about through a series of correlated spatial and interpersonal modulations that suggest a particular negotiation between public and private constitutions of the male postcolonial self within a colonial family romance that is at once intrapsychic and international in its scope.

In both films, memory—of personal experiences, the formative experiences of communities, and national histories—has a decidedly political valence. Memory's political potentials are explored in these films through the spatialized enactment of what could be termed "paternal melodramas," in which the conventions of more familiar nationalist melodramatic allegories such as *Cathleen ni Houlihan* or *The Dreaming of the Bones* are reinvented. In these contemporary reenactments of the nationalist melodrama, memory no longer passively retrieves and secures the subject's Oedipal relationship to the imaginary body of the mother (country); instead, memory actively redefines the subject's relationship to his own corporeal and psychic masculinity through the incorporation of symbolic paternal figures embodying the range of masculinities that emerged over the course of colonization, anticolonial resistance, decolonization, and the consolidation of postcolonial imperial relations.

These intrapsychic and interpersonal renegotiations of masculinity are spatially determined. Both films emphasize epistemological barriers within the first world that suppress the circulation of particular ideas, memories, and connections within the public sphere. In both films, radical subjective transformations are initiated through the unintentional transgression of epistemological barriers within the metropolis by postcolonial immigrants. These epistemological barriers, which invisibly structure First World space, are similar to those that separate opposing social spaces within the colony, a spatial dispensation that Frantz Fanon has referred to as the "colonialist topography."[4]

For Fanon, the colonialist topography specifies the asymmetrical and mutually opposed and opaque spaces that are brought into being within a colonized society at the onset of colonial domination, and which over time come to reinforce and institutionalize colonial relations within that society. As contemporary theorists such a Fredric Jameson have pointed out, however, the physical distance between the metropolis and the colony gives rise to an insuperable epistemological barrier for metropolitan subjects analagous to the absolute epistemological barrier within the colony that Fanon originally theorized. In his essay "Modernism and Imperialism," Jameson argues that:

> colonialism means that a significant structural segment of the economic system is now located elsewhere, beyond the metropolis, outside of the daily life and existential experience of the home country, in colonies over the water whose own life experience and life world . . . remains unknown and unimaginable for the subjects of the imperial power. . . . no enlargement of personal experience . . . no self examination . . . no scientific deductions on the basis of the internal evidence of First World data, can ever be enough to include the radical otherness of colonial life, colonial suffering and exploitation.[5]

Jameson's analysis emphasizes the emergence of absolute perceptual and conventional divisions between the imperial power and its colonies. As Jameson contends, this perceptual and conventional schism between the imperial core and the colonized periphery is, over time, incorporated into the First World. It would thus appear that an epistemological cleavage originally brought about by colonial violence at the imperial periphery has come to permeate and structure representation and perception within the metropolis. As these films suggest, an epistemological barrier between the world of the "settler" and that of the "native" persists within the First World even after colonial subjects relocate to the metropolis. The persistence of such a colonial, Manichean epistemology within the metropolis helps to account for the affect-laden power of the image of the displaced postcolonial worker in the metropolis for both First World and Third World audiences.

For audiences within previously colonized countries, on the one hand, the image of the homeless postcolonial emigrant renders visible the otherwise obscure injuries of neo-imperialism. This paradigmatic emigrant is typically male because his image also emblematizes imperialism's less quantifiable undermining of a normative (male) national identity. Within the metropolis, on the other hand, the presence of the dispossessed postcolonial subject calls attention to Fanon's colonialist topography as it exists, both concretely and metaphysically, within the First World. Because, as Jameson argues, the overall system of imperial appropriation, with its historical roots in colonial domination, are invisible from within the metropolis, the homeless postcolonial worker is constituted within the metropolis not merely as an alien, but as the harbinger of an alien and threatening epistemology that cannot be contained within the existing social order.

In the two films I consider in this essay, male postcolonial immigrants are involuntarily thrust into silenced, repressed lacunae within the British social order in which physical agency is nullified, but in which repressed personal and historical memories emerge, and new epistemological and interpersonal connections consolidate. In both films, liminal metropolitan spaces equivalent to the colonial shantytown operate as sites of opposition within which alternative narratives of paternity, and, beyond this, new inter- and intrasubjective relations may be forged. Both films thus bear out and extend the global significance of Fanon's assertion that the colonial topography, characterized by an absolute, binary dichotomy between the "lawful, orderly" settler town, and the "chaotic, ineffable" native village or shantytown, is in itself a potential anticolonialist weapon.

## Postcolonial Paternity

Just as the Victorian maternal melodrama "represent[s] social problems as emotional problems,"[6] thereby acknowledging certain structural problems while simultaneously recontaining them within an ahistorical domestic sphere, Jim Sheridan's In the Name of the Father exhibits an ambivalent impulse to recontain Guildford Four defendant Gerry Conlon's struggle against state-sponsored injustice under the rubric of "paternal melodrama." The film's unstable oscillation between the private and the public, the personal and the political, however, could also be interpreted as symptomatic of a more widespread problem involving the representation of masculine agency, or, indeed, identity, within a postcolonial context.

Many theorists, beginning with Fanon, have identified a fundamental Oedipal stumbling block that arrests the growth of colonized males: under colonial rule, fathers cannot bequeath to their sons an authorizing "Law of the Father" of which they are themselves bereft.[7] The title of Sheridan's film suggests that in order to visually narrativize Gerry Conlon's story, his character's masculinity must be secured through the successful negotiation of an Oedipal process of identification and individuation that is, if Fanon is correct, seldom if ever successfully negotiated in real life except in times of revolution.[8] As a medium, film may have demanded a teleological maturation sequence despite the fact that Conlon's autobiography, *Proved Innocent,* upon which the film is loosely based, does not. In his autobiography, Conlon's narrative beguiles its reader through the voice that tells it; throughout the autobiography, Conlon remains ironic and often playful, maintaining an appealing writerly detachment from the horrific events he relates. At times he addresses the reader quite earnestly and forcefully, but at these moments it is the momentary modulation in tone that moves the reader, not an accompanying sense of any cumulative, fundamental change in his character.[9] In Sheridan's film, by contrast, for technical reasons, the two modalities that characterize Conlon's autobiography, the ludic and the politically persuasive, must be separated out as stages in an overall process of maturation. Since the viewer must *see* Conlon undergoing exemplary instances of the brutality the book describes at greater length, but at a safer remove, Sheridan must separate the ludic Conlon and the more somber, earnest Conlon or risk undercutting the film's polemical potential. Hence, Sheridan's Conlon begins, as the film opens, as an exaggerated rendition of the ironic, irreverent man whose voice predominates in *Proved Innocent,* and grows in painful fits and starts into the earnest, politically angry but focused man whose voice is also present throughout the autobiography. This radical shift from modally produced effects to narratively produced effects gives rise to a masculine "coming of age" thematic entirely foreign to Conlon's preoccupations in *Proved Innocent;* many of the film's father/son elements discussed in this essay are not even implicit, let alone explicit, in the autobiography. Nonetheless, the film's father/son dynamics shed considerable light on the very real problem of postcolonial masculine identity and self-representation, and could even be seen as offering insight into the emergence of a new political praxis.

In the film, Conlon, a troubled Belfast youth, emigrates to London and is falsely accused of having helped to plant the IRA bomb that demolished a crowded pub in Guildford on 5 October 1974. After extorting fabricated confessions from Conlon and three of his associates: Paul Hill, Paddy Armstrong, and Carole Richardson, a British acquaintance, British officials go on to arrest and falsely convict Conlon's father, Giuseppe Conlon, and his aunt and cousins, the Maguires. The external strictures imposed on Conlon by the British state place him, in the film's symbolic economy, in charged, quasi-filial relationships with three older men: his father, Giuseppe, Joseph McAndrew, an invented, partly stereotypical version of an IRA bomber, and Charlie Burke, the homeless immigrant who spoke with Conlon and codefendant Paul Hill in a London park on the night of the bombing. The film's title alludes most directly to Giuseppe, a lifelong pacifist whose lungs, damaged by long-term exposure to lead paint in the Belfast shipyards, completely collapsed during his years of wrongful imprisonment. Conlon's efforts to attract public attention for the Guildford Four and the Maguires are an extension of the campaign Giuseppe started, and are therefore carried out "in the name of the father." Moreover, the film turns thematically on his loss of Giuseppe, first symbolically and then literally, to British imperialism. However, Joseph McAndrew and Charlie Burke complement Giuseppe's position in the film as an emblematic Irish father. Between the three of them, Giuseppe, Joe McAndrew, and Charlie Burke represent a range of possible male subject positions as these have been culturally inscribed in the course of British colonialism: pacifist and martyr, republican rebel, and disenfranchised victim.

In order to retract his loyalties from the system that has laid waste to his community, rent apart his family, tortured and wrongfully incarcerated him and destroyed his father, Gerry Conlon must psychologically break with Giuseppe's pacifist politics, which are, at early stages in the film, represented as masochistic. By adopting a militant, anticolonial father figure who models an alternative, oppositional relationship to British imperialism, Conlon breaks away from an immobilized father/son dyad in which he has repeatedly sought a legacy of masculine identity from a father whom he could only construe in terms of lack. In order fully to break out of the space of imperial invisibility to which the imperial order has relegated him, however, Conlon must ultimately remember and then recover Charlie Burke. Ultimately, Burke's characteristics—his abjection, his powerlessness to ameliorate his own condition, and his nurturing posture toward Conlon—are elaborated through changes in the representation of Giuseppe following Conlon's break with Joe McAndrew. Through a process of what could be termed recovery, in a historical as well as a psychoanalytic sense, undertaken at the behest of his biological father and guided by the political analysis and organizational gifts of a second paternal mentor, Conlon disinters a phantasmal third father, and thereby claims his own political agency and authoratively establishes a public voice.

As an Irishman of the same generation as the pacifist Giuseppe and the militant IRA volunteer who claim Conlon's conflicted loyalties, Burke represents a subset of Irish-born Catholic men that surely out-

numbers both pacifists and IRA volunteers. His complete political disempowerment within the British social order, almost unto the point of
erasure, is far less appealing than either the moral power inherent in
Giuseppe's stance, or the military and analytical power of the IRA volunteer. Conlon, however, is completely reliant upon Charlie Burke, as a
child is upon a parent, for Burke is the only living person whose story
can set him free.

Burke represents a third "father" to Conlon in the sense that he
most saliently embodies affective forces that both Joe McAndrew and
Giuseppe (at first) deny: the deep, intergenerationally transmitted humiliation and abjection that are colonialism's inescapable legacy. To
uncover and place himself in relation to Charlie Burke's story represents an alternative to either the passive and even masochistic impulse
to *ignore* colonialism and hope that it will go away, or the (largely unconscious but powerful) fantasy of a decisive military victory that will,
by punishing British transgressions, restore the dominant, invulnerable ideal of masculinity that British colonial domination simultaneously instilled and maimed within Irish men. This ideal of an
invulnerable masculinity was held out by the British as the valorized
criterion by which a people proves itself qualified for self-rule. Both
the pacifist and the warrior, when these positions have become all-
encompassing identities rather than chosen strategies, seek to *resolve*
the problem that is represented by Charlie Burke without ever actually
having to acknowledge it. In situating Charlie Burke as the key to
Conlon's own damaged political and, in a sense, personal selfhood, the
film structurally suggests that Irish men must confront the abjection
that the domination-obsessed British Empire has taught them, with
good reason, to abhor.

In the film, Charlie Burke represents Conlon's (and the audience's)
first shocking glimpse of the conditions of many Irish immigrants in
England. As such, Burke serves as a Tiresias figure, initiating both Conlon and the audience into a previously invisible underworld, and introducing us to that world's unfamiliar and harrowing logic. As a witness
whose testimony corroborating Conlon's alibi is repressed, Burke also
literally embodies the wrongs that the British state has committed
against Irish people, and which it seeks both to "forget" and to deny.

Burke's largely unrepresented story constitutes a ghostly parallel
to that of the Guildford four. In the case of the Guildford Four, three
male Irish emigrants and a British woman who had the misfortune of
befriending them had their lives, along with the lives of their families,
systematically dismantled and permanently derailed by a British jus-

tice system ravenous for scapegoats in the wake of the Guildford bombing. Burke, a ghostly foreshadowing of Conlon's own probable future before the British police intervened, was, like Conlon, victimized by British society because he was in the wrong place at the wrong time, and because he was Irish. As with Conlon, the British social order condemned Burke to a state of living death characterized by isolation, hard labor, and, as in the case of Conlon's own father, slow death. Because of his poverty and his undocumented status, Charlie Burke, and his confirmation of Conlon's alibi, were easily "forgotten" by the British state. The British officers who questioned Burke "forget" their meeting with him, thereby attempting to erase his words, perceptions, and his very existence from the public memory. Conlon, by contrast, remembers Burke because of what he represents—his own probable future as a displaced, unemployable "paddy" subsisting on handouts and refuse on the streets of London.

In its final scenes, the film's drama turns on the tangible and public production of Charles Burke, the Irish "father" whose existence and experiences must be made manifest if Conlon himself is to be "proved innocent." The visual character of lawyer Gareth Pierce's sensational production of the image of Charlie Burke in the climactic trial scene correlates with an established pattern of references to the gaze throughout the film. This pattern begins when Gerry verbally attacks Giuseppe, when he unexpectedly appears in the holding cell in which Gerry is being detained, for having shamed him when he saw him foul the ball in a football game for which he received a medal. Giuseppe's gaze is constituted as a shaming intrusion into his son's life, an intrusion that is now repeated in adulthood as his petty crimininality and his powerlessness within the British legal system are abruptly and unexpectedly placed before his father's eyes in excruciating detail. The tropos of the gaze recurs in the moments following McAndrew's sadistic (and entirely fabricated) assault on the Chief Warden, Barker, when Gerry demands to know why McAndrew can't look at him. McAndrew responds by staring levelly at Gerry, who dismisses his gaze by saying "I know how to look people in the eye without blinking too." In this scene, both the masochistic inability to look and the sadistic, contemptuous stare of uncompromising opposition are connected with shame and guilt. The averted gaze McAndrew initially exhibits is connected with Giuseppe's pattern of avoidance, his retreat to his cell in response to harassment by the other prisoners, his moral scrupulousness in the face of a brutally inequitable system, and his denial of the institutionalized prejudice that destroyed his lungs while he worked in the paint sheds of the Belfast shipyards, the only job a Catholic could get. Gerry's dismissal of McAndrew's unblinking stare, by contrast, constitutes it as a sort of trick that can be mastered; McAndrew's stare represents a projection of internal shame outward onto an external object that is constituted as utterly contemptible. Gerry knows this because he externalized his own guilt and shame over the fouled ball in a similar manner, by writing the name GIUSEPPE in the dirt and urinating on it.

These various strands are brought together in the first conversation between Conlon and Gareth Pierce, following Giuseppe's death. This scene is pivotal to the film's narrative construction, as the events of the first two-thirds of the film are retrospective, drawn from Conlon's taped testimony to Pierce, whereas the death of Barker and the subsequent reorganization of Giuseppe's and Gerry's relationship initiates a movement into an unframed "present tense" in which Gerry Conlon's "own" story, in which he appears as an agent rather than a passive object within the larger system, begins. In this interview, the first in which Conlon speaks directly to Pierce, Conlon tells her to keep the pressure up, saying "They fouled the ball and they're as guilty as sin. Believe me, if there's one thing I know about, it's guilt. Keep looking them in the eye and it's going to reveal itself."

This scene completes a process that began with Conlon's reconciliation with Giuseppe following his break with Joe McAndrew. During their remaining time together, Gerry comes to accept his father's weakness, and to cherish his peculiar point of view; he tells Pierce "he always saw the good in everyone." Significantly, Giuseppe is no longer depicted as averting his gaze; instead, like Charlie Burke, he now seems privy to aspects of the system that are invisible except from a position of abjection. Giuseppe's abject yet privileged perspective is exemplified in a poignant scene in which Conlon and his comrades play in the snow in the prison yard while Giuseppe, too sick to leave his cell, minutely observes an act of unsanctioned kindness: a guard, acting outside the parameters of his institutional role, is tenderly feeding a pigeon. In a voice-over Gerry recalls, "I tried to wave to him, but he was looking at something else." In accepting and embracing both his father's and his own frailty (he wordlessly accepts Giuseppe's judgment that he hasn't the maturity to take care of himself, let alone his mother), Conlon recognizes his own pervasive sense of shame and guilt as systemic and cultural rather than as symptomatic of individual failings. He accepts that the overriding need to win at *something* that led him to foul the ball did not originate in his own defective morality, but on a culturally inscribed sense of shame stemming from a pervading sense of emasculation for which the British state, not Giuseppe, bears the ultimate responsibility. As he tells Pierce, it was, in effect, the British state that fouled the ball. He recognizes that state's historical guilt in the guilt and shame that he himself has carried throughout his life. As his comment "if there's one thing I know about, it's guilt" suggests, the guilt he has struggled to deny, repress, or project represents a valuable form of inside knowledge, constituting his most effective weapon against a system that has cast him as intrinsically guilty and inadequate throughout his life.

The trajectory of Conlon's self-construction in this film suggests that the wounds of centuries of economic exploitation and degradation have left their traces within the subjectivity of Irish men. As Conlon's delicate negotiation between paternal paradigms suggests, only when the abjection that post-Enlightenment models of an autonomous masculine self so abhor is named, made visible, and perhaps ultimately embraced as an inevitable component of an alternative and less domineering mode of masculinity, will the humiliation imposed on Irish men through the double binds of British imperialism be resolved, and the haunting ghost of a vitiated, colonized paternity at last be laid to rest.

### Liminal Social Spaces in *In the Name of the Father* and *Sammy and Rosie Get Laid*

A pattern resembling the emergence of Charlie Burke in *In the Name of the Father* is also enacted in Hanif Kureishi's *Sammy and Rosie Get Laid*, another film exploring the lives of postcolonial immigrants in London. For the second half of this essay, I will use the narrative trajectory of *Sammy and Rosie Get Laid* to highlight narrative elements in *In the Name of the Father* that are relevant to my exploration of postcolonial paternity in the latter film.

Like *In the Name of the Father*, *Sammy and Rosie Get Laid* imaginatively explores events surrounding a violent contemporary eruption of Britain's colonial past while focusing on a troubled father/son relationship. The film's preoccupations with British justice, postcoloniality, and grassroots resistance parallel those of *In the Name of the Father*. Set during the Tottenham riots, which erupted in 1985 after British police broke in upon and shot dead an Afro-Caribbean grandmother, *Sammy and Rosie Get Laid* explores the reactions of Sammy, a British-born Pakistani accountant, and his wife Rosie, to the return to England of Sammy's father, Rafi. Rafi is a Pakistani politician on the run from his own past, a former anticolonial militant whose Oxbridge education and privileged class position led him to supplant the colonizers he had helped to oust rather than to dismantle the colonial power structure altogether. The narrative of emergence that is enacted in *In the Name of the Father* via the restoration of Charlie Burke into the public memory is paralleled in Kureishi's film by the growing visibility and corporeality of the ghost of a tortured and murdered union organizer who follows Rafi throughout the film. This expressionistic emergence of a corpse who, by the end of the film, is enabled to speak the truth of his own death, parallels the realist emergence of damning documentation concerning Rafi's past unearthed by Rani and Vivian, two Third World (Pakistani and Afro-Caribbean) lesbians. Unlike the film's other characters, who accept the vague, idealized narrative of postcolonial paternity that Sammy and Rosie construct, Rani and Vivian distrust the admiring outline of Rafi's political career conjured by Sammy and Rosie's unconscious, ambivalent wish for an admirable, worthy anticolonial father.

Whereas Charlie Burke and the mutilated ghost that stalks Rafi exist within a sphere of silence and invisibility equivalent to that of the colonial shantytown, Irish and Afro-Caribbean prisoners in *In the Name of the Father,* and punk and Rastafarian anarchists in *Sammy and Rosie Get Laid* both occupy more spatially concrete First World renditions of the shantytown: the imperial prison system, and the squatters encampment. These spaces both represent epistemic voids within the larger social order; both are spaces whose inhabitants' lives are invisible within the larger social order; in both cases, enormous wrongs can be committed against the inhabitants of these First World shantytowns with impunity. Yet, both of these spaces also provide privileged sites for the transmission of information and for the negotiation of alliances between members of heterogeneous postcolonial populations.

In *Sammy and Rosie Get Laid,* the anarchist village, base of operations for a band of modern day Diggers who transform the desolated landscape of a burned-out, inner-city lot into a flourishing garden of material and intellectual production, provides a site for the realization of a quasi-Oedipal friendship between Rafi and Danny, an androgynous, radicalized, Afro-Caribbean immigrant who also goes by the name Victoria. Rafi's identification with the British ruling class is so powerful that when he walks down the tree-lined avenues of a posh suburb with Danny, whom he met when Danny protected him from injury in the midst of a riot, he asks with genuine bewilderment why people are staring at them. Danny answers matter-of-factly "because they think we're going to steal their things." It is significant that outside the boundaries of the anarchist village, Rafi sometimes finds himself at odds with Danny, whom he constitutes at times as both a racial Other and a sexual threat.

For his part, Danny clearly seeks a teacher and a father figure in Rafi, whom he mistakenly assumes, as a veteran of Indian decolonization, to have been a Gandhian. In this moment of political and personal crisis (the woman the police killed "was like a mother" to him), he finds himself undecided on the crucial question of violence, and he is willing to admit his uncertainty, saying that he understands the appeal of violence, but worries about "what will become of all the beauty." Like Rosie, Rani, and Vivian, Danny also represents a new breed of theorist. That he is the product of a new generation and a new set of postcolonial conditions is made explicit in his bald statement to Rafi: "we have a kind of domestic colonialism here, because they don't allow us to run our own communities." The centrality of this statement to the film's overall concerns is evident in the film's penultimate scenes, which, in the razing of the anarchist village, brutally illustrate the precise extent to which the urban poor lack control over their own communities.

Through Rafi and Danny's discussions, parallels between Thatcher's England and colonialist India emerge, eliciting Rafi's dawning awareness of his own culpability, which is linked to his growing identification with the cause of the British underclass. He tells Danny: "If I lived here, I would be on your side." The anarchist village also constitutes a privileged site relative to history, for it is here that Rafi's dishonorable past, which is, like other dishonorable elements of the British colonial legacy, repressed within the larger society, finally catches up with him.

In *In the Name of the Father*, the space of public silence is a highly contested site; the silenced prisoners struggle to break out of it, first with a riot and a banner, and later with the burning toilet paper that commemorates Giuseppe's death, and that constitutes the prison community itself as its audience. British authorities, by contrast, work through close surveillance of prisoners and the careful policing of the circulation of information, both to oversee events and interactions within the prison, and to control the circulation of information from within the prison to the outside.

In both films, the opaque, contested spaces within British society represented by the anarchist village and the prison enable members of postcolonial First World groups to make contact with others who are struggling or who have struggled against similar forms of oppression in the Third World. In both, the atmosphere in which such encounters occurs is distinctly Dionysian in climate, typified by a throwing off of erotic and gendered prohibitions that signify a release from Oedipally inscribed notions of "decency" and familial and national "loyalty."

In *In the Name of the Father*, Gerry's departure from paternally transmitted norms of masculinity and national loyalty is marked by the scene in which he first drops acid with some of the Afro-Caribbean prisoners. They belittle British imperialism by parodying its operations as they devour an LSD-soaked cardboard puzzle depicting a map of the British Empire. Conlon and his comrades are enabled, in the course of the scene, to laugh at British imperialism, thereby divesting it of its symbolic power. Moreover, this scene contains the film's only brief acknowledgement of the potential for homoerotic bonds between prisoners. A fellow prisoner briefly caresses Conlon's chest, a gesture that Conlon receives with laughter, then rebuffs. This glimpse of homosexual eroticism's potential for advancing the cause of anticolonial solidarity is brief and muted. It is notable, however, because it occurs in the scene that precipitates Conlon's repudiation of Giuseppe's self-abasing morality and pacifist politics and initiates his movement into alternative, extrafamilial bonds.

Rafi's suicide at the end of the film similarly represents the culmination of Dionysic forces precipitated by contact between the present and the past, and between heterogeneous groups and histories within the anarchist village, a space outside the imperial order in which conventional social and chronological boundaries break down. His encounter with the tortured and murdered union organizer represents a violent "return of the repressed" (here, a double entendre). It occurs when Rafi seeks shelter in the anarchist village after he has been rejected by his former lover, Alice. Alice confronts Rafi with the ways in which his failure to return for her as he promised has left her life in a state of immobilized stasis by showing him the trunks that she had packed as a young woman, that have remained packed and gathering dust in her basement for decades. The breaking down of an epistemological boundary between his experience of his life and its consequences, and Alice's experience of it, is realized through the concrete, empirical nature of the evidence with which Alice confronts him. As the ghost that pursues Rafi stands ominously nearby, Alice makes visible to Rafi the humiliation, grief, and disappointment his casual abandonment of her in pursuit of political power has left her to deal with.

The sequence of events leading up to Rafi's death symbolically establishes his dissolution as corresponding to Fanon's call for the necessary "abolition of one zone," (either the settler's town or the native village), "its burial in the depths of the earth or its expulsion from the country." [10] Rafi undergoes a genuine epiphany when he chooses to defy the bulldozers that are razing the shantytown, and out of this insight he chooses to kill himself. His action indicates that he at last realizes the enormity of his own co-optation, the extent to which he has himself come to occupy the subject position of the colonizer. Insofar as Rafi is a metaphor for the Pakistani ruling class, his death coincides with Fanon's call for the dissolution through violence of the colonialist structure. His death may, however, have additional resonances. In the film, Rafi is associated with patriarchy as well as with both sides of colonialism. His first line of dialogue is to say that he associates England with "the smell of cunty fingers." His position as a sexual exploiter of women is as central to his placement within the film as is his position as a torturer of dissidents. Rafi's choice to commit suicide, rather than to redeem himself through a rebirth into a new, oppositional subject position in the London streets, may represent his understanding that under patriarchy the only available subject positions are victim and victimized, and that he is unable to step outside of this dichotomy save through the extinction of consciousness.

Significantly, both films depict a moment of filial identification with father figures who represent the military struggle against colonialism as prerequisite to a broader political coming to consciousness among young postcolonial immigrants in Britain. Both films represent armed struggle as a necessary component of the larger struggle to break down colonial divisions within the imperial center, as well as between the metropolis and the colony. Both films also, however, represent the military phase of decolonization as having a serious potential for outliving its own usefulness, and for ultimately perpetuating, at both the intrapsychic and national levels, models of masculinity and state authority that will serve to replicate the colonial topography rather than dismantle it if they are not supplanted by alternate models.

*In the Name of the Father* has been legitimately critiqued for its inclusion of a wholly fabricated scene in which Joe McAndrew turns a flame thrower on the chief prison warden in an act of pure, unilateral, and unstrategic malice. Critiques of this scene are certainly in order, especially when we consider the scene's resounding reaffirmation of a larger network of demonizing representations of the IRA within a world communications system that discovers the (always already) demonized IRA at the bottom of any and all political positions that resemble the IRA's socialist, nationalist agenda. The weird 180–degree pivot that this scene negotiates, however, also seems to respond to a deeper logic than that which director Jim Sheridan acknowledges when he claims that the scene was put in to prevent the film's being censored in England. This scene could also be seen as negotiating crudely what *Sammy and Rosie Get Laid* negotiates more gracefully: the problem of how to represent a sharply defined postrevolutionary anticolonialism that takes as its work the breaking down of epistemological, rather than merely material divisions between past and present, metropolis and colony, and postcolonial and "British" societies within Britain.

The endings of both *In the Name of the Father* and *Sammy and Rosie Get Laid* each suggest their own symbolic resolution to the problem of the collusion between patriarchal and colonial power relations, and the ways in which patriarchal power relations serve to reinstate colonial power dynamics even after ostensible decolonization is complete. In both cases, this resolution grows out of the space within the film that corresponds to the Fanonian shantytown. In both cases, it is within this space that symbols of the patriarchy, in one case Rafi, and in the other case the body of the warden, and simultaneously the moral credibility of the IRA commanding officer, are destroyed. Although neither film is able to depict the long-term deconstruction of the colonial topography within the metropolis, both seem to suggest that only from within the boundaries of the shantytown, and through the eyes of its denizens, can we honestly assess our own subject position, as Rafi does, and see clearly the truth that lies behind hegemonic mystification.

Both films seek to provide alternative models of male anticolonial resistance. Danny, the androgynous, nonviolent revolutionary who concerns himself with what will happen "to all the beauty" in the case of civil war, and who is depicted as parenting a male child, represents a new male revolutionary subject position that places itself outside of colonially instated binary oppositions through the expression of traits that are socially constructed as "female." Danny is, in effect, a representational revolutionary who challenges middle-class conceptions of property and identity, as the Diggers did, through a mode of living that violates bourgeois conventions at every turn. *In the Name of the Father* also shifts its emphasis onto representation by suggesting a covert but necessary connection between the injustices committed against Gerry Conlon, and the fate of Charlie Burke and thousands like him whose lives have been similarly derailed through ongoing spirals of British imperialism.

## Representational Resistance

In recent postcolonial cultural production, in works such as Jim Sheridan's *In the Name of the Father* and Hanif Kureishi's *Sammy and Rosie Get Laid,* the sentimental popular image of the homeless immigrant in the imperial metropolis is being redeployed. In these films, postcolonial immigrants in London appear as inassimilable traces of a colonial elsewhere that British society conventionally denies. Like ghosts or other gothic figures, postcolonial subjects in these films are simultaneously invisible to the society in which they live and move, and invested with a supernatural, disruptive *presence* that cannot be accounted for by or contained within that society.

The presence of formerly colonized subjects in Britain, working at the most exploitative jobs or homeless on the streets of London, bears mute witness to the long-term detrimental effects of colonial domination on formerly colonized countries. The relegation of postcolonial immigrants within England to literal and imaginary shantytowns allows most British citizens, however, to ignore or deny the significance of postcolonial immigration to England by rendering postcoloniality itself invisible. This invisibility also, however, renders the surveillance of the shantytown's inhabitants difficult, and thus makes the shantytown an important locus for connections between interlocking resistance movements. *In the Name of the Father* and *Sammy and Rosie Get Laid* thus call attention to the colonialist topography within the First World as a space in which and out of which the goals and terms of modern day oppositional praxis are currently being renegotiated.

As both films suggest, indigent postcolonial workers, caught between British injustices in the former colonies and British injustices in England, are as utterly if not as dramatically wronged as were the Guildford Four. For these immigrants, however, no legal or social recourse exists; letter-writing campaigns are seldom organized to expose and rectify the injustices that shape their lives, no mass-scale social movement has specifically taken up their case. Nonetheless, their stories, words, and persons constitute potent and embarassing evidence of unjust relations between Britain and its former and current colonies, as well as within Britain. Charles Burke and other men like him are symbols, in other words, of what the British Empire would rather forget. He is simultaneously the symbol of what young Irish men and women, enmeshed in intergenerational webs of British economic and military domination, must remember if their lives are to be restored to historical and social coherence. As *In the Name of the Father* suggests, the truths of these silenced and forgotten lives must be heard and made visible if justice is to be done, and if a system of imperial denial that perpetuates a splitting off of masculine identity into either masochistic or sadistic extremes, is to be permanently dismantled.[11]

# 7

# "Different Countries, Different Worlds"

The Representation of Northern Ireland
in Stewart Parker's *Lost Belongings*

## Jennifer C Cornell

Throughout the 1980s, representations of Northern Ireland in British
television drama impeded efforts to end the violence by encouraging a
form of "psychological withdrawal" from the North on the part of the
British public. By depicting Northern Ireland not only as "alien" but as
in fact antithetical to Britain in every way, these representations complemented a political agenda that sought to deny responsibility both
for creating the conflict and for failing to bring it to a swift conclusion.
Like the British government of the time, these narratives placed the
burden of conflict resolution on the Northern Irish themselves by
blaming the continuing violence on the refusal of the two communities
to make a sincere effort to resolve their differences.

Depictions of intractable Irish tribalism had been used for centuries to justify, and thereby elicit acquiescence for, social policies and
the perpetuation of British rule. By the mid-1980s, however, the Irish
economy was beginning to blossom, and Hibernia, depicted in Victorian caricature as a cowering maiden, had become both a coherent foreign power in her own right and, increasingly, much like Britannia, her
former defender. Moreover, given its apparent willingness to shoulder
the economic, social and political burden of the North, the Irish Republic could no longer be held responsible for encouraging or inflaming
the conflict there. Seen in light of these improvements, the deliberate
erosion of public interest in the North on the part of the British elec-
torate could be viewed as part of the larger effort to prepare the
ground for the eventual military and political withdrawal—in other
words, the end of British rule in the North.

With the signing of the Anglo-Irish Agreement in 1985, relations
between the two governments entered a new phase, culminating in the

71

1994 declaration of ceasefires by paramilitaries on both sides, and the subsequent inclusion of former extremists in official debate over the future of the North. Military and political withdrawal now seem inevitable, if not imminent. Yet despite the results of polls in Great Britain and Ireland that consistently show support for such a policy, its implementation remains a delicate matter. In the course of the thirty-year conflict, British taxpayers have invested heavily in Northern Ireland, both emotionally and financially, and an abrupt or overly eager departure now would be unseemly, given the number of casualties involved. Moreover, the British rhetoric of refusal to compromise with terrorism, at its most strident during Margaret Thatcher's regime, necessitates a cautious approach, not simply to save face, but also to serve as a warning to those ethnic minorities and political extremists whose relations with Britain remain less than cordial. With a degree of psychological distance among the British public, however, an apparent change of heart could be more acceptable, and could prevent withdrawal from being perceived as defeat.

Among those whose perceptions could be important are those Northern Irish who wish to retain their position within the United Kingdom. Given that historically, roughly 60 percent of the native population has been suspicious of any diminution in British presence, the people of Northern Ireland, no less than the British public, must be prepared psychologically for the possibility of withdrawal, if for no other reason than to prevent the bloodbath which many have feared could ensue should the troops be pulled out of the North. In keeping with the presentation of Northern Ireland as unlike Britain (and in tune with recent sociopolitical initiatives, such as those of the Cultural Traditions Group, which have sought to encourage Protestants to recognize and accept their "Irishness"), British television drama about the North has denied, whether explictly or by implication, the Unionist community's sense of self-identity, dismissing it instead as a kind of false consciousness.[1] Though it may be less an expression of solidarity than a pragmatic concession to political reality, the Loyalists' decision to match the Republican ceasefire could be viewed as evidence of the success of that approach.

## Stewart Parker's *Lost Belongings*

One of the most convenient vehicles for illustrating the way in which Northern Ireland and the Northern Irish are typically represented in contemporary British television drama is *Lost Belongings,* Stewart

Parker's six-part series for Thames Television (1986). Parker's heroine, Deirdre, is the daughter of a Catholic woman and her Protestant lover, for whom Deirdre's mother leaves her husband and son. When her parents die in a house fire, the young Deirdre is taken in by her father's brother, Roy Connell, a brutish man who constantly reminds her of her illegitimacy and torments her with his sexual advances after his wife dies. At seventeen Deirdre meets Niall, a Catholic boy with whom she begins a secret affair. When her uncle learns of the relationship and becomes abusive, Deirdre escapes with Niall to England, where he and his brothers are planning to launch their band.

In London Deirdre visits Alec Ferguson, a celebrated classical musician, who as a boy was a close companion of Deirdre's cousin Craig, Roy's eldest son, now a high-ranking member of the Loyalist Ulster Volunteer Force, or UVF. Having immigrated as a teenager to escape the violence, Alec has made every effort to distance himself from his roots. Toward this end he has married a Belgian and cultivates a crowd of international friends, one of whom is Gretchen Riley, a left-wing American archaeologist whose father is a fundraiser for the IRA. It is through her father's activities that Gretchen first meets Hugh, Deirdre's half-brother (from her mother's first marriage) and a high-ranking member of the IRA, who, Deirdre learns while in London, has recently escaped from prison and is in hiding somewhere in Northern Ireland. Also among Alec's associates is Simon Hunt, a failed English journalist with a liking for booze and marijuana who latches onto Niall's band and takes up residence with them in London.

The band has little success in England, however, and is forced to return to Belfast. Deirdre is fearful, but for Niall's sake agrees to go back. They move in with Lenny, Niall's eccentric cousin, who plays the saxophone, throws outrageous parties, and works intermittently for the BBC. Shortly after their return, however, Deirdre is kidnapped by her uncle with the help of Craig and his paramilitary associates. Back in London Alec's wife arranges for him to perform at the Ulster Hall, and so, under obvious and bitter protest, he too returns to Belfast.

Meanwhile Hugh has contacted Gretchen, who agrees to a rendezvous in Fermanagh. On her way there she meets Simon (who traveled to Belfast with the band) and Teddy Ridell, an old school friend of Simon's now working undercover for the SAS. With Simon and Gretchen as unwitting participants, Teddy and Hugh engage in a game of intelligence and counterintelligence that culminates in Hugh's ambush and execution at the hands of his own associates in the IRA.

Imprisoned by her uncle for days in a darkened room, Deirdre goes mad. She sets fire to the curtains and severely burns her hands; later, recovered physically but mentally unbalanced, she stabs her uncle with a pair of scissors and takes to the streets of Belfast, searching for Niall. When by chance she stumbles into Hugh's funeral procession, the discovery of his death sends her over the edge. As Alec prepares for his gala performance, Deirdre continues to run through the city, until she is knocked down by a van. At her request the driver takes her to her parents' old house, now occupied by Chinese students. There she faints, and the students send for the police. On its way to the hospital the car is ambushed by unidentified assailants and the driver is shot dead. Pregnant with Niall's child, Deirdre suddenly miscarries, staggers to the steps of a nearby church and collapses, while Alec responds to calls for an encore with earsplitting clangor.

It would be easy to ridicule *Lost Belongings* without reference to its themes or implications. In an effort to create symbolic figures who embody the complex and often contradictory factors that shape loyalties and identity in Northern Ireland (Deirdre is at once both Catholic and Protestant, for example, yet her native illegitimacy makes her a member of neither community), Parker has peopled his narrative with characters whose personalities are insufficently developed, whose histories are implausibly interwoven, and whose paths too often literally cross. Burdened with subplots that have no obvious bearing on its denouement, the narrative relies heavily upon coincidence, contrivance, and lengthy passages of exposition in which one character explains his or her relationship with another character to a third. Its themes lack subtlely, its imagery is often heavy-handed and predictable, its symbolism is repetitive and frequently trite.

Perhaps because of these shortcomings, the series presents images of Ireland—particularly in contrast with images of England—that are typical of contemporary British television drama. In keeping with the so-called official perspective on political violence,[2] for example, the conflict is either depoliticized (by personalizing or emotionalizing the motivation for violence), criminalized by revealing the objective of violence to be personal gain, whether material or psychological, or simply delegitimized by portraying the proponents of violence as either hoodlums, assassins, or utopian idealists. Few distinctions are drawn between Loyalist and Republican violence; in fact, an equivalence between the two is suggested by the very structure of events and relationships in the play: Deirdre's cousin Craig has his counterpart in her half-brother Hugh, Hugh's address to the "Sons of Patrick" in America harks back to an earlier scene in which Roy addresses the members of his local Orange Lodge, and the armed and hooded Loyalist paramilitaries who hijack Niall's van are indistinguishable from the Republican gunmen who ambush Hugh. Loyalist characters however, are distinguished by their lack of even the pretense of political motivation. When Roy uses the UVF to abduct Deirdre and wreak vengeance on Niall and his brothers, he is motivated not by political conviction but by sexual obsession. They are also more blatantly ignorant, uncouth, and barbarous than the Republicans portrayed: Roy, for example, toasts the Queen and addresses his lodge less than one hour after he rapes his neice.

As a representative of the traditionally oppositional perspective (he blames the British for making the war "ugly" and for creating conditions under which "terrible mistakes" are occasionally made; he argues with Gretchen about the efficacy of armed conflict, and repeatedly offers a political explanation for the Republican campaign—which she and others at once reject), Hugh, though less overtly bestial, is no more sympathetic a figure than Roy. Gretchen dismisses his arguments as empty, outdated rhetoric which attempt to mask the reality of the violence ("Tell that to your victims," she retorts when they first argue in America, repeating the phrase when they meet in Fermanagh). Hers is a particularly damning assessment, given that she shares his political objectives. Once Hugh's tutor in the Maze Prison, Gretchen later recalls her impressions of him then. He had "a great mind," she tells Alec's wife Regine, but "in one crucial part [it was] completely unteachable": that part was "full of blood, and blood can't think, you see. It can only cry out for more and more blood." The episode concludes with a sinister image of Hugh, his face half-hidden in shadow, crosscut with scenes depicting Republican assassinations for which, it is implied, Hugh has been responsible. The meaning of the sequence is clear: whatever his politics, whatever his potential for something better, in the final analysis Hugh is a killer.

Commonplace ("It was only a bomb," Niall soothes when Deirdre jumps at the sound of an explosion), ubiquitous (even the dance where Deirdre's parents first meet is marred by a vicious sectarian brawl), and unavoidable (both Alec and Deirdre flee to England but eventually each is forced to return), violence is also self-destructive. Even Hugh is ultimately a victim, betrayed by his own side moments after he admits to Gretchen that he has been informing on his fellow members of the

IRA in order to pave the way for "a real social program" that will "stop the killing for its own sake." Thus violence is not only treacherous and self-destructive, but an impediment to progress as well.

Just as the violence is depicted as homogeneous, apolitical, and futile, so are those engaged in it either criminal (like Roy), deranged (Riddell speaks of the "hereditary insanity" of the Irish, all of whom are "as daft as a brush"), or naïve (Lenny describes the hunger strikers as "poor, bloody demented folk heroes" and "deluded skeletons"). Though Parker suggests collective self-delusion as an explanation for Republican violence, he does not pursue the idea beyond Episode Four. Instead, the most developed and consistent argument regarding the use of violence presented by the series concerns the influence of environment and upbringing.

Reared in a home where sectarian prejudice runs high, Deirdre's younger cousins cannot help but be infected by it ("You just can't ask a civil question in this house," Colin's sister complains when an innocent query about the Pope provokes the boy to apoplexy). It is also inevitable that they become acclimatized to violence: while Deirdre is raped and beaten by her uncle, Colin calmly reads a comic in a downstairs room, apparently oblivious to her screams.

The same point is made more subtly through the contrast of Alec's background with Craig's. Craig's father Roy is a confirmed bigot, a UVF supporter who prefers "a good Loyalist tune" to Mozart, and who does all in his power to prevent Deirdre's escape from Northern Ireland. By contrast, Alec's parents are law-abiding (his father's a policeman), tolerant (even when hospitalized after an attack his father discourages Alec from thought of revenge, reminding him that it's only "a hard core of fanatics" that are responsible for the violence), respectful of education and the arts, and they encourage him to immigrate (his parents are "dead keen on Britain," Alec tells his music teacher).

Under these opposing influences, Craig develops an enjoyment of Orange parades and paraphernalia which is as obvious as his ability and willingness to fight, whereas Alec appears uncomfortable with the symbols of Loyalism, and violence literally makes him sick. Moreover, following their murder of a Catholic florist, their paths diverge. Both boys are arrested for the crime, but only Craig goes to prison, his fist raised defiantly as he goes; Alec is saved by the intervention of his parents and teacher. Scenes in which Craig is forced to adjust to prison life are crosscut with others depicting Alec's arrival in England, his preparations for his debut concert, and the rapturous applause he receives in its wake.

Despite this theme of the power of one's early experience to shape one's actions and allegiances as an adult, responsibility for the violence is nevertheless ascribed wholly to the Northern Irish themselves. As Teddy Riddell of the SAS explains, the "hereditary insanity" of the Irish may make them violent, but it is their willful refusal to recognize reality and work out their problems which keeps them "at each other's throats." For centuries they have been fighting over differences of cultural identity, he tells Simon, "when what they really belong to is one another, actually. They certainly deserve each other. But if they were ever to acknowledge that, we [the British] would be finished here. But they never will."

Importantly, this thesis is confirmed by Deirdre's friend Carole, whose sudden realization that she's "never really spoken to a Catholic before" fills her with disgust. Though Niall attempts to reassure her ("It's this place that's ridiculous, not you"), she insists on placing the blame for the state of the country firmly on the shoulders of those who live there ("We bloody vote for it"). By their own foolish actions, Northern Irish people have "lost nearly everything . . . everything that was human, every shred of human dignity. We don't even feel shame anymore." As Carole says bitterly, "Everyone is so busy playing cock of the walk" that the country has been reduced to a "dunghill."

England, by contrast, is a place of refuge, whereas the English themselves are frequently responsible for making escape possible: it is Alec's English music teacher who arranges for him to study there and lies to the police to enable him to go; it is an English professor of music who recognizes his talent and looks after him once he arrives. The contrast between the two countries is made explicit by the juxtaposition of scenes from Alec's life in both. In England he is a wealthy, respected musician living in a spacious, attractively furnished home; he has a beautiful, exotic wife and cultured, well-educated friends with names like Constance, Humphrey, Felicity, and Guy, whereas in Belfast he was "Buck Alec," living in one of countless small, dark, terraced houses and fraternizing with a UVF gunman. Such differences are symbolic of the social and cultural gulf that separates England from Northern Ireland.

Uniformly well-mannered and civilized, all the English characters (with the temporary exception of Simon) are sensible, reasonable beings to whom the ongoing conflict is simply irrational ("Why do you all feel this need to belong to the place and to have it belong to you?"). Their behavior stands in sharp contrast with that of the Northern Irish characters in the play. Roy and Craig are the most obviously brutish, though Niall and his brothers are equally uncouth, their loutish behavior at Alec's party (during which they shower each other with alcohol, stumble about in the rain and yelp Republican ballads, drowning the strains of classical music inside the house) being a case in point. Even the dissolute journalist Simon is morally superior to someone like Gretchen—an avowed Republican—by virtue of being "a democrat."

In Teddy Riddell, these consummate English qualities fuse to create an image of the British soldier that goes far beyond that of the level-headed professional depicted, for example, in A.F.N. Clarke's *Contact* (BBC, 1985). That Riddell is somehow extraordinary is evident from the moment he is introduced, and is repeatedly underscored by the contrast of his character with that of Simon. On the evening of Simon's arrival, for example, Riddell empties a bottle of gin and then insists on a trip to the pub, where he consumes an enormous quantity of beer and appears to become uproariously drunk. The following morning, however, he is up at dawn with no sign of a hangover, hunting rabbits with an automatic weapon and yet with such skill that the carcasses are unmarked. As a soldier he is unimpressed by the enemy and remains unflappable in the face of the panic and outrage of others. Moreover, he alone appears to have any insight regarding the causes of violence in the North, and of all the characters in the play—including the Northern Irish—is the only one to offer any explanation for or solution to the conflict.

It is Riddell who puts most clearly the thesis that the Irish and the English are distinct and incompatible beings, though evidence for that argument can be seen throughout the play. He describes Northern Ireland as a "no-man's-land," a "buffer zone" without which "it [the violence] all comes home"—"home," of course, being England. As such, Northern Ireland itself, together with its citizens, is demoted to an uncertain status, becoming somehow less than a country ("I always feel at home in a place where nobody properly belongs," Riddell tells Simon). Even Niall's words of encouragement are hardly positive. "Just stick with it," he tells Deirdre's disheartened friend Carole. "I mean, if we don't belong together, who does? I mean, who the hell would have us?" Given the horrific imagery of the final frames (Deirdre's car stops beside the still quivering body of a murdered horse, a sudden burst of gunfire kills the driver, and a blood-soaked

Deirdre stumbles toward the light of an illuminated cross), the prison officer's quip—"Let them kill each other if they want!"—delivered as the Maze erupts into riot in Episode Three seems as sensible a solution as any.

In Parker's series, it is the potency of Irish violence that is to blame for the difficulty Irish people experience in trying to assimilate in Britain. Moreover, mutual incomprehension between the various traditions—Catholic and Protestant, Northern Irish and English—makes genuine contact virtually impossible. In keeping with the conventions of British cinema, violence is characterized as a disruptive force that is typically placed in opposition to the creative forces of the home, the family, and romantic love.[3] What is most disturbing, however, is the implication that to reject the violence is not enough: only when they reject their identity as Northern Irish (as Alec Ferguson tries to do) can immigrants flourish in their new surroundings, and can "mixed" relationships thrive.

Part of the reason for the failure of romance to cross these divides is due to the fact that a normal (i.e., happy) life is impossible in Northern Ireland. All that is evil (or simply unpleasant) in *Lost Belongings* occurs in or because of Northern Ireland, while any suggestion that Northern Ireland can be peaceful, attractive, or normal in any way is eventually undermined. Television producer Gillian Pringle only half listens as Niall's cousin Lenny babbles about peat bogs and traffic management; her attention is held instead by the black-and-white photographs of rioting youths and burning buildings spread out on her desk. Though Simon arrives by bicycle at Riddell's cottage for a fishing holiday amid sunshine, birdsong, and lighthearted music, the same, picturesque cottage with its thatched roof and window boxes and brightly painted door eventually goes up in flames.

Northern Ireland's ability to corrupt, pervert, and prevent all that is positive is due at least in part to the apparent obsession of its people with the past, another of Parker's major themes. Deirdre herself functions both as a symbol of the past and as a victim of her own fascination with it ("I'm interested in the past," she tells Niall when he asks why she insists on scheduling their trysts at the Ulster Museum). Running through the city against the flow of pedestrian traffic and dressed in the costume of the aunt who died some fifteen years before, she returns to the Museum toward the end of the play to search for Niall among the mummified corpses on display there. Later she goes to "the Holy Land" in East Belfast to view the house in which her parents died, a pilgrimage she makes periodically even when sane, though it always reawakens painful memories.

Although concern with the past is portrayed as a particularly Irish pastime ("Sure, that's all they ever do here—talk about the past," Lenny tells Gillian), those who are not Irish yet still show an unhealthy interest in the past may likewise be taking a risk. When Gretchen (who, as an archaeologist, has turned an obsession into a profession) agrees to meet Hugh "for old times' sake," the consequences are dire. When Alec's wife Regine insists on probing her husband's past and reuniting him with the place of his birth, his worst fears are realized: almost instantly he becomes reembroiled in violence.

Their obsession with the past is just one aspect of the fundamental incomprehensibility of the Irish. As a Belgian, Regine cannot understand why people of different traditions cannot live together in peace; Simon, too, cannot fathom the scale and persistence of the conflict, especially when "the border is so arbitrary"; and both Gretchen and Simon grow disenchanted with the North as events taking place around them grow ever more complex.

Of course, confusion is inevitable, given that nothing in Ulster is ever as it seems. As in Douglas Livingstone's *We'll Support You Evermore* (BBC, 1985) and Anne Devlin's *Naming the Names* (BBC, 1984), flashbacks, dream sequences, and devices designed to convey the heightened sensitivity of dementia confuse and disorient the viewer, and blur the distinction between what is real and what is imagined. Moreover, the question of what is "real" is raised explicitly several times. At Lenny's party Deirdre tells Niall enthusiastically, "It's a dream! You're a dream!" to which he replies, "No, I'm not, doll; I'm real," and Alec's teacher draws the curtains as the grind and shadow of passing tanks interrupts his concentration during one of his lessons— "Music is the real world, Alec," she tells him, "not that barbarism."

The alien nature of Northern Irish society is but one aspect of the mystical, other-worldly quality of Ireland itself and the primitive character of its people. Riddell calls the Irish "uncivilized," their barbarism so deep "under the skin" that it "cannot be cured." When Simon runs into Gretchen in a Fermanagh forest, for example, she is surprised to see him, but he accepts coincidence and the unusual as fundamentally Irish phenomena. "It doesn't surprise me in the least, which is what I find really weird about this country." Carole, too, confirms the impression that Northern Ireland is an enigma to any but the Northern Irish. "What do the British really know or care about us?" she asks rhetorically, "and what does Dublin know? We're the only ones who know."

**Interpretations and Conclusions**

Whatever its intended benefits, the sociopolitical consequences of encouraging psychological withdrawal through images such as these have not been all positive. In both newscasts and screenplays, televised images of Northern Ireland produced a popular misperception in Britain by which the country and its inhabitants became synonymous with violence. Frightened off as a consequence of perceptions manufactured largely by the media, few British travelers visited the North during the last quarter century;[4] what is more, in the absence of direct experience, most have no means of challenging the images they receive. Given that virtually all those accused or suspected of violence in these plays are subsequently shown to be guilty, it is not surprising that so many immigrants from both sides of the Irish border have encountered some form of anti-Irish racism in Britain.

One of the few plays to explore this phenomenon is Morrison and Clarke's *Elephant* (BBC, 1989), a forty-five minute piece without dialogue consisting solely of a series of nineteen stylized killings. After each murder, the camera holds a shot of the corpse from the angle at which the body would eventually be discovered (a victim murdered in his car, for example, is seen through a side window; another, shot behind a service counter, remains half-hidden by it when he falls). Some of the deaths are more graphic than others, many are singularly undignified, and a few of the victims are more pathetic than others, but on the whole the viewer remains equally distanced from both victims and killers, unable, by the very nature of the piece, to identify strongly with anyone.

Although the first murder is deeply disturbing, as are the second and third, gradually the violence loses its ability to shock. Eventually, with each new scene, we begin to expect to see someone die, and our reaction to the deaths is no longer so visceral. As if it too has become acclimatized to, perhaps even bored with, the violence, the camera's hold on the corpses becomes ever more brief as the play goes on, while the alternation of day and nightime scenes suggests, as did *Contact* through the same device, that the violence is both ceaseless and unstoppable, as well as commonplace.

Furthermore, the play deliberately obscures the distinction between killers and victims. Indeed, it is difficult to distinguish between individuals, as the camera frequently follows from behind, obscuring faces, and all those depicted are male and roughly similar in age, deportment, and appearance, including costume. Nor is there a consistent pattern to the way the scenes are played out: sometimes it is the killer we see first, elsewhere it is the victim. In the final scene the distinction between killer and victim is more blurred than ever, and the clarification of roles takes place so quickly at the end that it is difficult to absorb. The credits roll over the sounds of passing traffic—sounds that can be heard after every killing, often from traffic that can be seen in the background behind the corpse or behind the killer as he walks away.

*Elephant*'s power is derived from its ability to recreate what Livingstone (through Sue Friday in *We'll Support You Evermore*) claimed was the general response of the British public to the violence in Northern Ireland, namely, boredom, apathy, indifference, and desensitization—in short, psychological withdrawal. It also effectively conveys the popular impression of the violence as uniform, self-destructive, and having no discernible cause or purpose. In this regard, the play could be said to reproduce the official view of the conflict, and to typify the treatment of the subject by the media. It does so, however, both consciously and deliberately, as a testimony to the inadequacy of such an approach. It also serves as an invitation to viewers to reconsider their own response to the violence by suggesting that those who choose to ignore it are as responsible for its perpetuation as those who are guilty of its use.

Whether Irish characters appear as obvious terrorists or merely as fanatical in their social alignments and political beliefs, both depictions have had and continue to have consequences for the peace process in the North. By suggesting the impossibility of a lasting, peaceful solution because of the Irish national character, these images have obstructed the efforts of those working for an end to the violence, and have made reasonable discussion to overcome differences all the more difficult by exacerbating a climate of cynicism and distrust. Moreover, by misrepresenting felt identities as correctable illusions dependent upon circumstance and therefore negotiable—even if only to hasten the process of reconciliation—the genuine complexities of the problem continue to be obscured. After all, the sociopolitical aspirations that divide the two communities are no less salient now than they were before the gunmen lay down their arms.

It is therefore essential to expose the viewing public to stories that speak from across the wide range of cultural, social, and political traditions in the North. In the past, fictions with a Northern Irish setting have tended to portray the deployment and consequences of the violence there to the virtual exclusion of the more mundane aspects of daily life; Stewart Parker's own *Iris in the Traffic, Ruby in the Rain* is a

notable and beautifully rendered exception, in which the literal crossing of paths confirms the possibility of genuine contact. More recently,
Margo Harkin's *Hush-a-Bye Baby* (Channel 4, 1990) has depicted Republican nationalism as a dynamic, creative force within the community in Derry, while Owen O'Neill's *Arise and Go Now* (BBC, 1991)
juxtaposes familiar stereotypes with complex characters who defy easy
categorization in an unusual blend of humor and horror. Though depictions of Loyalism remain largely negative, Alan Bleasdale's *No Surrender* (Channel 4, 1986) is one of the best of the more "progressive"
plays. Set in Liverpool on New Year's Eve, it tells of the events that
ensue when two senior citizen groups, one a division of the Orange
Order and the other of the Ancient Order of Hibernians, are double-
booked into a second-rate night club owned and operated by local
racketeers. As that synopsis suggests, and despite the arrival of a Loyalist gunman who threatens Billy McCracken's daughter and her
Catholic husband back in Belfast, the real ugliness in the play is home-
grown. Indeed, the shots of Liverpool we see look remarkably like
those commonly used to identify Belfast—grim concrete housing es-
tates disfigured by graffiti, garbage, abandoned cars, and belligerent
youths. If McCracken, once a Loyalist killer himself, has transformed
at all it is due to his own strength of character and not to the influence
of living in England. What is most striking, however, is the play's subtle recognition of the deep social, cultural, and even psychic significance of Unionism for those who claim it as part of their identity. Thus
the cry of "No Surrender" becomes a statement of determination to resist despair as well as a refusal to ignore, let alone submit to violence.
Likewise John Forte's *Henri* (BBC, 1993) is a rich and beautiful testament to the vibrance and validity of Protestant culture in the North, his
child heroine a talented musician, receptive to new influences and creative possibility while at the same time a bright and dignified representative of her community, rightly proud of who she is.

In the main, however, realistically complex images such as these
remain outnumbered by those that rely as much as ever on oversim-
plicity and stereotype. This imbalance is at least partly responsible for
what seems to be an ever growing problem of self-image in screenplays by Northern Irish writers, a "preoccupation about the bad impression" that will be conveyed ("particularly to the English") by
representations of the North in the [visual] media.[5] Although it would
be foolish (and insensitive, with more than three thousand dead) to un-
derestimate the influence of the Troubles on Northern Irish culture and
society, it is a fact that for most people that influence has been more

tangential than direct, and much more subtle than the images above suggest. For most of the population, the violence of the past quarter century has been an occasional inconvenience, not a daily threat, something that regularly disrupted the traffic but rarely put their lives at risk. A normal life has always been possible in Ulster; crises of varying proportions and character arise and are dealt with heroically, inadequately, or not at all; there are many moments of tenderness, cruelty, and loss that are unconnected to the Troubles though every bit as real. Yet stories that are played out regularly on television against other settings are rarely told by Northern Irish dramatists. Perhaps because it has been defined by violence by those outside its borders, Northern Ireland has developed a native artistic culture in which those who address that violence, however indirectly, are often suspected of demagoguery, while those who refuse to do so are frequently accused of copping out, of closing their eyes to the realities of Northern Irish society and pretending that it is something more "normal" than it is. This atmosphere, an overconcern with the way Northern Ireland is seen outside the province (while paying little heed to how the Northern Irish see themselves), and the remarkable number of characters in the plays above who find artistic freedom and self-expression only after moving to England (a manifestation of the mystique of immigration that took root in the Irish artistic consciousness long before Joyce) are all part of the same fabric that keeps the people of Northern Ireland smothered, nationalist and Unionist alike, unable to develop a truly pluralist and peaceful society. If the current ceasefires do hold, perhaps the generation of artists who have "grown up with" the Troubles will begin to forge a new, comprehensive identity in which all may find cause for celebration.

# 8

# "I Kinda Liked You as a Girl"

Masculinity, Postcolonial Queens, and the "Nature"
of Terrorism in Neil Jordan's *The Crying Game*

## Maria Pramaggiore

In *The Crying Game* (1992), conflicts involving sexuality and Irish nationalism echo postmodern and postcolonial understandings of identity as a process of negotiating claims of gender, sexuality, race, and
nationality. As in many of Jordan's previous films, including *In the
Company of Wolves* (1984), *Mona Lisa* (1985), *High Spirits* (1988) and *The
Miracle* (1991), things are never what they appear to be: any attempt to
equate race and nationality, on the one hand, or gender and sexuality
on another, meets with disaster. In other words, reading the body's
"natural" attributes as markers of identity fails because vision is unre-
liable and incomplete, because "nature" is no longer stable.

Given contemporary debates about the efficacy and limits of identity politics, it is not surprising that the film's postmodern obsession
with the terrain of the body appears to eclipse the long-standing and
bloody dispute regarding geographical territory and political autonomy in the six counties of Northern Ireland. This religious/political
conflict appears that much more difficult to resolve because the Irish
Troubles themselves are grounded in modernity and colonialism. The
conflict presupposes national and religious identities that permeate
both public sphere politics and private concepts of subjectivity. In the
film, the politics of nationality are confounded by the complexities of
postcolonial identities, by the problematic incommensurability of race
and nationality, by the unreliability of all appearances. The postmod-
ern/postcolonial subject cannot guarantee the existence of, much less
the security of, modernity's territorial or bodily demarcations.

Gloria Anzaldua has developed an important and often-cited
metaphor of borderlands—sites where indeterminacy and excess are
powerfully articulated, where identities are experienced as both/and,
not either/or.[1] *The Crying Game*'s erogenous and geographical zones

are such borderlands where national, racial, and sexual identities resist historical and cultural equations between skin color and privilege, between sex organs and sexuality. A number of critics have celebrated the film's postmodern tendencies, arguing that *The Crying Game* pries sexuality and gender apart and, therefore, that it destabilized identities generally. Caryn James claims that the film "made transvestites the trendiest of heroes."[2] "Cross-dressing," she writes, "resonates with social and political implications . . . [t]he point . . . is not about trading sexual identities but about breaking down simplistic superficial notions of them."[3]

Judith Halberstam concurs, arguing: "the fact that Dil is anatomically male throws all other identities in the film into doubt."[4] In general, according to Halberstam, the film "is a scathing critique of identity politics: accordingly, its backdrop—IRA terrorism—must be read in light of this critique. If gender identities are uncertain, and if sexual instincts often lead us astray, then how much less reliable are concepts such as national identity?"[5]

Echoing Halberstam's point, David Lugowski writes: "in true Hollywood fashion, questions of what seem to be political are collapsed into the realm of the 'personal.' The most obvious casualty is the film's treatment of the IRA; any sort of violent goings on around the world would have sufficed equally well."[6]

Finally, Kristen Handler claims that "nationalism and racial difference become pretext and backdrop for a drama of sex, identity and desire . . . the film isn't ultimately very interested in politics as such."[7]

Admittedly, the melodramatic narrative of coincidence, secrets, and delayed gratification does privilege sexual over national politics and its resolution celebrates redemption through a Christian-inspired self-sacrifice in the name of true love. However, I am particularly interested in Halberstam's and Lugowski's assertions that IRA terrorism is a "backdrop" to the film. In the remainder of this essay, I will pursue two questions: first whether IRA terrorism is just a backdrop for, or, instead, is a context for—and is thus implicated in—the film's depiction of struggles around gender, sexuality, race, and nationality. I argue that Fergus's crisis of masculinity connects politics and sexuality in *The Crying Game* and motivates the plot shift from political thriller/war/buddy film to romance. I will claim that Irish-British postmodern/postcolonial warfare is crucial to the film's rendering of Fergus's "male troubles." The second, and related, question I am interested in exploring is what sort of representational field in terms of gender, race, and sex we arrive at in the film's conclusion: in other words, in a film primarily concerned with identification and masculinity, what happens to racial difference and sexual difference?

## Militancy and Masculinity

The Irish Republican Army and stringent requirements for its volunteers produce a crisis of masculinity for Fergus, the masochistic protagonist whose name somewhat ironically signifies "manly strength." Fergus rejects Irish nationalist political activity and reasserts his masculinity in the realm of heterosexual romance, although he encounters complications in this arena as well. Unlike Fergus's, Jude's monstrous amalgam of femininity and masculinity is predicated on the conflation of sex and politics.

Whereas sexual and political confusion characterize Fergus, religious/political fanaticism and sexual excessiveness mark the film's representation of Jude, the fanatical female IRA volunteer turned high-tech killing machine for whom violence is synonymous with sexuality. Fergus uses his participation in—and inability to carry out—Jody's assassination, his responsibility for Dil, and his relationship with Jude to establish an identity. Finally, however, it is Jody's model—a paradigm of masculinity in relation to which Fergus both identifies and experiences desire—that provides Fergus with the means to do so.

In an essay on John Singleton's *Boyz in the Hood*, Robyn Wiegman convincingly makes the case that feminist critics need to shift our frame of reference away from the scene of woman/women and toward issues of difference among men. She argues: "the homogenizing tendencies of patriarchal discourses have been strangely reinscribed by feminist theory's own attention to the monolithic logic provided by sexual difference."[8] Wiegman is most interested in how the discourse of sexual difference has shaped representations of African-American males and masculinity in U.S. film. In *Boyz in the Hood*, for example, she argues that black masculinity is not coterminous with patriarchy.

*The Crying Game* prohibits any simple yoking together of masculinity—"white" or "black," English or Irish—and patriarchy as well. Cleavages erupts among, between, and within male characters and concepts and components of ideal masculinity, not least among those components being heterosexuality. Jody, the black British soldier—perhaps targeted by the IRA because of their racist perceptions of the ease with which they might entrap him with a willing female body—is a sexually rapacious "animal" in Jude's words, and also Dil's devoted and protective lover. Fergus is committed to what he sees as a simple "cause"—getting the British out of Northern Ireland—yet cannot participate in the impersonal violence the IRA deems necessary to accomplish that task.

Patriarchy governs but does not wholly determine relationships between and among men in the film, asserting itself most prominently as a punitive and misguided British military technology, a technology that consumes the bodies of its colonial subjects. Although patriarchal masculinity in *The Crying Game* appears to reside in the last bastion of male dominance, the military, and paramilitary, ultimately this latter culture of combat does not provide an unproblematic narrative of male bonding in wartime. In the context both of post–World War II revolutionary movements in former colonies and of gay, lesbian bisexual, transgendered liberation movements within North American and European nations, the homosocial fraternity of the military, state sanctioned or otherwise, becomes "suspect" both on political and on sexual grounds.

The importance of the terrorist context to the film—the reason why postmodern warfare is not merely a backdrop to the film's events but is critical to its exploration of sexuality—is that Fergus is unable to establish his masculinity as an IRA volunteer partly because of changing perceptions regarding the psychology of the military brotherhood, partly because of Ireland's legacy as an English colony, and partly because of the "nature" of guerrilla warfare. Terrorism has become the postmodern, post–Cold War paradigm of armed struggle, and its representations in popular media and culture and, perhaps, in the popular imagination, invariably include the breakdown of the modern, "rational" politics of the nation-state by fundamentalist religious sects and tribal factions. *The Crying Game* insists that irrationality characterizes both "sides" of such deadly conflicts by counterposing the rigidity of the IRA and its overwhelming demands to the anonymity with which killing is carried out by the British Army.

The particular type of solidarity and dedication required by the IRA prove too demanding for Fergus, who fails to establish his masculinity as a soldier on several counts. He is too solicitous of the prisoner, too willing to personalize him and to condemn the verbal and physical abuse directed at Jody by Jude and Peter in favor of a friendship of sorts. Suspected of being soft and unable to carry out his assignment, Fergus indeed does fail to execute Jody. Fergus's failures are cast in sharp relief against Jude's willingness to inflict violence on Jody and, much later, in relation to Peter's desire to carry out orders, despite the cost. Fergus's reason for agreeing to the suicide mission, in contrast to Peter's last minute act of bravado, is to save Dil from the long arm of the IRA. Jude's status as a woman warrior and Fergus's conflict between interpersonal and Republican politics prevent the inscription of the combat scenario as a male coming-of-age narrative. The structure and ethical ambiguities of postmodern warfare will not permit Fergus to realize himself in the context of battle. Rather, it is his relationship with Jody, the catalyst for his reappraisal of both his nationalist politics and his sexual identity, which serves as the scenario of male bonding and identification. That Fergus both identifies with and desires Jody becomes apparent in later sequences in which Fergus dreams of Jody playing cricket, looks at a picture of Jody while having sex with Dil, dresses Dil in Jody's cricket clothes, and assumes the role of Dil's protector. It is in retreat, through the romance with Dil, not the nebulous battlefield of postmodern warfare, that Fergus seeks to prove his masculinity, to be the man that Jody was.

The IRA volunteers are overdetermined by their religious fervor, which partly defines their unambiguous "Irishness." Jude and Peter, whose names recall the first Christian cult of the Bible, are cast as disciples in a self-destructive passion play. In London, Jude menacingly reminds Fergus to "keep the faith," after her offensively aggressive attempt to seduce him turns into an equally dangerous assignment to kill an English judge. Jude's role invokes masochistic fantasies of the controlling woman/mother and also reproduces stereotypes of national and sexual identity. An Irish woman, Jude's role as agent of emotional excess is consistent with certain historical representations of Irish women in early U.S. cinema. Her devotion to the cause echoes stock female characters that date back as far as silent cinema.[9] Popular Irish films (which were as popular as Yiddish films) depicted strong matriarchal figures with an absurd devotion to religion. Jude is also problematic because she instrumentalizes the sexual, using sex in the service of politics, making her a better soldier than Fergus could ever be. Although Jude tells Fergus, "there are some things I wouldn't do for my country," when he asks her if she "gave it" to Jody, she certainly does not distance sex and politics when she approaches Fergus in London. More dangerous than their putative leader Peter, Jude uses sexuality to entrap Jody, to reinstate a political relationship with Fergus in London in an overt power play, and to threaten both Fergus and Dil in order to secure Fergus's participation in the assassination. Jude's transformation, accomplished like Fergus's, by crossing water, signals not only her withdrawal from Fergus's erotic orbit but also her complete immersion in the technology of warfare. The surfaces of her hair, her clothing, and her body as well as the settings in which Jude is framed suggest that, ironically, she has rejected the rustic, backwoods of Ireland in favor of the ultramodern (or postmodern?) delights that can be found in the colonial capital of the British Empire: London.

## Shifting Identities and Romantic Triangles

The narrative organizes itself around the metaphorical and literal crossing of water; crossings that signify transformations of various kinds. The opening crane shot moves in sweeping and circular fashion across the river, closing in on the carnival where Jude entraps Jody, the black British soldier whom the IRA has targeted. After he is kidnapped, Jody is taken back across the water by the IRA. In Jody's tale of the scorpion who negotiates passage on the frog's back, the passage is never completed because the scorpion, in keeping with his nature, stings the frog halfway across. Jody's trip across the water from England to Ireland is similarly truncated—he never returns to England—when he is captured and killed.

After Jody's death, Fergus himself "goes across the water" to take up residence in London as "Jimmy." Fergus's grief and guilt at Jody's death force him to question and ultimately to abandon his political commitment to the IRA. It is not in Fergus's "nature" to continue to contribute to the kind of violent death Jody experiences nor to "widow" any more "women" like Dil. When Fergus leaves Ireland, he "puts away the childish things" of the Bible verse he recites to Jody in response to the scorpion and frog story. Fergus sheds his Republican politics in his movement across the water, telling his friend, "I have to lose myself for a while." In mythology, it is Fergus's fate to wrestle with water, telling his friend, "I have to lose myself a while."

Fergus's soldier self is never recovered; his mourning of Jody the soldier changes his own sense of himself. In the manner described by Freud in "Mourning and Melancholia,"[10] Fergus incorporates Jody, the lost object, forging an identification with him and also, I would argue, reflecting upon him as an object of desire. Fergus's shape-shifting is signaled not only by his name change and haircut, but also in a brief shot of his face covered with dust. This temporary but dramatic change in skin color suggests he is now an alien in racial and ethnic terms, like Jody, an alien postcolonial subject living in England. Similarly, Jude's transition is manifested in outward signs; new hairstyle, new clothes, and a polished sophistication that reflects her relocation from rural Ireland to urban London.

A second structuring device further links Fergus and Jody across racial and political differences. This device is a shifting romantic triangle. In the opening carnival scene, Fergus watches Jody and Jude: we at first may read him as a jilted lover of Jude's or, perhaps, as a provincial passerby who disapproves of the interracial couple. The triangle established here by the mutual looks of Jude and Fergus at Jody sets up the political conflict as a struggle over sexuality and race as well. We learn that Jude and Fergus are involved with each other sexually and politically and that Jody—their enemy, the unlikely representative of English colonialism—is captured because of both sex and politics. He is a British soldier who is also susceptible to Jude's charms.

Jody is not only a man, of course, he is a marked man, a black man. In the film's insistence on Fergus's personal and political transition from IRA volunteer to romantic leading man, issues of cultural and racial differences among the men are subordinated to questions regarding sexual definition. Vanessa Place argues that, despite the apparent antiessentialism represented by Dil, the discourse of "true nature" haunts the film. Place argues that the film's message is that race is superficial to or irrelevant to "nature," whereas gender and sexuality are potentially disruptive. Place summarizes her view in the following pithy statement: "those who would have *The Crying Game* be a treatise on the omnipotence of true love cheat themselves of the effects of a black man's penis in a white man's face."[11] I would argue that the erasure of racial difference is another symptom of the problematic of masculinity in the film, a device for solidifying even different masculinities across race and culture in a manner that pits true masculinity in opposition to biological women. For example, consider the web of relationships among Jude, Jody, and Fergus: Jude and Fergus are lovers; Jude entices Jody for sex for political purposes and tells Fergus later that she had to pretend Jody was Fergus in order to be able to tolerate the encounter with Jody. Jude's conflation of Jody and Fergus both signals and then sutures racial difference; a classical structure of the fetish. The reason why she has to pretend, she suggests, is because Jody is black and she finds him repulsive and animalistic. But the easy superimposition of Fergus and Jody subsumes their racial difference into their presumed masculine, heterosexual sameness; their ability to be aroused by a woman.

The solidarity between Fergus and Jody lies at the heart of the film and organizes the film's representations of masculinity. More subversive than the black man's penis in the white man's face, in fact, is the black man's penis in the white man's hands—Jody's penis. The relationship between Jody and Fergus links sexuality, race, and power and precipitates Fergus's crisis of masculinity.

Fergus and Jody forge an identification through their gazes at both Jude and Dil. When Jody and Fergus look at the photograph of Dil that Jody carries with him, Dil supplants Jude as the object of their interest. The canted angle during this scene, its triangular reframing of the two men suggests a literal resituating of the vertices of the romantic triangle and places Dil in Jude's position. Fergus's posture mirrors Dil's place in the photograph, however, for he stands over Jody just as Dil leans over Jody in the photograph. The composition can be read in several ways: as a foreshadowing of the way that Fergus will attempt to replace Jody in relation to Dil (he looks at Dil as Jody does) or as Fergus adopting a position in relation to Jody as Dil—Jody's lover—is situated in the photograph.

Racial difference is once again signaled and then smoothed over in their discussion of Dil. Fergus's desire for Dil, mediated through Jody, is manifested without reference to race, despite the conversation Fergus and Jody have already had regarding race and nationality. Fergus remarks, "She'd be anybody's type." His statement clearly contradicts Jody's experience as an Afro-Caribbean English subject and soldier stationed in Ireland. Jody complains that Ireland is "the only place in the world where they call you nigger to your face." Fergus tells him not to take it personally, wholly missing the point that racism is not personal. Fergus's attraction to Dil, the film suggests, is color-blind, based upon a system of simplistic sexual dualism: men desire women.

Throughout the film, Fergus's involvement with Dil is mediated through Jody—through photographs of Jody, through Fergus's dreams of Jody during sex with Dil, and finally when Fergus dresses Dil in Jody's cricket clothes in order to disguise Dil. Fergus's conflict over his feelings for Dil (after he finds that Dil possesses a penis) is in fact a struggle between his homosocial and homosexual desires, a struggle that stems from his simultaneous identification with and desire for Jody. Carole Anne Tyler and Eve Sedgwick, among others, differentiate between two models of male homosexuality: one defined by sexual difference, the other by gender distinction. In the model of sexual difference, homosociality is not clearly distinguishable from homosexuality, and identification and desire are not mutually exclusive but reinforcing. I would argue that this model characterizes Fergus's relationship with Jody—that is, Fergus both identifies with and desires Jody, evidenced by his dream of Jody during sex with Dil and his mimicry of the cricket game he observes from his work site.

Jody himself is perhaps the most indeterminate of all the characters: a West Indian from Tottenham, Jody's political, national, and sexual identities are the most fluid and therefore perhaps the most disturbing in terms of the aesthetics of narrative closure and the politics of identity. Jody figures the British colonial presence in Ireland, but neither his national nor sexual identity is capable of being recuperated by traditional definitions of race, citizenship, or sexual orientation. Jody plays cricket, thus appearing to be an assimilated colonial, yet his usurpation of the sport of the colonizer can be read as mimicry, which Homi Bhabha writes is menacing "in its double vision which in disclosing the ambivalence of colonial discourse also disrupts its authority."[12] Jody's pitch is the "googli," equivalent to a knuckleball in baseball. Thus his mimicry of the colonizer's sport is also performed with a twist that can undermine the colonizer's authority: his pitches are never what they appear to be. Jody further articulates cultural differences and disrupts the authority of the colonizer when he praises the black man's version of the game as it is played back home in Antigua, just as Fergus argues that the Irish sport of hurling is best. The men share cultural legacies of domination at the hands of the British.

We encounter Jody in the context of a sexual liaison with Jude and as a devoted lover of Dil who asks his captor to take care of his lover after his death. Yet Jody must be described in retrospect as perhaps bisexual, as neither heterosexual nor homosexual; he establishes a strong homosocial bond with Fergus, is in a homosexual relationship with Dil (arguably), and looks forward to a sexual encounter with Jude. His sexuality has nonspecific objects; his politics are similarly indeterminate. "You guys never get a break," he says to Fergus, and calls him "brother" shortly before he is killed. The implicit gender neutrality of Jody's name (paralleling that of Jude's) suggest that both figures pose a challenge to strict categories of gender and sexual identity. Jody's indeterminacy and Jude's excessiveness both contribute to Fergus's quest for and crisis of masculinity.

### Women and the Spectacle of Male Masochism

Earlier, I referred to Fergus as a figure of male masochism, by which I mean to say that *The Crying Game*'s representations of masculinity correspond to the historical conventions Steven Neale identifies in his 1983 essay, "Masculinity as Spectacle." Neale argues that the "male body cannot be marked explicitly as the erotic object of another male look: that the look must be motivated in some other way, its erotic component repressed."[13] He cites narratives involving sadomasochistic themes and fantasies as typical avenues for representing male bodies as spectacle while simultaneously repressing the erotic component.

Certainly, Jody's incarceration, torture, and death permit spectators as well as on-screen males like Fergus to look at his black male body. And Dil, who tells Fergus it's all right to hit, just not on the face, confirms stereotypes of gay male masochism and narcissism. But Fergus himself provides the most complicated example of male masochism in the film.

According to post-Freudian theorists of masochism, the masochist needs to be dominated, a need that supersedes the need to suffer. Masochism is characterized as voluntary submission to a woman, generally the powerful mother, toward whom the masochist has ambivalent feelings. The mother is both love object and controlling agent. The characteristic of masochism that both Freudian and later theorists identify is that in fantasies, although the masochist assumes a variety of roles and is in fact somewhat indifferent to sexual difference itself, the masochist (unlike the sadist) never assumes the position of authority, the parental role, the role of punisher.

Fergus's discomfort with masculine/phallic power and his readiness both to court suffering and to allow others to assume control (primarily Jude and Dil) mark him as masochistic. In the midst of the shifting configuration of masculinities in the film—Jody's apparent indifference to sexual difference, Dil's disdain and desire for Jude's female body, Fergus's renunciation of Jude's sex and her politics—the film's only biological woman is objectified both overtly as a woman and covertly, through the devices of male spectacle. In her early scene with Jody, her body is the object of the camera and of Jody's interest. By the end of the film, Dil verbally dismembers and literally disembowels Jude's body.

Jude is excessively and gratuitously violent and her violence is overtly linked to sexuality, as Neale's analysis of male spectacle would predict. In other words, Jude is susceptible to objectification both in terms traditionally linked to female representation, as a sexual object in the first scene, and in terms of her role as a masculinized member of a terrorist organization where bodies suffer violence in order to be explored cinematically. Jude is masculinized not only in terms of violence but also in terms of her gender identity. When she arrives on her motorcycle at the IRA hideout, she may be read as a man until she takes her helmet off. When she dresses in preparation for the assassination of the judge, it is less a reverse striptease than a paramilitary readiness exercise. Judith Halberstam writes that "femininity in this film is always powerful (the female terrorist is the IRA's most lethal weapon), while masculinity is oddly manipulable and unstable. When Fergus cuts Dil's hair to make her into a sad-looking boy, it appears that masculinity or maleness is defined as castration."[14] Yet it ultimately is for her female body that Jude is killed.

### Re- or De-Masculinization?

The second romantic triangle (Jody, Fergus, Dil) and the final romantic dyad of Fergus and Dil both eliminate Jude, the only biological woman and the most potent political force in the film. This fact, together with several observations I have made, link the treatment of masculinity in *The Crying Game* to Susan Jefford's discussion of masculinity in her book on the "remasculinization" of America through Viet Nam War films.

Jeffords argues, among other things, that the narratives of numerous Viet Nam war films develop a model of male bonding across race, age, ethnic, and religious differences that differs in important ways from previous cycles of war films, most notably World War II films. In Viet Nam War films, as opposed to World War II films, the male bonds do not dissolve when the soldiers come home. Instead, women are eliminated and self-sufficient male communities are sustained "stateside." Jeffords further argues that racial difference is consistently eradicated, and gender differences are used to divert attention and tension away from racial conflict. In these films, Jeffords claims, gender and sexuality are the locus for the renegotiation of U.S. masculinity.

I want to briefly suggest the ways in which this model is relevant to *The Crying Game*, a film whose exploration of masculinity is intertwined with terrorism: postmodern, postcolonial warfare. There are certainly similarities between both the realities and the various discourses surrounding the two military conflicts. Articles in British publications discussing Northern Ireland, for example, often use the same rhetoric the American press used and continues to use in relation to Viet Nam—that self-imposed constraints limit the ability of the colonial power to win the war. "The British Army, which is professionally superb, could of course win a straight shooting war against the IRA if it was ever ordered to fight one."[15] Further parallels relate directly to identity issues insofar as Irish Catholics in Northern Ireland are often presumed to be members of the IRA because it is impossible to distinguish between the "regular" population and terrorists (as in Viet Nam)—a seeming plausible justification for mass murder of civilians during the Viet Nam War.

The structure of representation in *The Crying Game* conforms in many ways to Jeffords's model. Jeffords discusses the fact that women are often portrayed as sexually aggressive (prostitutes in Viet Nam

War films) while "masculinity remains passive and subject to the explicit sexual overtones of women who represent only sex."[16] In other words, masculinity is under attack not by other men, with whom bonds are formed across race, age, ethnicity, religious difference, but from women, who represent an overpowering sexuality.

The elimination of Jude does not necessarily leave us with an all-male homosocial environment, however, as Jeffords's Viet Nam model would predict. The film presents us with a variation on this narrative through the figure of Dil, whose sexuality conforms to that of the "invert" of classical sexology—that is, the psyche of a woman in the body of a man. In other words, Dil is biologically male, which the film takes pains to point out, but is not interested in homosociality. Fergus's masochistic relation to the controlling mother/woman figure is apparently resolved when the controlling female figure—first Jude, then Dil—no longer threatens biological sexual difference. In this film then, male bonding still requires violent spectacle, such as Jody's violent death. Male bonding also requires the partial erasure of racial difference, and it still requires that women be disallowed from the bastions of male power, notably the military and the prison. Yet in the character of Dil, the film offers a model where the classical invert is invited to be a member of the fraternity and thus provide the masculine world with difference and sameness.

This reading of sexual and national politics in *The Crying Game* is an attempt to struggle with the connections between conflicts for geographical and bodily territories and to emphasize that these struggles are not distinct. *The Crying Game* links problematics of sex and gender, race and nationalism through a crisis of masculinity that is unresolvable through a traditional narrative of wartime heroism and romance. The attempt at resolution involves the "hero's" strong bonds of identification with and desire for another man. Fergus's relationship with Jody must be forged across race, culture, and sexuality. Fergus assumed Jody's role as Dil's protector, thus realizing his identification with Jody. Dil's feminine gender identity—despite her "penis"—allows for the possible reinstatement of Fergus's masculinity. Masculine sameness does not necessarily produce a homogeneous cultural order, according to Robyn Wiegman, "regardless of the extent to which certain social arrangements (such as the military) operate by and through the mythos of an undifferentiated masculine structure."[17] In the final scenario of the film, Fergus finds himself in an overtly all-male environment, the prison, and the mutual desires of Fergus and Dil are indefinitely deferred—although Dil has calculated Fergus's incarceration down to the day. This homosocial environment has been attained through the violent destruction of Jude's female body and is controlled by the patriarchal, technological colonizer: the British government. Fergus is finally able to understand the multiple possibilities for masculinity because of his rejection of IRA politics, his strong identification with Jody, and his desires for Jody and Dil.

# 9

## Neil Jordan's *Miracle*

From Fiction to Film

### Kathleen Gallagher Winarski

Like most Irish artists, Neil Jordan grapples with the great ghosts of
Ireland's past, but he is not intimidated by Irish tradition. Rather, Jordan explores Irish literature and culture as an artist who challenges tradition to express and to enrich his own vision, which is rooted in his
past, but headed toward a future that will, by its nature, push the artist
beyond all boundaries. For Jordan stretching the boundaries of tradition means liberating his fiction—breathing new life into Ireland's stories of family and nation through film and its ability to create intricate
and subtle textures of characterization and feeling.

In *The Miracle,* a quiet, subtle film, Jimmy, the film's teenage hero,
expresses his joy in the discovery of his mother and in the renewal of
his father's love while the wild animals from the Bray circus run loose
on the shore. This, the film's final and most striking image, is an allusion to Yeats's poem "The Circus Animals' Desertion," and Jordan's in-
vocation of Yeats is as deliberate as his summoning the ghosts of Frank
O'Connor and Brendan Behan in *The Crying Game.* From O'Connor's
"Guests of the Nation," Jordan took the heart of his film, as he struggled with what O'Connor saw as the irreconcilable conflict between
friendship and duty. From *The Hostage* he took Behan's theatricality.
*The Hostage* is a chaotic play in which expressionism and theater of the
absurd are mixed with exuberance and wit as Behan comments on the
power of the national drama to intrigue and to destroy. Behan's outcasts—Free Staters, Republicans, Irish, English, homosexual, heterosexual, transvestites, and whores—all find their way into Jordan's film.
Jordan's conversation with Yeats, however, is more subtle as he transforms Yeats's circus animals, which the poet described as "Those
stilted boys, that burnished chariot, /Lion and woman and the Lord
knows what," into real and metaphoric animals.

In the poem Yeats has been led away from true feeling by the imagination: "Players and painted stage took all my love,/And not those things that they were emblems of." He must return, not to that rich world, but to its source, where he finds "Old kettles, old bottles, and a broken can,/Old iron, old bones, old rags"—the pain and the poverty of the human heart. Perhaps because of his age, Yeats thought of going back to what was not "complete" and, therefore, not "masterful" as a painful reversion to process during a time of waning energies. Where Yeats saw desertion, Jordan sees liberation and the flight of the circus animals as the release and not the diminishment of creative energies. However, like Yeats, his use of the image is multilayered and includes the strange creatures of the imagination, the dark powers that would repress them, and the responses of the artist to both. Because of that complexity, their release is a beautiful and terrifying fantasy brought to life as well as a metaphor for the richness of the heart's liberation.

*The Miracle*, however, does not begin with Yeats's poem but in one of the most Irish of genres—the short story. Although Joyce and O'-Connor would certainly recognize the quiet desperation of his characters, there is in the collection *Night in Tunisia* a style that is Jordan's own. Marked by his skill as a filmmaker, the stories are spare, visual, tactile—sensual but remote, set in landscapes that mirror the alienation and sensitivity of their protagonists. The voice of the omniscient narrator is quiet as he passes through, with the camera's peculiar combination of distance and intimacy, the mind of his characters, noting the seemingly trivial placement and texture of objects, the changing light, and the colors of sky and sea. Although Jordan deals with themes familiar in Irish fiction—the repression of the individual by Irish culture and the Catholic Church and the emotional deprivation in Irish family life—there are glimmers of hope in his stories as his characters' fears and disappointments are sometimes resolved in friendship, the love of music, or in the reconciliation of parents and children. *The Miracle* evolves slowly from the characters and themes first introduced in *Night in Tunisia*.

His short stories often deal with boys on the verge of adolescence, for Jordan, a crucial stage in adult development. More than a time of sexual initiation, these are the years when young boys discover who they are, and a time when they may find the courage to be themselves, free from the constraints of religion and politics. The stories develop unconventionally. With no traditional plot or characterization, they are paced to reflect the passage of time as it is experienced by the boys, who, although intelligent and sophisticated, are inarticulate, almost primal in their raw sensitivity to people and place. Although they talk little, they often meditate and daydream, and metaphor and symbol become the means for Jordan's exploration of their feelings.

Most of the stories take place at the shore during summer vacation, the landscape of sea and sky appropriately reflecting the deep and subtle changes the boys are experiencing. Sky and sea, symbols of the unconscious and of flux and transition, are the chaos from which their feelings originate. They are haunted by in-betweens—twilight, in particular, fascinates. The boy in "Night in Tunisia" "taste[s]" twilight "as he would a sacrament": "The tincture of the light fading, the blue that seemed to be sucked into a thin line beyond the sea into what the maths books called infinity, the darkness falling like a stone." Twilight merges opposites, sky and sea. However, in their gray, lonely landscape, horizons are limitless and empty. Jordan explores, as well, the breakthrough into consciousness of what is pushing unremittingly upwards from the unconscious, described best in a metaphor again from "Night in Tunisia": "The sea had the movement of cloth but the texture of glass. It flowed and undulated, but shone hard and bright."

Lonely, curious, afraid of the sexual energies that will shape their beings, they search the long summer days and nights for adulthood. Jordan takes us back into the world when we struggled to find ourselves among all the twists and turns, fantasies and fears of our sexual nature—repressing what we feared as deviant, afraid of the rejection inherent in difference.

The stories "Seduction" and "Sand" come from the earliest stages of adolescence when the boys struggle with the sexual fears rising from the depths of the unconscious. The two boys in "Seduction" have been friends for several summers, but when they meet again, they are now rivals as well: "We loved to talk in monosyllables conscious of the other's envy, a hidden mutual delight underneath it like blood." With their carefully greased hair, they are all ducktails and bravado as they pursue the local whore, a fat, rather unattractive blonde woman, who has been rumored to swim nude. This peculiar woman (middle-aged in "Seduction" and a girl in "Night in Tunisia") entices and frightens. As a symbol, she represents the archetypal "Terrible Mother" as well as the power and mystery of sex. In "Seduction" she resembles a kewpie doll and a Medusa: she "turned her head towards me, looking at me straight in the eyes. And in the green irises underneath the clumsy mascara there was a mocking light that frightened me. I thought of the moon with a green mist around it like the Angel of Death in *The Ten Commandments*." Threatening and remote, she signals the crucial absence of a maternal, loving woman in the boy's life. His father is present briefly. While the boys prowl the strand hoping to find the woman, they hear his voice: "My father was calling my name from the drive of the guest-house. His voice seemed to echo right down the beach, seeming worried and sad."

The boys wait all night but the woman does not come. He notices his friend is crying as he has been, "weeping for the innocence of last year," and, in a gesture of love almost maternal, he wraps his coat around the boy: "He shivered and moved in close to me and his head touched my chest and lay there. I held him there while he slept, thinking how much smaller than me he was after all." The story ends with a peculiar but not unusual incident as they splash in the water.

> Then I felt myself slipping, being pulled from the legs and I fell in the water again and I felt his arms around my waist, tightening, the way boys wrestle, but more quietly then, and I felt his body not small any longer, pressing against mine. I heard him say "this is the way lovers do it" and felt his mouth on my neck but I didn't struggle, I knew that in the water he couldn't see my tears or see my smile.[1]

The moment articulates the anxieties about growing up which, in Jordan's world, includes an intimate bonding—erotic and emotional, but not always sexual—with another. With boys so young, sexual confusion and experimentation are not uncommon. Whether this is a homosexual experience is not of primary significance, however, since Jordan is tracing the fundamental but frightening energies that shape human character. In the "Introduction to *The Crying Game*," Jordan talks about a subtext—"an erotic possibility, a sense of mutual need and identification" that could prove to be "salvation" for the story's protagonists. Fergus and Jody are able to love each other through Dil, but Fergus's love for Dil is complex—emotional, intense, but not, physical. In the transitional world of adolescence, a world of discovery, that two boys love each other is for them a mystery and relief from the burden of loneliness and isolation.

"Sand" is a far more disturbing look at innocence when it becomes corrupted by experience. A young boy is jealous of his sister's apparent worldliness: "He felt that somewhere he knew as much as she, but when he came to say it he could never find the words." In an act of revenge, desire, and perversity, he trades her for a ride on a tinker's pony. The boys laugh about the bargain although the younger boy is only dimly aware of its consequences: "The joke had changed into another joke, a joke he didn't understand, but that made it all the more funny."

The boy, ruled by instinct, is willing to sell his sister for his pleasure. However, he is responsible enough to save her from possible rape and alert enough to strike up a bargain: " 'You won't—' he asked. 'I will,' she said. 'I'll tell it all.' The boy knew, however, that she would be ashamed." Through the story's imagery, Jordan brings up from the unconscious disturbing suggestions of homosexuality and incest. Without a knowledge of evil, then, the boy would remain in a dangerous state of innocence. That experience is necessary is made clear in the story's final image. "His hands were wet with the donkey's saliva and to the saliva a fine film of sand was clinging. When he moved his fingers it rustled, whispered, sang."[2] However, in spite of what happened to his sister, for the boy, forbidden pleasure has become more attractive.

The boy in "Night in Tunisia" is a gifted musician who rejects his father's world of big bands and dance halls. Although his father, too, has grown tired of playing "in the world of three-chord showbands," he is "galled" that his son, who "could be so good," refuses to play the saxophone. He has decided instead to play a broken piano to earn the goodwill of the older boys on summer holidays. However, he rejects their music as well, and "the brashness they were learning, coming over the transistors, the music that cemented it." Their rebellion makes him think of the "odd melancholy of the adulthood they were about to straddle, to ride like a Honda down a road with one white line, pointless and inevitable."

He is awakened not by Elvis but by Charlie Parker playing "Night in Tunisia," a raw, sensual, jazz instrumental: "He heard the radio crackle over the sound of falling water and heard a rapid-fire succession of notes that seemed to spring from the falling water, that amazed him, so much faster than his father ever played, but slow behind it all, melancholy, like a river." He has found his music—not the show tunes his father has been forced to play to earn a living, not the rock and roll of his peers, but jazz—cool and sad, structured and improvisational. On the broken piano he tries "to imitate that sound like a river he had just heard." The girl he has been stalking, a friend of his sister's, appears mysteriously, responding to the sensuality of the music: "Her eyes were on his hands that were still pressing the keys and there was a harmonic hum tiny somewhere in the air. Her eyes rose to his face, unseeing and brittle to meet his hot, tense stare." A few years before she was like a sister, and their nakedness under a rough blanket was daring but childlike.

The older boys mock this girl, who is rumored to be a prostitute. However, the girl's stare stays with the boy, and he agrees to accept his father's money as a reward for learning to play the alto sax. Even as he contemplates buying the girl, he daydreams about an Eden full of women: "All of them on the dawn golf-course, waking in their dew-sodden clothes." For the boy, women are Eve and Venus, women as instinct and emotion. When he can discover no Edenic fairway, he starts to teach himself to play: "As he played he heard voices and sometimes the door knocked. But he turned his back on the open window and the view of the golf-course. Somewhere, he thought, there's a golf-course where bodies are free, not for monetary gain."

He thinks of himself not as Adam, an innocent in this Paradise, but rather, as a lifeguard "dark sidelocks round his muscular jaw, a megaphone swinging from his neck, that crackled." Rumors have circulated that the girl has attempted suicide by drowning. In the last few moments of the story he imagines himself kissing her, "her open mouth like it was for the lifeguard when he pressed his hand to her stomach, pushed the salt water out, then put his lips to her lips and blew," an imitation of making love and making music. The girl is a muse who calls his music forth from the primal energies that Jordan has shown to be both creative and corrupting. In the story the words "money," "whore," and "venal" are balanced precariously against "saxophone," "music," and "melody."

In "A Love" the boy has become a man of twenty-five or twenty-six, and the struggle of a father and son over woman, with which this story begins, has become simply a reminiscence, a conversation between two former lovers.

The couple began their affair when he was fifteen and she was thirty-nine. They have arranged to meet years later (he has discovered that she is ill) on the day of Eamon de Valera's funeral. De Valera, Irish politics, and the Civil War are the subtexts of "A Love," a story of the civil war in the family and in the nation that was begun, to Jordan's thinking, by de Valera's notions of what Ireland should be. His policies have lead to a stultifying conformity—what Jordan would call a beast, "an animal that was huge, murderous, contradictory." He thinks of his lover's reputation: "I wondered what deity it was that would label you old maid or spinster when you had once pressed that happiness on me. Then I heard the band outside, so loud now, and the cortege was passing and the band was playing the old nationalist tunes to a slow tempo."[3] Once, she had been courted, correctly and conventionally, by the boy's father, "a widower, a natural partner," but she fell in love with his son. The culture created by de Valera would repress such a woman. The beast demanded conformity, even as she talked to him of "other countries where women are young at the age of thirty-nine and boys are men at fifteen." It is this beast that pressures all three, the polite and distant father, the beautiful, single woman, and the lonely teen-ager, playing "James Dean" to her "Ava Gardner."

As a boy, he had never known his mother, but he imagines her from a faded photograph, and an ancient story surges up from the unconscious.

> And all the time for me there was my father lying underneath, cold most likely, and awake and I wanted him to hear the beast I was creating with you, I wanted him to hear it scratching, creaking through to him from above, for your body was like the woman he must have loved to have me, I had seen her in those brown faded photographs with a floppy hat and a cane, in a garden, like you but fatter, with a lot of clothes that came off, the coloured dresses and blouses first, then the white underclothes, dampened under the armpits, between the legs.[4]

He wants his father to remember and himself to possess and to know his mother. For there is another beast, the passions emerging from the unconscious, that is as angry and destructive as de Valera's repression of individuality, and his lovemaking with the older woman is an act of revenge, lust, but of love, as well.

The civil war in the family ends one night with "four bangs and four rapid thuds" from her father's Civil War pistol into the door of the toilet, where his father sits "each shot wedging, hardly piercing the mahogany." The son cannot kill his father and possess the woman they love nor the woman she resembles. Ten years later, however, he does possess her completely, but she is no longer beautiful. Dying of cancer and embarrassed by her age, she still allows him to rekindle and to let his memories die. "Then I looked at you and saw the eiderdown rising each time you breathed and your body clenching itself every now and then as if you were dreaming of pain. And I knew it had ended but I still thought to myself, maybe tomorrow."[5] It is toward tomorrow that Jordan turned to create *The Miracle,* a film that explores and resolves many of the themes raised in the short stories, particularly those of creativity, freedom, and responsibility.

Although Jordan is an impressive short story writer, his short stories are *The Miracle* in embryonic form; their climaxes not epiphanies but quiet transitions into the next stage of development. Through color, light, music, a skillfully told story, and an inspired choice of actors, he transforms stories that are "masterful" but not "complete" into a brilliant film.

*The Miracle* opens with the camera following the face of a beautiful, blonde woman, mysterious behind her sunglasses. She is friendly. She smiles, points, gestures, and murmurs something incomprehensible while Wynton Marsalis plays the jazz standard "Stardust," as a sensuous instrumental. The heart of the film is here, in her face shaded the colors of an old photograph and in the music, at once sexual and sentimental.

She is the subject of much speculation by Jimmy and his friend Rose, the two teen-agers who spot her on the strand at Bray. Friends and rivals, brother and sister, theirs is the most balanced and fruitful relationship in the film and the relationship that has been missing for the boys in Jordan's short stories. Rose wants to be a writer, and she keeps a notebook of their observations, including Jimmy's enchantment with the mysterious blonde. He and Rose try to puzzle out her life. Jimmy thinks she is French and has run away from a "strange and fascinating past," and as the long summer days pass, he grows more attracted to the woman who is often caught as she emerges from the water like Venus, startling, and unexpected. In the film, the "Terrible Mother" of the short stories has been transformed into the less threatening, more maternal, although sexually provocative, image of the seductive older woman.

Jimmy lives with his father, a saxophonist in a local show band; his mother is dead. However, like the younger boys in the short stories, he feels a strange kind of loneliness as if something were missing. Rose has a family but prefers Jimmy's father, who although he drinks too much and is only a mediocre musician, cares about his child, unlike her own, indifferent father.

Jimmy has agreed to play in his father's band to earn money. He is far more talented than the other members of the band, and he is attracted to jazz and not to their tired renditions of big band tunes. From "Night in Tunisia," Jordan adapted the rivalry between father and son that he expresses through the metaphor of music. Jimmy and his father quarrel, as they often do, their musical tastes just another example of what separates them, and he quits the band. The circus has come to Bray and he gets a job playing the saxophone for the contortionist. Rose, half jealous of his fascination with the older woman, takes up with the animal trainer, a wild-looking boy around her own age.

Jordan's camera follows Jimmy closely as he stalks the woman through Dublin. Part of what makes a Jordan film so enjoyable is his love of scene and texture; even the most ordinary situation, a walk down a Dublin street or a ride on the DART (Dublin Area Rapid Transit) is created with an extraordinary beauty and a sense of mystery. The excitement and color of the Olympia Theatre, the circus at Bray, and the bustling "theatre on the strand," form the backdrops of this love story, as does the sea—its presence serene and majestic against the commotion on the shore.

Jimmy discovers that the blonde woman is a singer, star of *Destry Rides Again,* a musical at the Olympia. That the woman is somehow connected to his father becomes more apparent after he found the couple in a heated discussion during a break in the musical. Father and son fight over the woman as years of loneliness and disappointment find expression in fisticuffs and angry words. Although his father warns him to stay away, Jimmy pursues the woman more insistently. She refuses his advances, but she is attracted to the boy in spite of their age difference. Their scenes together are beautifully filmed. The sexual tension rises, and their flirtation moves dangerously close to seduction, although it is not clear who is seducing whom.

During a short scene, Rose and Jimmy wander into a chapel to discuss their troubles with God. Jimmy insists he has no reason to believe in God, but he and Rose light a candle anyway. Jimmy prays for seduction, Rose for a miracle. The statue of the Sacred Heart stares down at them, silent and inscrutable. Rose's prayer is answered.

There are a number of miracles in the film, including a rebirth. Jimmy's mother is resurrected when his father reveals that the beautiful blonde actress is his mother, which Jimmy knew the moment he saw her. In the story of Oedipus, revelation lead to terrible tragedy, but in *The Miracle,* knowledge leads to peace because of the presence of a father in his son's life. His father is the lifeguard from "Night in Tunisia." In spite of his drinking, he has raised a son he is proud of and has sought to protect, and he saves his son from a life like his. He hated his wife because the other thing—love—was too difficult. Things will be different for Jimmy; he and his father can now talk of love and hate and of his beautiful mother. Communication and not confrontation generates the growth of both characters.

The encounters with his father have been inside the narrow hallways of their house, often on an ill-lit stairway, with a dim light filtering through curtains and the sounds of the waves at Bray audible. When Jimmy confronts his mother interior scenes are quickly shifted to Bray Head, to the strand at night, lit by the bright lights of the circus, or into the moonlight—bright and clear in a murky sky. On Bray Head, she confesses her love for Jimmy and her disenchantment with his father. As she turns from him, she falls asleep, looking eerie and beautiful in a light that seems to dissolve her into the earth. She has become mother and muse, and Jimmy draws inspiration from her confession.

Rose, too, has sought an awakening. Hers is a confrontation with her sexual nature, and her plan to "tame the brute" is deliberate and conscious. By taming the animal trainer, a character who embodies all of Jordan's beasts—the authority that would crush and control and the "animal grace" of sexual passion—she must walk the line between sexual experience and corruption, which the boy in "Sand" was not able to do. In a brilliant fantasy scene, Rose's face filters through the circus contortionist's, and she picks up a rose with her teeth while her face and body dissolve into an elephant's eye, small, piercing, with long, feminine lashes. Here Jordan plucks Blake's dying rose and insists that loss of innocence is not tragic. However, this dark area—the price of creative freedom—is not one that Jordan explores in the film, the end seemingly justifying any means in a world where truth is hidden and control and repression the norm.

Rose releases the circus animals by seducing the animal trainer and stealing his keys. An elephant arrives in the chapel as Jimmy tries to explain his parents to God. Later, when she and Jimmy chat and the animals run loose on the strand, Rose insists that the elephant had nothing to do with her plan.

However, the elephant, symbolic of memory, the past, of strength, and of the libido, upsets the serenity of the small Catholic chapel and suggests the need for a balance between the individual as a complex of repressed and conscious emotions, desires, and the demands of church and state. This not a battle between self and society because, as Jordan established in "A Love," they are both bestial. *The Miracle* is not about the abandonment of religion and community, but it is about the need to be free from the beasts of respectability. In Jordan's world, worse than uncontrollable passions are the beasts of conformity and repression. The final miracle is, of course, the film itself. Jordan brings to his lost paradise all the beauty, the pain, and the wisdom of life itself.

Jordan finds his circus animals not in the myths of Ireland's past, which Yeats cherished, or in its stories of revolution and resistance, but in the ordinary world of Ireland's teenagers, in the Irish family, on Bray Head, and on Dublin's streets. Where Yeats would capture and sublimate experience into a magnificent artifact, as is shown in the final moments of *The Miracle,* Jordan would have process, passion, and art exist simultaneously. For Jordan, to return to the heart is to acknowledge a richness that only film can capture fully—only film can bring all of his circus animals to life.

# 10

# Man's Mythic Journey and the Female Principle in *My Left Foot*

## Douglas Brode

At first glance, *My Left Foot* appears to be a "one-of-a-kind" film. Certainly, the premise of Jim Sheridan's 1989 Oscar-winner (Best Actor Daniel Day-Lewis and Best Supporting Actress Brenda Fricker) is far from ordinary for a commercial venture. The motion picture was based in part on Christy Brown's 1954 autobiography, in part on the novel *Down All the Days* (1970), as well as on several other works relating the unique fact-based tale of an Irishman born with cerebral palsy who overcame his body's severely limited motor abilities to become an award-winning artist and writer, despite the fact that he could wield a paintbrush and type only by literally using his left foot. The film (directed and coscripted by Jim Sheridan with Shane Connaughton), when first screened on the arthouse circuit, raised expectations about the possibility of a renaissance for Irish film in the 1990s. The comparison, of course, was to the preceding decade's new wave of intriguing motion pictures that all but poured into the United States from Australia beginning with *Picnic at Hanging Rock, Gallipoli,* and *Breaker Morant,* and for several years drew the attention of international cineastes to films hailing from Down Under.

Could *My Left Foot* be the harbinger of a similarly unexpected but appreciated flurry of significant films from Ireland? Certainly, such post-*Foot* projects as *Into the West, The Crying Game,* and *Michael Collins* all attest to the ever-growing significance of Irish cinema in the 1990s. Though these films are all rich in themes considered specifically Irish in nature, and set against backdrops that are strikingly Irish, each film ultimately reaches beyond such local limitations owing to an underlying universality of ideas and emotions that transcends the particulars of story and setting. Certainly, that is true of *My Left Foot.* Though casual moviegoing audiences of the late eighties were overwhelmed by what they originally believed to be a simple, unadulterated biopic of a remarkable man, Sheridan and his collaborators purposefully forsook the effective but limiting docudrama approach. On the surface, the film is true enough to key details from Brown's life: his working-class background, his initially being misdiagnosed as a retarded child when in fact his dysfunctional body enslaved a brilliant mind, his hunger to prove his worth as an artist and as a person, his need to win romantic love as well as intellectual respect. But, as is always the case with a motion picture, the character's entire life had to be compressed, simplified, crystallized for the sake of a comprehensible 103–minute movie; moreover, as I have already suggested, the filmmakers drew less on Brown's life as history than on the life as it had already been mythologized by Brown himself and others in previous works that served as Sheridan's source material. Although the filmmaker clearly wanted to capture the essence of Brown's story, he was in no way enslaved by a dutiful belief that it was his responsibility to remain artistically invisible while doing so.

In the process of making his selections from a wealth of material, Sheridan borrowed, consciously or otherwise, from the approach of John Ford. That Hollywood director was, up until the current interest in Ireland as a cinematic setting that began with John Huston's final film, *The Dead* (1987), the most influential of world-class filmmakers who have approached Ireland as setting, subject, and source of stories. Indeed, many of Ford's American historical films have been heavily influenced by Irish of the immigrant variety (the frontier army in *Fort Apache*, Boston politics in *The Last Hurrah*). Often, Ford went straight to the source, in such films as *The Informer, The Quiet Man,* and *The Rising of the Moon*. In these films, Ford offered mythical, romanticized visions of Ireland, created by an American of Irish descent. The movies—owing to the quality of moviemaking and commercial popularity—formed a collective vision of Ireland in the minds of Americans and, for that matter, moviegoers the world over. Like Ford, Sheridan understood the need to choose what critics of today like to call a "through-line," eliminating much fascinating anecdotal material to create a straightforward narrative that is both emotionally involving and intellectually stimulating. Once such an organizational approach is assumed, "realism" becomes a style, a look, a tone, ultimately an illusion for a film that appears to be taking place in the real world, but actually has its roots in basic, conventional, even ancient forms of traditional and ritualistic storytelling.

In this context, the uniqueness of Christy Brown's situation provides the specific variation necessary to make an old theme vital again. The nature of that theme is clear from the way in which Sheridan chose to structure and frame his material: a "current" situation that allows for, indeed necessitates, a recalling (and reinterpretation) of the past story as key moments, ripe with meaning, pass through Christy's mind. A dignified, professorial type (old pro Cyril Cusack, with little to do or say but whose very presence, with its echoes of a host of previous movies, sums up vast symbolic import for what occurs) lords over a benefit for cerebral palsy victims. Christy has (as a person who overcame any preconception that the disease must necessarily be limiting) been persuaded to attend by friend and mentor Eileen (Fiona Shaw). We do not yet know any of this; all we see, for the time being, is Christy as he travels by limo to the appointed mansion. A nurse named Mary (Ruth McCabe) attends to Christy while, in a private drawing room, he waits his turn to speak and receive an award.

As he does—and as Mary, fascinated to learn that the man in her care has written about his life, reads the book *My Left Foot*—Christy thinks back over the life that has brought him here. The process—for him, for the filmmakers, and for the viewer—is complex. The obvious response is to believe that what we see unfolding on-screen, in a series of flashbacks, is a random selection of incidents, accurately remembered and realistically rendered, as they casually pass through Christy's mind at this moment of what Gail Sheehy would call a "passage" in his life. In fact, though, such a reading is naïve and incorrect. We must take the immediate situation specifically; it is (as we will learn by the movie's end) Christy's intense awareness of Mary reading Christy's book that causes him to selectively recall the past. In another situation, he might visualize the past incidents quite differently, might for that matter recall different incidents altogether.

What Sheridan's film shares with us, then, is Christy's vision of his life as he conceives it at that moment before he all but throws away his opportunity for public esteem in front of an upscale audience compulsively and desperately to pursue an unlikely romance with a working-class woman. If he is to woo her and win her, he must appear to her as something of a hero-figure. That is of extreme importance, since Mary has made it abundantly clear that she has a date for later in the evening with an ordinary man of her own class. In casually overheard conversation between Christy and Mary, we grasp that she is mildly attracted to this man, though hardly in rapturous love with him. Christy, then, can compete, and to do that, must prove irresistible. If this is not possible in terms of looks, then—like a knight of old winning the fair maid—he may accomplish his aim as a result of his deeds. The actual autobiography by Brown is too humble to suggest there was anything truly heroic in nature about his accomplishments, only that he knew what he wanted to be and set out to become precisely that: accepted as a respected man of letters. But the Christy of Sheridan's film, nervously watching Mary read the "realistic" account of those incidents, now recalls them (and visualizes them for us) as he hopes she will interpret the bare facts.

This situation, then, provides a fascinating cinematic variation on the literary device of the "teller" of the tale and his relationship to the "listener." Numerous studies of Conrad's novels have remarked on the effect that the personality of the hopefully sympathetic listener has in shaping the second-hand story, even as it is related by the narrator; the "ear" is as significant as the "voice." During our experience of viewing Sheridan's movie, we watch as Mary reads, though the dramatic or comic sequences taking place on-screen are not representations of what she finds in his words, rather what Christy hopes she will be inspired to envision as a result of them.

The story that subsequently unfolds on-screen is what Joseph Campbell would refer to in *The Power of Myth* as one of the endlessly satisfying variations on the hero's journey. (Let's not forget that the film begins with a physical "journey" of sorts.) Like England's Arthur and endless other hero-figures, Christy Brown is raised in humble surroundings but early on senses his difference from everyone around him. He must remain true to this vision of himself as unique and apart if he is to overcome his seemingly impossible adversary, his own "dragon." After many temporary setbacks, he eventually does just that and, in so doing, rises to truly heroic stature; now, he must at last win the hand of the fair lady and achieve national recognition. Christy's award at the benefits ceremony, in which Cusack's character transforms into a modern variation of some ancient Celtic king, is the contemporary equivalent of knighthood bestowed. The overcoming of Christy's cerebral palsy—not the disease, which can never be banished entirely, but the apparent limitations caused by the disease, which he heroically manages to overcome completely—represents the defeat of his adversary, the slaying of his own "dragon." All Christy needs is his fair lady—if not a Guenevere, then at the very least an Elaine of Astolat—for the story to end with a happily-ever-after sense of closure. Then, and only then, will we have a fairytale for adults—or, more precisely, a modern myth in which the ancient notion of the hero's journey is played out believably (if somewhat less realistically than our first impression might suggest) in a contemporary setting, in this case Ireland.

From the film's first flashback, Sheridan makes clear that Christy's hero-journey will be made possible only through the presence of the female principle. Despite the film's reputation as a groundbreaking work in the modern Irish cinema, Sheridan relies on stereotypical images of women and men that are at best quaintly traditional, at worst dehumanizing in their simplistic revival of screen clichés. These images pass back beyond the films of John Ford, who consistently romanticized them with gusto and genius, further on still through Irish literature, both serious and popular, to the oral tradition. On the night when Christy is born, his father Paddy (Ray McAnally) wanders into a local pub, insists on a brew he cannot pay for, then punches out a fellow lout who dares to joke about Paddy's offspring. In contrast, Paddy's mother Mary (Brenda Fricker) is presented as such a conventional representation of the long-suffering Irish wife-and-mother that her name rings with religious symbolism.

If these elements attest to the John Ford influence, other golden-age Hollywood directors also impacted on Sheridan's version of the Christy Brown Story. It is not John Ford but George Stevens from whom Sheridan borrows as he visually delineates the "worlds" in which Paddy and his wife move. Sheridan relies on *Shane*, perhaps the most impressive of Irish-influenced westerns (even the title reverberates with a sense of the old sod reborn on American soil) for his visual symbols. In Stevens's 1952 film of that Jack Schaefer novel, the farmer played by Van Heflin is constantly seen entering the home from his work in the fields; the doorway serves as his identifying symbol. His wife (Jean Arthur) appears a prisoner in her humble house, peering out at the male action which she is at best peripherally related to; the window is her identifying symbol. The house itself, their common ground, is the place he returns to, feeling something of a stranger, and the only place where she exerts any sense of control, empowered (a predecessor of the heroine in *Like Water for Chocolate* some forty years later) by those acts of cooking and cleaning she constantly performs.

In *My Left Foot*, Sheridan effectively revives both those visual motifs. Mary is almost always observed through a glass, if not necessarily darkly; Paddy staggers in, exhausted from work or drunk from the pub. Immediately, we notice that their crippled son (Hugh O'Conor, playing Christy as a child) recoils from the father and is drawn to the mother. The near-Neanderthal male cannot relate to the one among his offspring who happens to have been born "different." But his mother—with her generous, supportive mother-love for a child, however sad his condition—nurtures him, and he responds. Importantly, Christy's first "heroic" act in the film is to save his mother's life; when, during an illness, she accidentally falls down the stairs in her home, Christy with great difficulty manages to crawl to the door and kick loudly until someone hears and help arrives.

In context, this seems a unique moment in a unique movie; in fact it is a satisfying variation on the age-old notion of the male hero figure proving himself, early on, by rescuing a woman in distress. Christy's heroic action goes unappreciated; owing to his inarticulateness, the neighbors loudly proclaim that he has "the mind of a three-year-old." One particularly nasty neighbor-woman, a foil for Christy's own Madonna-like mother, goes so far as to announce this in front of the child. We see the pain in Christy's face; but we also see that, rather than some sad victim, he is spurred on to prove himself. There follows the scene in which Christy's older sister attempts to solve a math problem ("What is a quarter of a quarter?") and, significantly, turns to her father—the paternal male—for help. In a narrow, ignorant, self-aggrandizing, and dismissive manner, Paddy asserts that there is no such thing ("a quarter is a quarter"). Christy, however, quickly calculates in his mind and seizes a piece of chalk with his left foot to scribble the answer on the floor.

There is more than a suggestion of an Oedipal situation in Sheridan's scene: Christy, competing with the father he wishes would go away so that he would have his mother all to himself. No one grasps what he is trying to do, or understands how desperately Christy needs to communicate. The sister, who possesses a strong if incomplete element of mother Mary's female principle—the positive pole in this picture, as it has been in traditionalist movies ever since the work of D. W. Griffith—comes the closest to understanding, while the brute father remains completely uncomprehending. Christy realizes, though, that if he is to break through, it will be to a woman, not a man, be it his father or any substitute father-figure. Understandably, then, the "good father" from the church, supposedly the possessor of eternal knowledge, only attempts to frighten Christy with antisexual rantings and ravings: "You can get out of purgatory; you can't get out of hell." If Christy is frightened by religion, he is also terrified of its antithesis: on Halloween, when the neighbor boys dress up as devilish creatures of the night, Christy once again recoils in horror.

Yet during his hero's journey, Christy senses that he must compete in this world of men. So during a street soccer game, he plays—and wins—by biting an adversary on the leg, rewriting the makeshift rules to his own advantage. In a later scene that recalls the drunken barroom brawls of Ford's *The Quiet Man,* Christy manages to fight alongside his father and brothers when they take on another family's men in a pub fight. When the Brown family is all but freezing to death during a harsh winter (Paddy, let go from work, is the impotent raging male who cannot provide for his family), it is Christy who devises a scheme whereby his brothers may steal coal from a passing truck. Christy wins the respect of men thanks to his machismo, which is intellectually sharp enough to surpass his obvious physical limitations. Still, he is sensitive (as the other men are not) to his mother's moral rejection (her name is, after all, Mary!) of coal won through dishonest means, as well as her insistence that such devilish coal should not be burned in their furnace. When the men insist, and the coal does indeed burn, the mother's power for moral uplift in her home—her corner of the universe—is momentarily diminished. Understandably, we view her sitting in a cold outer room, consciously refusing herself the desperately needed warmth. Meanwhile, the others—the less moral men—crowd about the furnace for warmth.

Christy's ongoing desire to operate as part of the rugged male community, intriguingly balanced by his now necessary reliance on those women who most strongly project the female principle, is next witnessed when the teenagers play spin-the-bottle. One attractive young woman, Rachel, tries to win a kiss from a handsome lad, only to have her spun bottle accidentally point directly at Christy. She makes the best of what she considers a bad situation and kisses him sweetly on the cheek, proclaiming: "You're the nicest of the lot." But he mistakes her kindness—a potential-motherly gentleness that naturally derives from her female sensitivity to his difficult situation—for romantic love. So Christy meets with his first great rejection: Rachel returns the beautiful paintings he creates for her in his first awkward attempt to win a woman through his art.

But if Christy learns a lesson from this unpleasant and embarrassing experience, it is not that he will forever be cut off from the warmth of romance, destined to know only mother-love from women who will serve as surrogates for his own mother. He does not want this, absolutely refuses this, and so—with a hero's intensity—fights to overcome this treatment as fiercely as he did the limits of his palsy. At this point in the flashback, Christy's sister becomes pregnant by a boyfriend; the father's reaction is Irish-machismo (he wants to throw her out on the street) while the understanding mother arranges a hurried marriage ceremony. Then, in one of the many crosscuts to the present story, Christy asks the nurse Mary for a light. "Don't you think I'm your mother because I'm looking after you for the evening," she insists.

In fact, that's the last thing in the world Christy wants from her, despite the fact that she shares his mother's name, and offers him salvation, even though in her tartiness she is clearly more of a Magdalene than a Virgin Mother. Christy knows that he is at another point in his life now: then he was a boy, now he is a man. From his first Mary, he wanted, needed, demanded motherly support; from this Mary, he wants, needs, demands respect and a sense of mutual attraction, however unlikely a possibility that may be. Mary's abrupt statement impacts on Christy's mental selectivity as he immediately slips back into his highly subjective recollection (and recreation) of the past. At this point, we watch as the mother's role in Christy's life reaches a crescendo. It was she who somehow saved the needed money to buy Christy a wheelchair (the father would have spent it on necessities or, more likely, brew); it was she who saw something in Christy's paintings and showed them around; it was she who finds Dr. Eileen Cole and brings her to the home. "You're a great painter," Eileen announces, as she takes charge, or at the very least shares the mother's business of helping Christy make a meaningful life for himself.

Eileen (an Irish form for Elaine) is the transitory bridge between the two Marys, though Christy cannot know that yet, or that he even needs to cross such a bridge, though in fact most every hero does just that: a physical bridge that represents the emotional gulf he must pass over on his way to self-realization. So Eileen assumes the role of the mother Mary but is mistaken by Christy (at his awkward in-between stage between boyhood and manhood) for a woman who will play the role in his life that Mary the nurse will eventually assume. Whenever Eileen exits the humble home with Christy, the mother is seen through the second-floor window, glancing down. Visually, Sheridan reminds us that Mary the mother is the catalyst who made this happen, though she is unable to share much of Christy's newfound life in the art world. However, her female-principle must (and will) be continued, and in an unlikely person: Cyril Cusack is seen, in the framing story, photographed through the window in his mansion, peering down at the approaching Christy. Through the editing of parallel images, he is presented to us as a man who can carry through on the female principle heretofore represented first by Christy's mother, then by Eileen. Not all men are like Paddy; this man is able to offer loving support.

Christy, however, is still horribly frustrated. He has misinterpreted Eileen's gregarious, enthusiastic friendliness (she has an unconscious habit of plopping down on the bed beside him) as sexual attraction. At one point in Christy's development, he appears to have it all, possessing both sides of the female principle he so hungers for: Eileen, curled up on the bed with him, seemingly a possessable romantic figure while also a stimulus for his intellect, spurring him on to read Shakespeare; in the next room, his mother, ironing, washing, cooking, and cleaning. Christy has the traditional housebound woman for his mother, the ultramodern career woman as mentor and intended wife.

Which only sets Christy up for his greatest crisis. On the night of his artistic success, Christy loudly announces his love for Eileen at the party that follows; awkwardly, she announces her plans to marry the art dealer whose gallery houses Christy's work. At that point, Christy becomes as drunk as his father has ever been. "You're not my mother," Christy screams at her. "Never forget that." Meanwhile, the unlikely parallel between Paddy and Christy—two seemingly polar-opposite males—has already been firmly established. At precisely that moment when Christy was hard at work, studying Shakespeare, the father was seen quoting Hamlet's "To be or not to be" speech; shortly thereafter, Christy all but makes that speech literal when, in his despair at ever knowing romantic love, he considers suicide with a razor.

"You get more like your father every day," his mother exhorts. "Hard on the outside; putty on the inside." Even the least likely and most artistic man will gradually move backward toward that Neanderthal pole, much to the chagrin of the sensitive woman who would nurture his "higher" elements, only to express disappointment when he regresses, despite her positive influence. Yet whereas Christy's nature is male enough to be all too capable of such regression, he has been too carefully nurtured by the mother to succumb without thought. His mother's words express precisely the fate Christy consciously wants to escape from, so he sets out to do just that. When all the Brown men spontaneously enter into a contest as they lay bricks to build a new room, the mother secretly exhorts the brothers: "Let your father win. He needs it." Christy and the others do as told. The father's rare moment of warmth afterward is the closest he can come to breaking out of his hard Irish male attitude; "That's the nearest he'll ever come to saying he loves you," the uneducated but instinctively wise mother explains. If there is a certain sense of reconciliation between father and son here, it is tinged by Christy's realization that he does not want to be like this man. Or, at least, does not want to be entirely like him. A balance must be possible between that part of him which, for better or worse, is like his father, and the female principle existing within himself (just as it exists within Cyril Cusack's character) that he can acknowledge and accept, as his own father could not.

So Christy must overcome his difficult reaction at earning eight hundred pounds for his writing; "More money than your father earned in a whole year," his mother sighs. But success as an author as well as a painter is not the apex for Christy. He must with difficulty accept Eileen as a loving friend rather than the lover and friend he hoped (and dreamed) she would become. He must accept her invitation to speak at the benefit. And he must continue drinking with Mary the nurse, pushing her to cancel her date for that night and spend the evening with him instead. At this key moment, Christy at last strikes a balance between his father's machismo and his mother's sensitivity. He drinks too much and shouts at Mary, embarrassing her as well as the gathered people in the next room. He attempts to make his acceptance speech in front of Eileen and the others, then is gratified to see that Mary—who slipped out the door when her official duties were finished—has chosen to return. We do not need to hear any words telling us that she has stood up her date to spend the evening with him; in the visual language of the cinema, we simply see this.

Christy is last seen with Mary, on a hill overlooking what appears to be a lovely stretch of Irish countryside. In fact, the place is the peninsula of Howth, offering a view back on the Dublin Harbor. Anyone familiar with Irish geography knows full well that the setting is urban/suburban, yet Sheridan frames his shot to make such city elements all but invisible, cut out of his frame through careful camera placement. What the shot evokes, then, is the countryside far to the rural west, the areas surrounding Kerry and Mayo, which those multitudes who know Ireland not through direct experience but through motion pictures associate with John Ford's *The Quiet Man*. In fact, Christy and Mary look, even sound remarkably like John Wayne and Maureen O'Hara in that film. Their raucous give-and-take, which has itself given way to romantic love, leaves us with the dramatically satisfying sense of closure this film has been moving toward all along. The unlikely hero has found his proper balance between his father's rugged masculinity and his mother's sensitivity. In so doing, he has slain the final dragon and won his fair maiden, if not the one he first hoped for (he is in the good company here of Tristram and numerous other hero-figures), then instead the one fate delivered to him as compensation. He has completed his hero's journey, which is why we feel a sense of satisfaction leaving him at this point. The originality of the plot specifics and situation, which provide the all-important freshness any variation on a theme must boast if it is to strike us as successful and worthwhile, cannot mask our collective reaction that this is, in terms of essential dramatic structure, the oldest story of all, here given a new and (on the surface, at least) original lease on life.

# 11
## Huston and Joyce
Bringing "The Dead" to the Screen

## Moylan C. Mills

For twenty years during the mid-passage of his life, film writer and director John Huston resided in western Ireland. Huston, an Irish-American by heritage, loved Ireland, and he loved the work of James Joyce above all. It is fitting, therefore, that the last of his thirty-seven feature films should be an adaptation of Joyce's celebrated short story "The Dead," the final piece in Joyce's 1914 collection *Dubliners*. Huston had long wanted to bring this story of middle-class Irish celebrating the feast of the Epiphany to the screen and was finally able to do so with the collaboration of his son Tony during the winter and spring of 1987.

Huston had always been attracted to literature for his films. Most likely this interest in books stemmed from his being bedridden for a prolonged period at the age of twelve with life-threatening heart and kidney problems. He spent a great deal of that time reading. In fact, he is reported to have read three or four books a week into his early eighties. At any rate, many of his films have been based on novels or plays, including *The Maltese Falcon, Moby Dick, The Treasure of Sierra Madre,* and *Prizzi's Honor,* as well as *The Red Badge of Courage, The African Queen, Reflections in a Golden Eye, Key Largo, The Night of the Iguana, Fat City, Wise Blood, Under the Volcano,* and *The Man Who Would Be King.*

The conventional view of film adaptations from literary sources has generally been that of theater and film critic John Simon, who states unequivocally that "no great work of literature can be turned into a comparable movie."[1] I would argue, however, that Huston's film, on close examination, provides a refutation of Simon's patronizing approach to films based on literary works.

When Huston embarked on his project to film *The Dead,* most Hollywood wise guys were skeptical, not because they agreed with Simon's lofty view, but because Huston was dealing with James Joyce—and all of that strange stream-of-consciousness prose—*and* with a story that depends for its ultimate effect on nuances of perception and on long passages of interior monologue. How does a film director translate that kind of material to the screen? Where's the beef? That is, where's the action?

Huston's adaptation, however, is not the first time that "The Dead" has been used as the basis for a film. In 1953, Italian director Roberto Rossellini created an English-language film loosely adapted from Joyce's story. *Voyage in Italy*, also known as *Strangers*, features Ingrid Bergman and George Sanders as a couple who try to sort out their deteriorating marital relationship during a trip through Italy. *Voyage in Italy* was a critical and commercial failure that had minimal distribution in the United States. Recently, increased interest in Bergman's work with Rossellini during her exile from Hollywood has generated additional attention for the film.

The film that emerged from the Huston/Joyce connection has been hailed by almost every critic and reviewer—but not the aforementioned John Simon—as an outstanding artistic achievement. To illustrate, Denis Donoghue in a lengthy critical examination in the *New York Review of Books* concluded that "the film [is] superb in the most comprehensive regard";[2] Richard A. Blake, writing in *America*, pointed out that Huston "has orchestrated all the parts into what can only be called a masterpiece";[3] and Richard Shickel in *Time* magazine called the film "sublime."[4]

Joyce's story is, on the surface, quite simple. A group of Dubliners gather for the annual Epiphany dinner dance and musicale at the apartment of the elderly sisters Kate and Julia Morkan and their middle-aged niece Mary Jane, all of whom have taken a major part in the musical life of the city. Among the guests at the party are Gabriel and Gretta Conroy. Gabriel is the Morkan sisters' favorite nephew, and it is Gabriel who will carve the goose, look after the drunken Freddy Malins, and present the celebratory toast to the hostesses. Gabriel, a university professor and book reviewer, seems troubled, tense. He is nervous about his speech—will it be too highbrow? will he appear clownish? He is also accused by one of the guests of being a "West Briton," that is, sympathetic to the English view of the Irish question. And finally, after returning to the hotel where he and Gretta are staying for the night, Gabriel discovers that the reason Gretta was so taken by the singing of the ballad "The Lass of Aughrim" at the party is that the song was sung to her by a young man with whom she was in love long ago as a teenager, a young man for whose early death she feels somewhat responsible. Quite shattered by this confession, especially by Gretta's revelation of her strong emotional attachment to her young suitor, Gabriel, at the close of the story, reflects upon the inexplicable connections between the living and the dead as the snow falls soundlessly, blanketing the Irish countryside and the abodes of the dead and the living alike.

The story is one of nuance, mood, and reflection, and John and Tony Huston are faithful to these aspects of Joyce's work, as well as to the overall structure. Tony has said that he first wrote a literal film script of the story and then adapted that script to take into consideration the screen medium.[5] For instance, he has cut out most of Joyce's initial exposition and begins the film immediately with an establishing exterior shot of the Morkan household, then cuts quickly to the guests arriving at the party. Through close-ups of Gabriel, the viewer can see that he is a bit "edgy." Huston, however, has deleted most of the interior monologue that would explain his behavior. Gabriel's uneasiness is presented instead by his wary, preoccupied manner caught by Huston's camera. A brief scene in the men's lavatory between Gabriel and the amiable drunk Freddy Malins has been added to underscore another of Gabriel's habits, his sense of responsibility as he attempts to tidy up Freddy to keep him from ruining the party and upsetting the Morkan sisters.

Tony Huston has added one new character to the cast, a Mr. Grace, an expansive English professor who works at the university with Gabriel and who recites for the partygoers a translation by Lady Gregory of a traditional Irish poem called "Broken Vows." This lament by a young girl for a boy who has disappointed her in love is a favorite of Tony Huston's and was inserted to trigger Gretta's remembrance of the lost love of her youth. This remembrance is further sharpened when she later hears the ballad "The Lass of Aughrim" sung by Bartell D'Arcy, a well-known local opera singer who is another guest at the party. Tony Huston has pointed out that he invented Mr. Grace for the singular purpose of introducing the poem, the recitation of which is intercut with several striking shots of Anjelica Huston, playing Gretta, as she responds ruefully to the tale of unrequited love. Tony Huston has, thus, introduced the "lost love" theme earlier in the film; furthermore, he has given added emotional weight to Gretta's feelings without violating the essential truth of Gretta's character.

Other changes include the lengthening of the operatic discussion during the dinner, thus providing the singer Bartell D'Archy with a larger role and also pointing up his romantic interest in his dinner partner, Miss O'Callaghan. Tony Huston has also enlarged the roles of

Freddy and his sour disapproving mother, adding a bit of comic relief to the proceedings. Another addition is a wink that Miss Ivors, the Irish Republican who accuses Gabriel of being a West Briton, gives Gabriel during Mr. Grace's poetry recital. The wink suggests that Miss Ivors, though critical of Gabriel, finds him attractive. In fact, the film script more than the story suggests that Gabriel finds Miss Ivors attractive, too. This sexual tension underscores the unspoken eroticism, kept in careful check, that informs the gathering and that motivates Gabriel's later ardor for Gretta when they return to their hotel after leaving the party. Another change involves the placement of the "Johnny-the-horse" story. In the film, it is during the carriage ride to the hotel, not earlier as in the story, that Gabriel relates the tale of his grandfather and his crazy horse, Johnny. Tony Huston has said that he shifted the story of Johnny in order to show Gabriel, sensing Gretta's distant mood, trying to break through to her with a bit of levity and failing, thus, providing the audience with a cinematic equivalent to Gabriel's inner voice as set forth by Joyce.

Another cinematic addition occurs when Aunt Julia is persuaded by the revelers to sing "Arrayed for the Bridal." Once the possessor of a fine, rich voice, Julia makes a brave try at the song and pulls it off, although it is obvious, despite the too lavish praise of Freddy Malins, that her voice is well past its prime. However, the Hustons, to their great credit, resist the temptation to emphasize the comic aspects of the scene and instead treat the moment with tenderness and understanding, as did Joyce. During the song, Huston's camera moves about the empty private rooms of the Morkan apartment, creating a montage of heirlooms and old cherished photographs of long-dead family members, suggesting the ever present leitmotif of living and dead that runs throughout the film and story.

The montage that accompanies Julia's song finds its equivalent later, during the film's closing moments, when Gabriel, standing at the hotel window, not lying in bed as he does in the story, observes the snowstorm. A series of shots of various locations around the country under siege by the snowfall, overlapping with stately serenity, unfolds on the screen. It is during this montage that Gabriel in voice-over arrives at his own private understanding of his interconnectedness with the dead who have gone before, as well as with those still living. Thus, the structure of the film, even more than that of the story, points up certain correlations: the recital of the poem followed later by the singing of the ballad by D'Archy; the cinematic montage during Julia's song followed by the concluding montage as Gabriel stares out the hotel window; and Gabriel's half-mocking, half-serious toast to the Morkan women followed by his concluding heartfelt and bittersweet thoughts on the universal condition. The overarching design, then, of both the film and the story is the journey from the first section, with the hustle-bustle and good fellowship of the dancing and dinner undercut by the accompanying intimations of needs unmet and desires unfulfilled, of disappointments and regrets amid the gaiety—to the second section, with the tearful confession, the rueful reflection, the bittersweet knowl-edge of mortality and eternity: from the specific to the universal, the epiphany on the day of the Epiphany.

Tony Huston has described how difficult it was to shoot the con-cluding moments of the film. Joyce's great final monologue was first eliminated entirely, and only the cinematic montage overlaid with the plaintive strains of "The Lass of Aughrim" was used. This approach did not work. The Hustons then tried using a third-person narration of the Joycean words during the montage. This approach failed also. The third and subsequently successful solution was to have Gabriel voice the words—slightly rearranged by Tony Huston—while the montage accompanied by the ballad played on the screen. The other problem with the ending focused on Anjelica Huston's confessional scene. This confession by Gretta to Gabriel of her youthful love occurs immedi-ately before Gabriel's reflections and helps to motivate them. Anjelica, John's daughter and Tony's sister, was very apprehensive about doing this scene, her most important and crucial moment in the film. The scene was shot, according to Tony Huston, "about twenty-seven times."[6] Finally, John Huston thought that they had a perfect shot, only to discover that the camera had caught the edge of the set during this so-called final take. When she was told that she would have to do an-other run-through, Anjelica became hysterical. Her father decided, therefore, to go with the take that included the questionable footage, and, in fact, audiences have never noticed the mistake.

The style of the film is simple, sparse, elegant. The camera glides effortlessly from one group to another during the party, catching the guests and the hostesses most often in medium-close and close shots, using the theory of proxemic distance to create empathy for the charac-ters. Interspersed with the many close shots are judiciously placed reestablishing long shots of the parlor and dining room and of the exte-rior of the Morkan household. Because of budget limitations—*The Dead* cost $3.5 million to produce in an era when the average film cost $15 to $20 million to make—the interiors were shot in a warehouse in Valencia, California, whereas the exteriors were shot in Dublin using the actual house where the events are supposed to have taken place when Joyce wrote the story in 1907. (Incidentally, shortly after the filming, the house was torn down.) Huston, by the way, in an opening title, places the date of the film's events as occurring on 6 January, 1904, perhaps to allude to the celebrated Bloomsday, 16 June, 1904, of Joyce's *Ulysses.*

In an era when many filmmakers—in order to appeal to a public that has surrendered its powers of concentration to the rat-tat-tat style of television commercials—have kept the length of most of their shots to five seconds or less, Huston has the audacity to hold his shots in the closing section of the film to over a minute or more—a long time for a film shot—thus, correlating his cinematic style with the elegant dying fall of Joyce's story and allowing his performers to develop a continuity of character in the way that they would on stage, where there are no "cuts" in the interaction. And his actors take every advantage provided by Huston's directorial style. Donal McCann, the excellent Irish actor, brings great understated passion to his role as the sensitive, puzzled Gabriel. Anjelica Huston, perhaps a bit too statuesque for the role of Gretta, nevertheless, gives a fine, muted portrayal of a woman whose memories of a long-ago love have been stirred by the events of the evening. The supporting players, including Donal Donnelly as Freddy and Cathleen Delane and Helena Carroll as the Morkan sisters, are perfectly cast and create the right sense of verisimilitude needed to bring Joyce's story to life.

Another sequence that is handled very differently in the film is the staircase scene at the close of the party. In the story, Gabriel stands in the shadows of the downstairs hallway, gazing at a female figure standing also in half-light, transfixed at the top of the stairs listening to Bartell D'Arcy sing "The Lass of Aughrim." Gabriel, profoundly moved by the emotional intensity of the woman's intent stillness, realizes that the woman is Gretta. He is quite overwhelmed by the almost spiritual power of the moment and by his sense of wonder that this mysterious figure is his wife. In the film, the scene is played, not in shadow, but in full light, in a series of medium-long and close shots. As if to compensate for keeping his star fully lit throughout the scene, rather than in shadow, Huston has provided a stained glass crescent window to frame Anjelica and has draped her head with a pale-colored shawl. The muted colors of the glass and the shawl transform Gretta into a kind of Madonna-like figure, thus suggesting the quintessential female symbol that Gabriel sees in the figure of his wife at that moment.

This staircase scene is a subclimax in the story and in the film, for it underscores Gabriel's intense longing for an emotional and physical union with his wife and sets in motion the subsequent hotel room sequence in which Gretta reveals her long-ago love and the strong feelings brought forth on hearing Bartell D'Arcy's plaintive song. At first glance, it would seem that Huston's alterations to the scene might dissipate its pathos and mystery. However, the director and his colleagues have utilized cinematic techniques that not only keep the underlying intensity of the scene intact, but also allow the meaning to be expressed more clearly to an audience that may be unfamiliar with the story.

For their color design, Huston, his production designer, Stephen Grimes, and his costume designer, Dorothy Jeakins, use a muted palette of beiges, tans, and dark grays with cream and rose highlights, a combination perfectly in tune with the faded wallpaper in the Morkan apartment. This design creates a sense of looking at an ancient sepia photograph and provides an exact correlation with the nostalgic, reflective mood of the story. And Huston's cinematographer, Fred Murphy, unerringly catches this muted ambience with his soft-focus photography of the well-used interiors and the snowy Dublin streets.

Both Hustons have taken enormous pains to remain faithful to the spine and essence of Joyce's story. This fidelity is remarkable, for when most filmmakers adapt a short story to the screen, they feel the need— and perhaps in some cases rightly so—to embellish and add to the story. Alfred Hitchcock, for instance, in his adaptations of *Psycho* and *Rear Window,* used only the bare plot outline of each story in structuring almost entirely new works. Not so Huston. His obvious love of Joyce's work prevented him from making radical and possibly damaging changes, especially in his re-creation of the final moments of the story, that is, Gabriel's recognition—building all evening—of his disgust and disillusion with the petty follies of his fellow Dubliners and his simultaneous recognition of his inescapable connectedness with them and with all humankind, living and dead. Film and literature critic David Denby has called this great concluding monologue "bitterly eloquent" and "without equal in all of English literature."[7] And Huston's "snowfall" montage—both bleak and serene—that accompanies Gabriel's salient recognition captures with superb cinematic grace the Joycean insight.

There is no doubt that Huston probably misses some of Joyce's vitriol. Joyce is leaving these people and this country forever, and *Dubliners* is his sad, angry farewell to the Irish who, mired, as he felt, in their own limitations, so misunderstood him. Joyce can leave Ireland—

Gabriel, his surrogate, says, "I'm sick of this country"—but he can never truly get away from the signal events that took place in early-twentieth-century Dublin and that forever shaped his life. No matter his anger and disappointment, Joyce dissects the hopes, anxieties, and frustrations of his countrymen with penetrating insight and compassion. It is this compassion in *all* its complexity that John and Tony Huston have underscored in their version of *The Dead*.

Unfortunately, John Huston did not live to hear the acclaim for his film nor to know that he had won the New York Film Critics prize for best director once again and that he had also been nominated for an Academy Award. He died before *The Dead* was released, while working as an actor in a film version of Thornton Wilder's *Theophilus North*, directed by Tony. However, it is more than fitting that John Huston's last film should be one of his best—perhaps his best—and also the one that is closest to his Irish roots and soul.

# 12

# Cathal Black's *Pigs*

Ambivalence, Confinement, and the
Search for an Irish Sense of Place

## Jim Loter

Irish literature and verse has an obsessive fascination with naming places—it indicates a veritable "topomania" which belies an almost desperate attempt to seize upon some sense of permanence and meaning amidst a history of upheaval, flux, occupation, and destruction. In *"Genius Fabulae:* The Irish Sense of Place," Patrick Sheeran writes: "It is well-nigh a truism that Irishness and a sense of place go together."[1] The paradox of this prominence of placehood in Irish self-identity is that "while we credit ourselves with a strong sense of place, the places themselves are allowed to go to wrack and ruin."[2] Sheeran notes with irony that given the history of Ireland and the current littered state of its landmarks, countryside, and cities we should be properly speaking of a sense of "placelessness."[3] But Irish culture is defined, he continues, by this very paradox—by a sense of placehood that is not predicated upon the construction of enclosures, monuments, or structures but by a placehood that exists primarily through representation—"by being known and being talked about."[4] It is within this paradox that Cathal Black's *Pigs* (1984) operates, and it is the tension between a stable placehood and the tumult of unsettledness wherein *Pigs* locates the ambivalence that defines modern Irish urban culture. This ambivalence reveals not only a facet of Irish national identity, but challenges widely held assumptions about placehood within the field of cultural studies. The Irish sense of place described by *Pigs* breaks with the Western philosophical standard of placehood as rootedness or groundedness that finds its pinnacle in the writings of Martin Heidegger and informs geographical analyses throughout the century.[5] Furthermore, the nominality of Irish placehood offers a positive alternative to the leftist critique of place found in the influential work of David Harvey.

*Pigs* ends with an enigmatic and seemingly gratuitous shot of the Wellington Bridge in Dublin. The lingering, picture-postcard image encapsulates this filmic parable about a group of unemployed drifters who settle for a time in an abandoned Georgian townhouse. It exists as the second bookend to the film's opening shots of ruined houses, burning cars, and anachronistic horse riders. In *Poetry, Language, Thought*, Heidegger writes: "The bridge swings over the stream "with ease and power." It does not just connect the banks that are already there. The bridge designedly causes them to lie across from one another."

The bridge gathers to itself in its own way earth and sky, divinities and mortals.[6] The unity of those four concepts—earth, sky, divinities, mortals—for Heidegger constitutes "the fourfold," and "mortals *are* in the fourfold by *dwelling*. . . . Dwelling preserves the fourfold by bringing the presencing of the fourfold into things."[7] The bridge serves as a metaphor for totality, "indeed, [the bridge] is such *as* the gathering of the fourfold which we have described."[8] The irony in this reading of the bridge is apparent if we turn to Sheeran once again. Sheeran invokes Heidegger to set Irish placehood *against* "the general European sense of place."[9] The German philosopher, according to Sheeran, "provides us with the deepest, richest definition of dwelling when he points out that it includes both *aedificare* 'to build' and colere 'to cultivate'. . . . In this sense, one might argue, the Irish . . . have never truly dwelt in Ireland."[10] Far from this final image's being gratuitous, therefore, the bridge suspends a span of irony over the entire film that precedes it. It is a synecdoche that embodies *Pigs*' main themes and critiques of spatial representation and organization. Heidegger is criticized as he is invoked. *Pigs* problematizes the possibility of a stable, authentic place: if the characters in the film truly attempt to hatch out an identity through dwelling, it can only be temporary and transient—one derelict stop on the road of Becoming.

For geographer David Harvey, Heidegger's disillusionment with traditional philosophical dichotomies and his mistrust of modernity and technological universals led him to search for permanence over transitoriness, for Being over Becoming.[11] Modernity (as well as Postmodernity) is characterized by the phenomenon of "time-space compression," which is a term, Harvey claims, that signals "processes that so revolutionize the objective qualities of space and time that we are forced to alter, sometimes in quite radical ways, how we represent the world to ourselves."[12] The period of intense "compression" at the time of the industrial revolution gave rise to "a universalizing machine rationality as an appropriate mythology for modern life."[13] Heidegger notes his dismay with Modernity in "The Thing." "All distances in time and space are shrinking," he fears.[14] In contrast to this unsettledness, Harvey explains that Heidegger "proposed . . . a counter-myth of rootedness in place and environmentally-bound traditions as the only secure foundation for political and social action is a manifestly troubled world."[15] The ease with which Heidegger was able to adopt the principles of National Socialism to his philosophy (and vice-versa), however, indicates to Harvey that this grounded, static sense of place and identity is worse than ineffective. Heidegger eschews instability, and since, as Harvey explains, "part of the insecurity which bedevils capitalism as a social formation arises out of . . . instability in the spatial and temporal principles around which social life might be organized," a sense of grounded place is anathema to further attempts to "bedevil" the dominant order.[16] Place is, in every sense, reactionary.

In "Power-Geometry and a Progressive Sense of Place," however, Doreen Massey questions two of Harvey's major premises. First, she queries, "Why is it assumed that time-space compression will produce insecurity"?[17] Harvey merely takes for granted that anxiety is universal in the face of flux and forgets, she claims, that "different social groups and different individuals are placed in very distinct ways in relations to these flows and interconnections."[18] Second, and relatedly, Massey wonders on what methodological grounds Harvey's Heideggerian conceptualization of place rests. "If it had not started off from there [Heidegger]," she states, "perhaps it would never have found itself in this conceptual tangle in the first place."[19] Massey states that all cultures have some sense of placehood, and she specifically asserts that this sense varies among different social groups. In a sense, then, Massey and Sheeran agree that Heidegger's notions of place are limited and that other, less concrete senses are available and practiced by people. Sheeran claims that this less concrete notion—this "nominal sense of place"—is particularly Irish.[20] I maintain that as Heidegger uses the image of the bridge to stress the importance of the "gathering" and, hence, the importance of a singular, static place to Being, *Pigs* ends with the bridge to disrupt the very notion of a singular sense of place in Irish culture.

The ruined townhouse in which the protagonist Jimmy sets up housekeeping stands for a distinct and particularly repressive period in Dublin's history as the British capital of colonial Ireland. As a liminal space, a temporary respite for its inhabitants between social positions, the Georgian townhouse is akin to a bridge, though, as we shall see, a bridge in a different sense from Heidegger's. The Georgian squat is a forgotten ruin of a formerly glorious and majestic townhome; it is a standing symbol of both the height of British dominance in the eighteenth century and the decay of Irish cities over the last two hundred years. While Jimmy explores and "redecorates" (by hanging a tattered lace curtain over a formerly boarded up window), the omniscient camera remains mainly indifferent to his actions, and lingers on Jimmy only sporadically before it passes over decaying reminders of the house's once-proud stature in the British Isles: a faded photograph, a smashed transom window, graying walls, peeling paint. The Georgian past is not forgotten in *Pigs* but remains the path one must take to understand the present state of decay. Sheeran writes, for example: "It is sometimes alleged that the ease with which Dublin has been destroyed has to do with the urbanised peasants who have been in control of its destiny since independence. Such creatures, lacking the civility of an urban tradition, could hardly be expected to take care for the city."[21] In *Pigs*, however, the ruin of the house predates Jimmy's arrival and lingers after he departs. The source of the decay of Dublin, therefore, is shifted away from these uncivilized "urbanised peasants" and to the forces that have historically marginalized them.

One by one, more characters arrive to this renegade dwelling—this forgotten place for forgotten Dubliners. The house becomes a nexus through which the marginalia of society can pass and momentarily linger outside of institutional space. The travelers through this house seek a process that they can join—an alternative, progressive community to fill the various voids left in their lives by indifferent urban Ireland's systems and bureaus. According to Sheeran, the Irish sense of place "is a quality of awareness that occurs at a fracture point; between being rooted and being alienated, being an insider and an outsider."[22] In *Pigs*, Jimmy, George, Tom, and the rest are the alienated outsiders who find brief roots inside the unlikely shelter of the townhouse. The house is, then, a veritable "ship of fools" to which the dispossessed, unfit, and insane are drawn before they are finally confined. "Confinement," Michel Foucault notes, "that massive phenomenon, the signs of which are found all across eighteenth-century Europe, is a 'police' matter. Police . . . that is, the totality of measures which make work possible and necessary for all those who could not live without it."[23] Indeed, this "totality of measures" eventually encompasses even the dwellers in *Pigs*. The gutted, gray, and gloomy Georgian monument in which the crew settles is a signifier of that time of high repression, policing, and aristocratic domination of Ireland by the British; it metonymically demonstrates that repression, policing, and domination did not follow the British back over the sea but changed masters who speak now with Irish accents.

The foundation on which the community is built in Black's film is the desire for autonomy and freedom as much as it is a pessimism that is always aware that "the center cannot hold." The urban landscape of *Pigs* fulfills the conditions and stylings of postmodern architecture—the pastiche, the borrowing from the past, the creation of a palimpsest rather than a plan—yet is decidedly bleak and dystopian in outlook. "The places are broken," Sheeran also writes, "the names remain." [24] Jimmy, George, Tom, Ronnie, Orwell, and Mary are the names that circulate throughout the filmic space, frustrated by the failed promise of modernity. They squat in what becomes a "heterotopia"—a particular space that allows resistance to the bodily domination demanded by authoritarian institutions. For Foucault, the site of the body holds the power of resistance by way of the liberation of human desire. Each of the characters in the film is defined in relation to his or her body. The variety of desires and pathologies that is manifested gives rise to different methods of control that, in the end, subsume the characters. This simultaneous leap of scales in *Pigs*—the outside Dublin of oppression lifted to the "totality of measures"; the inside world of resistance reduced to the level of the body—allows the film to offer a spatial politics that organizes the house itself into a new kind place, and proposes a body politics as one possible path of liberation. In the space between the body and the totality, then, the characters of *Pigs* attempt to create and maintain a community that mirrors the proposed place Massey outlines in her article. The ultimate collapse of this community, however, demonstrates the extreme difficulty of holding such a place together in the midst of powerful state apparatuses. This half-success/half-failure results in an additional nuance of ambivalence that is absent from Massey's "progressive" place. That ambivalence, I argue, is an element that makes the place figured by *Pigs* particularly Irish.

In "Stability and Ambivalence: Aspects of the Sense of Place and Religion in Irish Literature," Seán Ó Tuama suggests that ambivalence is a primary characteristic of Irish identity, especially vis-á-vis urbanity. "Cities and towns," he writes, "have historically been the creations and preserves of invading colonists, and the consequent sense of alienation of the native population may help to explain some of the difficulties many Irish people still have in identifying fully with urban life." [25] Ó Tuama identifies in Irish poetry of the last four hundred years a profound and overwhelming obsession with the ancestral land of Ireland.

He sees the conflicts resulting from the linguistic shift from Irish to English in the nineteenth century as contributing particularly to this sense of ambivalence. Yearning for an Irish past in the language of the conquerors produces a strange tension. "It can be said then that while passion for place remains an integral part of the poetry . . . the sense of all the historical, mythological, ideological, familial associations . . . tends to disappear."[26] This response to the imposition of a foreign language, value system, and politics can take on the power of dissent. Ó Tuama explains:

> The most common form of this dissent . . . is ambivalence, or half-belief. . . . Such half-belief has always existed, I believe, as a necessary condition for survival, not alone in primitive societies but in all deeply-rooted communities. Liberal intellectuals, floating free of community ties, do not always appreciate why members of deeply-rooted communities are very reluctant to change their received dogmas—dogmas in which, quite often, they only half-believe. This reluctance is to be attributed, I think, to an intuitive understanding that while some simple acceptable dogmas are necessary for ordering human affairs, a deep reservation exists always about the ability of any dogma . . . to give satisfactory answers to the basic questions concerning life and death.[27]

Hence, even the strongest, most steadfast declarations of "Irishness" are internally conflicted, unstable, under question, and incomplete. Turning from this quality of Irish ambivalence to Massey's framework for a nonstable, non-Heideggerian "power-geometry," we can see how *Pigs* maps out an Irish sense of place.

Massey's first point about progressive places stresses that "places can be conceptualized in terms of the social interactions which they tie together."[28] *Pigs* presents the house itself as not a place in the traditional sense of the term but more as a process that remains outside of concrete space and time and demarcated only by its inhabitants. The film contains no establishing shots to aid in mapping the position of the house in relation to any Dublin landmarks or any of the other places described in the diegesis. Likewise, nothing exists to set a specific period to the film. In the final segment, the arresting officers mention that Jimmy's social welfare fraud has continued from 11 January to that day, 9 December. Thus, the film has covered the span of one year in eighty minutes, and it seems irrelevant which year that is. Space and time, in this sense, are constituted as a function of operations and processes, not established boundaries, walls, or conventional definitions.

"Places do not have to have boundaries," Massey continues. "Definition in this sense does not have to be through simple counterposition to the outside; it can come . . . precisely through the particularity of linkage *to* that 'outside.' "[29] The boundaries and walls of the house in *Pigs* are deconstructed primarily through the use of sound. Early in the film, after all the residents arrive, Ronnie awakes and turns on loud, industrial music that pervades the house, seeping through the walls, hallways, and staircases. Jimmy is particularly disturbed by this music, and several shots show him stuffing a pillow over his head to drown out the cacophony of noises invading his room. Ronnie, Tom, and George each leave, and Jimmy is woken again by their footsteps. Finally, his chances of a peaceful slumber completely destroyed, he rises to answer a knock at the door that illustrates a particular "linkage" to the outside—he sends a social census taker away. The characters are able to pass freely into and out of the house, yet the outside "threat" in the guise of a welfare quantifier is rudely told to go away. Indeed, it can be inferred, the social worker's attempt to identify and account for the inhabitants would disturb their tenacious grip on the temporary freedom they enjoy. Power requires knowledge, as Foucault reminds us, and this act to deny that knowledge to the representative of the state reinforces the idea that Jimmy is carving out his own nook outside of institutional control. The survey taker is thus denied access to the flows and processes that constitute the place of the disenfranchised.

In a later scene, Ronnie's record and Jimmy's radio fight for dominance throughout the rooms of the house. Tom lies awake in bed as the disturbing mixture of music invades his room. He becomes frightened and whimpers paranoically when Ronnie's mates arrive and create a din outside that resonates through the walls. In the next segment, Tom confuses the seepage of sounds with the sounds of George's urination. Tom rushes into Jimmy's room and accuses George of "pissing through my ceiling." When Jimmy investigates, of course, there is no evidence of unusual bathroom habits so Jimmy advises Tom to take his tablets. This "notion of places as social relations," Massey claims, "facilitates the conceptualization of the . . . arrival of the previously marginal in the . . . centre."[30] The marginalized characters of *Pigs* attempt to create a center for themselves without clear boundaries, but are eventually forced to abandon their well-intended dream for the defined and structured enclosures recognized by the state. The traditional distinctions between private and public are not easy to shake.

"Third," Massey continues, "places do not have single, unique 'identities'; they are full of internal differences and conflicts."[31] Clearly, the heterotopia described by *Pigs* is not singular and certainly contains its share of differences and conflicts. The house retains trappings that link it to its original "identity" as a Georgian townhouse, yet the characters and their personal traces (Jimmy's lace curtain, Tom's pin-up, George's telly) create a decentered, fragmented persona for the structure. Such a place can actually be defined by its conflicts, Massey proposes: "a conflict over what its past has been (the nature of its 'heritage'); conflict over what should be its present development."[32] The effort to preserve Dublin's Georgian homes provides a nice extradiegetic sense of this variety of conflict. In *Georgian Dublin*, Kevin Kearns describes the difficulty of engaging public support or governmental funding for preservation efforts. Kearns seems unproblematically concerned with the "fragile heritage" of the eighteenth century homes and explains that "preservationists face an exasperating challenge. They must combat the formidable obstacles of inept governance, commercial greed, public apathy and sheer ignorance which militate against the welfare of Georgian Dublin."[33] Kearns recounts the official conflict imbricated in the facades of Dublin's gutted reminders of British high imperialism; *Pigs* illustrates the peripheral conflicts that operate behind the scenes. It is through these latter conflicts that the squatters' community and sense of place are described.

Finally, Massey insists that her previous suggestions do not dilute the importance of a particular sense of place. "The specificity of places is continually reproduced, but it is not a specificity which results from some long, internalized history."[34] The house that Jimmy, George, Tom, Ronnie, Orwell, and Mary eventually occupy is figured to both precede them and exist for the future after they depart. Before Jimmy enters in the opening scene, for example, the camera that had followed him perches in a nook behind an eyebrow window inside the darkened dwelling. Jimmy enters and as he explores his new surroundings, the camera obliviously lingers over artifacts and details irrespective of his point-of-view. The identity, however, unstable, of the house is established; it predates Jimmy's arrival and will carry on after he leaves. Indeed, as he is driven away in the final scene, the camera pauses to lovingly crane around the house once more before it jumps to Jimmy in the police car. The "specificity" of which Massey writes is neither in the anonymous place nor in the individuals who occupy it; specificity is in the unique combination of the flows and interactions across space and time. Place is defined not because of boundaries or maps, but rather in

"the focus of a distinct *mixture* of wider and more local social relations." [35] *Pigs* at once invokes these elements and demonstrates the difficulty of maintaining the delicate combinations of flows that can
produce a progressive place. The ultimate submission of each character to the same institutions (in slightly altered form) from which they
earlier escaped demonstrates the difficulty—if not utter futility—of
this politics.

The final scene of the film demonstrates that, eventually, clinging
to this place is futile. Alone once again in the house, a dejected Jimmy
flies into a rage and attacks the last remnants of his prior life—his marriage. Screaming "You fucking bitch!" he rips his wife's red clothes
from the dressing screen, tears at them, and pounds the floor in frustration. This final abandonment of the past and destruction of the last
shreds of personal commitment to any institutional space only opens
the door for another totalizing force to take its place. After Jimmy re-
gains composure, two police officers enter the house and arrest him for
defrauding the social welfare system. It seems that despite his attempts
to shake off the memory of his wife, the legacy of having once be-
longed to the realm of the state still binds him to the social responsibility he has ducked throughout the film. "Criminals!" declares one of the
arresting cops. "All of you!" Jimmy's tenure in the in-between place of
the house has come to an end; the dominance of the police continues
and sucks him back into a correctional space. The final shot of Jimmy is
taken through the window of the police car. The glass acts as both window and mirror so that Jimmy's face, sealed into the automobile, is
seen covered by the translucent reflections of Dublin's buildings as the
car speeds past. Jimmy is now, once again, part of the official, recognized city now figured by reflection onto his body—and he must pay
for his deviance. The difficulty of maintaining such a tenuous sense of
place is rendered absolute.

George's illness can be likened to Jimmy's "criminality" in that
each embodies a condemned, socially unacceptable condition that al-
legedly requires corrective measures. "Sickness," writes Foucault, "is
only one among a range of factors, including infirmity, old age, inability to find work, and destitution, which compose the figure of the
'necessitous pauper' who deserves hospitalization." [36] A phlegmy,
hacking cough is the bodily manifestation of George's ailment: it greets
Jimmy at the door when George arrives through the "pissing rain,"
and it lingers on the soundtrack after he leaves his room for the last
time. This evidence illustrates that neither the hospital in which he previously resided nor the unappealing Council Flats into which his

"heart problem" has allowed him access will do any real good for him. Nonetheless, he accepts the free flat the state has provided him and completes his transition from one institutionalized space to another with a short holdover in the dingy, disenfranchised space of the Georgian townhouse. As George bids farewell to Jimmy, he pronounces that the rest of the tenants "are either mad or bent." Jimmy counters him by warning: "You're like everyone else in the house. You live in a dream." George packs up his things (except, significantly, his telly) and leaves to brave reality once again. George thus acquiesces, finally, and declares that the imposing, depressing Council Flats—little boxes of prescribed similarity, homes of homology—are "better than this place."

For Orwell, however, difference is embodied literally, formally, and figuratively. His presence indicates the film's ultimate position that the only politics that cannot easily be co-opted is a politics of the body. Reading Orwell as a productivist figure that promises the path to revolution, or even social hope, however, presents its own problems and reinforces the film's carefully construed unstable attitude of ambivalence. Though Orwell's "ruthlessness" (as George describes it) may enable him to rise through society and become a pop star despite his lack of talent, this success comes at the expense of his prostitute girlfriend's bodily freedom. Orwell is both colonizer (of women) and colonized (as a Jamaican) and thus repeats the same struggles of the other characters but on the scale of his body. Whereas Jimmy, George, Tom, and Ronnie each grapple for control of their bodies as they are ensnared between two institutionalized spaces, Orwell's fight is mapped onto his black skin and signifies the eternally recurring nature of the struggle. Hence, he is able to slip in and out of the transient place of the house and move to another, presumably, for he carries the dichotomies of control and controlled with him always. Even if he attains his desire, George postulates, "he'll find someone else" to replace Mary. There is no true, absolute path to liberation in the closed system *Pigs* represents—personal freedom is always at the expense of someone else's. This attitude is aptly summed up by the ambiguous title of the film: "Pigs" refers to the police as well as to the inhabitants of the house.

The attempt to forge a noncultivated sense of place (such as those described by Doreen Massey and Patrick Sheeran) is problematized in the bleak, funereal quality of Cathal Black's *Pigs*. The ambivalent attitude that permeates the film casts neither dispersion nor glory onto this sort of endeavor and, therefore, allows a space for both frustration and hope for the quest to establish a community that resists incorporation by the totalizing and homogenizing institutions of state power. On the road to becoming revolutionary agents of desire, the characters each succumb to the promised stability of singular, recognized identity. The Georgian house that acts as a liminal container for the social interactions and processes of its temporary inhabitants remains open for future attempts to hash out a truly liberating political space of resistance.

# 13

# An Elephant at the Altar

Religion in Contemporary Irish Cinema

## Pamela Dolan

There is a moment in Neil Jordan's film, *The Miracle*, which seems to me a wonderful visual summary of the ambivalent attitude of Irish film toward religion. One of the film's protagonists makes good on her promise to set free the visiting circus animals and, while the other animals are shown romping about her little Irish seaside town, the elephant suddenly appears in the local Catholic church. It is so absurdly large and primal that it has the unlikely effect of laying bare the shabby, cramped artifice of this "sacred" space. The elephant, rather than being made to look silly in its inappropriate surroundings, takes on an almost prophetic aspect; it is a wise and totemic creature whose disappointed eyes have seen and understood both the greatness of which humanity is capable, and the utter tawdriness that it usually achieves.

This scene is funny and achingly poignant all at the same time, and while it is certainly irreverent, it is hardly sacrilegious. Having viewed a large number of films that can, in some sense, be called Irish, I have found this a fairly typical approach; that is, these films display an attitude toward religion that is neither as sentimentally pious nor as intellectually critical as one might expect.

Janet Roach wrote an article for the *New York Times* in 1994 that served as an unofficial announcement to mainstream observers of literary and popular culture that Ireland had arrived on the movie scene. This fact has hardly been a secret to observant moviegoers, who have granted such films as *The Commitments, The Crying Game,* and *In the Name of the Father* a respectable measure of commercial and critical success in this country. Yet Ireland is still, as Roach puts it, "far better known for its pubs, poets, peat fires and bloody, intractable Troubles than for its contributions to contemporary culture. But in recent years, the Irish film industry has suddenly and surprisingly reached a kind of

critical mass."[1] Academics as well as film critics have begun to catch
on to this trend. At a 1994 Irish studies conference, David Lloyd tack-
led head-on the issue of how Ireland is represented by recent films
dealing with the topic of the Irish Republican Army, including close
readings/viewings of *Patriot Games* and *The Crying Game*.[2]

Lloyd, a Dublin native and an associate professor of English at the
University of California at Berkeley, posited that modern Irish society
has been divided into three spheres: the domestic, the public, and a
third sphere, the identity and definition of which are still being negotiated, but which for now can be labeled the sphere of "the other." During the formation of the Irish Republic, according to his theory, the
church was relegated to the domestic sphere (resulting in a "strangle-
hold on women"), and the public sphere remained dominated by the
language and politics of the English colonizers and their descendants.
This dual colonization, by the church on the one hand and the Anglo-
Irish elite on the other, continued the long-standing tradition of conflict
between colonizers and colonized that is played out so often in Irish
art and literature, including the early nineties spate of movies about
the IRA. A possible location of the third sphere would be the pub;
James Joyce's work, for example, illustrates the pub as a "homosocial
sphere" where neither women nor church dominate. Lloyd further argues that the dual colonization process has contributed to the stereotyping of the Irish male as feminized, which may in turn lead to the
violence that is so often portrayed as a tragic inevitability in Irish history and society[3] (this theory, incidentally, throws an entirely new in-
terpretive light on the gender-bending and bloodiness of *The Crying
Game*).

I would like to borrow and build on the basic premise and terms of
Lloyd's thesis, but with one crucial caveat: I do not think Lloyd has
given enough weight to the role of religion in Irish history or culture.
(And to be fair to Professor Lloyd, when I spoke to him about this
paper he entirely agreed that in that particular address religion had not
been given its due.) Clearly, politics and religion often overlap, and in
Ireland as elsewhere the official arm of the church has from time to
time extended its reach farther than hearth and home. Furthermore,
the private and spiritual aspects of religion tend to be ignored by any
purely social analysis. Surely there is more to religion than the oppressive colonization of the domestic sphere by the Catholic Church, sym-
bolized again and again by ominous black-clad clerics in the films of
the recent "Irish invasion." Is it either fair or accurate to reduce religion
in Ireland to a kind of caricature of a colonizing force of oppression? Is

not religion also a more personal, even intimate, and potentially liberating force in people's daily lives, and does not this force, this ultimate concern, take other forms than mere rote piety and obedience?

I will argue that both the oppressive and the liberating power of religion is in evidence in the recent influx of Irish films. I have chosen as my texts three films that are not specifically "about" religion; these are not movies like *Chariots of Fire* or *The Mission* that consciously choose religion as a subject matter. Instead, in all three of these films, *The Dead, The Playboys,* and *My Left Foot,* religion is a given reality in people's lives that must be dealt with for the stories to be authentic; to employ a worn but still accurate simile, it is like a current in a river that moves the water along but is itself essentially invisible, except for the ripples it produces on the surface when it meets with a rock or some other obstacle. Many of the obvious conflicts that an American audience might expect in any treatment of religion in Ireland—sectarian violence, for instance, or at least denominational conflict—are almost entirely absent. There is conflict here, often in the arena that Lloyd's thesis would project (that is, the conflict between women and the church for control over the domestic sphere), but there is also a true and unself-conscious celebration of the role of religion in the everyday lives of a people and a country.

Very little work has been produced on the religious interpretation of film, an area that merits further theoretical grounding and research. Religion is often defined as a person or people's "ultimate concern," and popular culture has no more relevant outlets for the concerns of our society than the media of film and television. Some hold that society creates and is responsible for what appears on screen whereas others worry that just the opposite is true, but either belief should encourage serious-minded people to carefully examine just what metanarratives are being created there.

My method of analysis is primarily a literary approach to film, in part because that is where my training and expertise lie, but in part too because I find Irish films particularly susceptible to this kind of analysis. The United States is, according to some observers, becoming the first industrialized, "postliterate" society, so dependent have we become on images for information and entertainment. Ireland may in fact be moving in this direction as well, but at the moment there remains a deep-seated relationship with language in Irish society. Filmmaking is still a relatively new phenomenon there, whereas storytelling has roots that go far back into the pre-Christian era, and I think the characteristic Irish reliance on the spoken and written word is still evident in Irish films. Jim Sheridan, the director, has been quoted as worrying about whether the influence of television is changing Ireland "from a verbal society to a visual one," but even he concludes that "tale-telling is very much a part of the Irish tradition."[4]

All three of these films have a strikingly literary tone: *The Dead* is an intensely faithful adaptation of a James Joyce short story, *The Playboys* has its roots in the stories of Shane Connaughton, who also wrote the screenplay, and *My Left Foot* is itself the story of a writer and is based on his autobiographical writings. Language has a rightful precedence and power in these films, and will be analyzed accordingly. That said, it is my belief that there is an element to religion that is by its nature metalinguistic, or beyond language. Therefore I have attempted to remain alert to nonlinguistic clues that can help me locate the religious sensibilities of these films.

Joyce's short story "The Dead" has been a pivotal piece of Irish literature since its publication, and John Huston's film of it, released in 1987, marks for me the beginning of the new era of film in Ireland. It is a film of stunning simplicity and integrity, and a faithful adaptation of its literary precursor that pays particular attention to the nuances of the Irish version of the English language. Joyce's well-known antipathy toward the Catholic Church comes across clearly in this version, but so do some of the subtler, more complex feelings he has toward his fellow middle-class Catholic Dubliners. The men are shown to be mostly passive figures, either literally or figuratively dead (or dying) under the constraints of their bourgeois and Catholic upbringing. The women, however much they may live under the same system of constraints, are shown to be somehow more alive, either bucking against those constraints and pushing them to their limits, or living within them while trying to enrich their own narrow lives and the lives of others through the arts of music and hospitality, or sustaining themselves with the warm memory of passions long since buried and gone.

The movie takes place entirely within the confines of a dinner party and its immediate aftermath, a party given by a trio of music teachers, two elderly spinsters and their niece, pillars of middle-class Catholic Dublin society. Huston repeatedly focuses on conversation rather than action, particularly on conversation that is about the art of music, and yet the audience quickly learns that the less acceptable topics of religion and politics lurk around every pause, and can only be avoided by the skillful interference of the hostesses. Two of the performances-within-performances that are so crucial to the plot of the film have distinctly religious overtones. The first (which is, incidentally, not in Joyce's story) is a translation of an Irish poem called "Broken Vows" which ends with the line, "And, my fear is great, you have taken God from me." The second is Aunt Julia's rendition of "Arrayed for the Bridal," which makes an ironic comment on the state of the Church, as Julia represents a remarkably old and withered bride of Christ. Using Lloyd's metaphors of colonized spaces, this film takes place within the domestic sphere, in which the women dominate over the men. But Huston allows us to see too that the women have in turn been dominated by the Church, and that the relationship does not rest easily with them.

Molly Ivors (Maria McDermottroe), for one, refuses to remain confined in the sphere to which she belongs. Early in the film she agrees to dance with Gabriel (Donal McCann), but she inappropriately uses the opportunity to scold him for his politically regressive views. She calls him a "West Briton," which she significantly defines as "someone who looks to England for our salvation, instead of depending on ourselves alone." Later, she causes scandal by leaving the party early to attend a Republican (that is, the political party in favor of the creation of an Irish state) meeting. The sisters remark nervously that she will be the only woman there, which does nothing to deter her. As she leaves, the others are called away to the table, at which point the domestic sphere visually and thematically reasserts itself and Molly is never mentioned or seen again.

Aunt Kate (Helena Carroll) herself voices frustration with the church's treatment of women when she complains that Julia's singing was never fully appreciated by the church choir in which she participated for many years. She refers to a purported papal mandate that replaced the women's choir with an all-boys group, saying, "I suppose it is for the good of the church, if the pope says so, but it's not right and it's not just." Her niece Mary Jane (Ingrid Craigie) had suggested that the women sang for the honor of God (not the good of the church), and now she chides Kate for being critical of the pope. Kate responds quite heatedly: "I don't question the pope's being right. I'm just a stupid old woman, I wouldn't presume to do such a thing. But there is such a thing as common, everyday politeness and gratitude." Mary Jane interrupts what promises to be a very interesting tirade by suggesting that Kate is just irritable because she is hungry. Again, the domestic sphere is reasserted and used to smooth over any untoward opinions (as expressed by women) in the area of politics or religion. Kate's comments bring to the fore the conflict between women and the church for control of the domestic sphere, and perhaps suggest even a measure of insecurity that the church exhibits toward women by excluding them from all but the most passive and silent participation in the Mass.

It seems at this point that nobody has a kind word to say about the Catholic Church, until an odd conversation takes place between the very drunk Freddie Malins (Donal Donnelly) and the only Protestant dinner guest, Mr. Brown. It is mentioned that Freddie will soon be making a visit to a monastery, which leads to a discussion of the various forms of asceticism practiced by the monks, including their maintaining silence and sleeping in coffins.

Mr. Brown, although impressed by the monks' reputation for hospitality and generosity, cannot understand these ascetic practices, and wants to know the logic behind them. Freddie launches into a rambling discourse on penance and indulgences, explaining that "the monks are trying to compensate for all the sins committed by all the sinners in the outside, external world." His mother, for the first time in the film, looks on at her son approvingly, but when Mr. Brown tries to continue his line of questioning, Mrs. Malins effectively ends the conversation with the comment: "They are very good men, the monks. Very pious. The coffin is to remind them of their last end." Here a woman is shown getting to the heart of the matter when it comes to the issue of religion, grasping it in a way the men seem incapable of. Mrs. Malins, a pious woman, becomes the mouthpiece for Joyce's condemnation of institutionalized religion, his sense of the enervating effect it has on Irish society, and his characterization of it as a symbol of death.

One of the strongest visual reminders of religion in the film is the moment that ultimately becomes the catalyst for Gabriel's epiphany. Mr. D'Arcy begins to sing "The Lass of Aughrim" just as Gretta (Anjelica Huston) is descending the stairs to leave. The camera lingers on her as she looks up, rapt, listening to D'Arcy's tenor floating down. She has a white scarf wrapped around her face, from which a beatific light seems to shine forth, and she is framed by the stained glass window behind her. John Shout calls this "Huston's most daring use of real time" and comments that "Huston alternates only three shots—close-ups of Gretta and Gabriel, and, in a madonna effect, a staircase shot of Gretta against a stained-glass window. The effect is to canonize Gretta . . . and, given the purity of the music and the iconography, to introduce a new solemnity."[5]

This solemnity, of course, is used to introduce the final scene, the scene of the epiphany. After Gretta reveals her first, youthful experiences of love and death, both embodied in the person of Michael Fury,

Gabriel looks out on the falling snow and meditates on the meaning of the various signs of mortality that have confronted him that evening. More important in this last scene than the sense of martyrdom that Michael Fury's love-inspired death creates is the train of thought that the story of his death evokes in Gabriel. His contemplation takes the form of a voice-over, a first-person narration, while illustrative images flash across the scene. Huston offers seemingly artless images of snow lying on Celtic-cross grave markers, snow against castle ruins and a Norman stone tower, snow on bare and thorny branches, snow falling into a black seascape, and finally just snow, snow falling against a blue-black background, before the final fade to black. Gabriel thinks aloud that, "One by one we're all becoming shades. . . . Think of all those who ever were, back to the start of time. . . . Snow is falling, falling in that lonely churchyard where Michael Fury lies buried, falling faintly through the universe and faintly falling, like the descent of their last end, upon all the living and the dead." Shout construes this final sequence as representing Gabriel's understanding of his own inadequacy and a sense of commonality with other Irish,[6] but I find this interpretation insufficient and not entirely convincing. A gradual understanding is not, after all, an epiphany, and moments of epiphany are the leitmotif of Joyce's *Dubliners*, of which "The Dead" is the final, crowning achievement.

The story, as has been repeatedly noted by critics, takes place on the feast of the Epiphany. The characters in the film comment on this fact in the opening sequence, relating it to the exchange of Christmas gifts and the gifts of the Magi to the Christ child. Huston uses this opening to remind the audience that the whole thrust of the story will be the epiphany granted to Gabriel Conroy in the final scene. An editorial in *Christian Century* seems to me quite close to the mark when it describes an epiphany as "a gift from beyond" and this particular epiphany as a "revelatory moment" or "a sense of 'connectedness' in which the protagonist finds himself related to all the living and all the dead in the midst of his ordinary life."[7] The sense of connectedness achieved is something larger and far more profound than mere nationalism (a force for which Joyce, the quintessential expatriate, had little use). This moment can only be described as religious, leading me to believe that his religious sensibility was something that Joyce, an excommunicant who reportedly continued all his life to attend Mass at Easter for the "aesthetics" of the experience, never entirely relinquished. He may have believed that the authoritarian policies of the church threatened to strangle all the latent creativity of the Irish people, but such a political belief could never entirely sever his emotional connection to the aesthetic and communal experience of being Catholic.

A religious sensibility and aesthetic also enliven and enrich the film *The Playboys*. This is one of the movies around which the question of "what makes a film Irish" has centered.[8] It stars two American actors (Aidan Quinn as Tom, one of the playboys, and Robin Wright as Tara, the unmarried mother around whom the story revolves), received American financing, and was directed by the Scottish-born Gillies MacKinnon, who has been quoted as saying: "*The Playboys* is not an Irish film. I see it as an international film set in Ireland."[9] However, written and closely supervised by Shane Connaughton (an Irishman) and filmed in his own home town, this film portrays archetypal Irish themes about exile, emigration, and man's relationship to the land, as well as the eternal conflict between prudishness and generosity of spirit, in characteristically Irish ways. These themes are all played out against the backdrop of a conflict between the church and the more secularizing forces in society.

The film also fits neatly, almost literally, into Lloyd's colonized-spaces metaphor. The interiors of houses in the film are all feminized spaces, controlled by women, and it is only in the pub that we see men freely interacting with one another. The church and the outdoors are the two other spaces that the film explores, and much of the story centers on the drama of the priest trying to extend his influence beyond the boundaries of the church door, to the point of wishing to control people's behavior and even the forces of nature.

Sexuality, nature, and magic, often as embodied or experienced by women, are all posited in opposition to the institutional Catholic Church. The opening sequence sets up many of these oppositions, as the camera focuses on the progress of a blind woman slowly making her way toward the well in the village green. As church bells toll, the audience sees the villagers filing into Mass, each dipping his or her hand into the holy water fonts. Ireland has many "holy wells," places that have been focal points of worship and legend for many centuries. As they were adopted by early Christians they came to be associated with certain saints, but they have never entirely lost their "pagan" resonance either. MacKinnon's camera allows one to be cognizant of the multiple religious meanings of water in Irish culture, as it moves from the well to the holy water. Another layer of meaning is then added. While the Mass is going on around her, the very pregnant Tara's water breaks, a shockingly public and earthy announcement that she is about to become a mother. Later in the film, when Tom and Tara finally come together as a couple, they take a boat out on a lake and end up falling into the water. An easy visual metaphor for falling in love, of course, but it is interesting that Tom has just finished calling the lake "heaven." A new life in Christian baptism and the most primal forces of nature itself are all caught up in these images of water.

There are other forces of nature at work, sometimes frankly sexual ones, as in the scene of horses mating. Tom's magic tricks also seem connected to nature, as he pulls an egg (an almost hackneyed sign of fertility) from behind a child's ear and a dove from under his hat. The dove flies up and lands on Tara's window sill, as if to bring her to Tom's attention, and him to hers. Later, when the two make love, the dove is shown roosting near Tom's trailer.

These natural and mystical forces find their primary opponent in the person of the rigid, authority-obsessed village priest, Father Malone (Alan Devlin). He openly confesses to being afraid of change, something that must have seemed very much in the air in the Ireland of 1957, and he also comes across as being terrified of sex. His church lacks all the positive elements of religion—creativity, passion, and even magic—that are so abundantly alive in the world around him. For instance, when Malone attacks the troupe of performers, or playboys, who come to town, his attack is not based on their supposed immorality, but occurs because they trespass on the church's traditional territory of miraculous healing. During a magic act, Freddie says, "The dark shall be defeated," and suddenly the blind woman from the opening shot cries out, "I can see!" Someone else in the crowd shouts, "That man is a miracle-worker!" The priest immediately denounces him and calls in the police to restore order. The villagers become quite devoted to the idea that Freddie can heal them, though (as the woman has in fact regained her sight—the film wisely never ventures a rational explanation as to how), and Freddie is all too happy to take advantage of their credulity. The priest ultimately disavows the miraculous nature of the event and censures the entire performance, proclaiming from the pulpit, "There is a rational explanation for everything—unless God and the church declare otherwise. . . . The artist has a kind of power for good or ill, but God's power is paramount!"

Early in the film Tara makes a disparaging remark about one of the villagers, noting that he's "just like all the other men in this place. Scared to death of the priest." Her sister replies, "Scared to death of you, more like," thereby declaring the lines along which another battle will be drawn. Tara and Father Malone play out this conflict throughout the rest of the film, but Tara's character is not portrayed as godless or even antichurch; she seems mostly concerned with being true to herself and fighting off the hypocrisy of conventional society, whether it is being advanced by the church or by anyone else. At one point Malone scolds her with the words, "You can't fly in the face of God. . . . Sergeant Hegarty, you could redeem that man." Tara replies with an assertion that might almost be her creed, or at least a key to the theme of the movie: "We can only redeem ourselves." She is a sympathetic character, a single mother fending off the almost persecutorial oppression of the priest and the prying villagers, and engaged in an increasingly desperate battle of wills with the threatening, looming Hegarty, to whom she cries out in one of her few shows of weakness, "Brendan, you're crucifying me!" Although there are echoes of martyrdom in this cry, the film is not a tragedy, and Tara's character is allowed to be a free spirit, a noncomformist perhaps, without any undue sacrifice being required of her.

Tara's relationship with Tom is in and of itself an escape from these forces of oppression, even before she decides to actually leave the village—and perhaps Ireland—with him. Their passion is playful and natural, not erotic in the usual violence-laden way of Hollywood romance. As a couple, they are symbolically aligned with the more benign aspects of nature and magic. Their innocence is underscored by a scene that takes place during the hay gathering. The entire village community is working out in the field together when suddenly one of them exclaims, "Jesus, Mary, and Joseph!" and the camera pans to a shot of Tom appearing over the crest of a hill, leading a donkey along behind him with Tara astride it, her baby in her arms. The three have become an ironic tableau of the Holy Family. This scene works at several levels, primarily as a visual pun on the ubiquitous, everyday blasphemy of the Irish. Perhaps, too, Connaughton intends a more meaningful insight, a comment on the kind of Catholicism that produces followers who are supposed to affirm the doctrine of the Virgin birth, but who cannot accept an unwed mother in their own midst without allowing their disapproval to erupt into a potent mix of voyeurism, suspicion, and hostility.

Shane Connaughton also cowrote the screenplay for *My Left Foot: The Story of Christy Brown,* the film perhaps the most credited with breathing life into the Irish film industry. It is the true story of Christy Brown (Daniel Day-Lewis), a poor Dublin boy born with cerebral palsy whose body was entirely out of his own control, with the exception of the eponymous left foot, and who nevertheless became one of Ireland's most acclaimed painters and writers of this century. Although the film was widely regarded by Christian reviewers as the uplifting story of a man's soul overcoming bodily limitations, it is a much more complicated—and better—film than that description might lead one to suspect. It displays the by now familiar mistrust of organized religion, and confirms the validity of Lloyd's metaphorical scheme of things. Here too Irish domestic life is shown as the domain of a strong woman dominated by an oppressive church, and it seems to be human relationships, rather than traditional piety, that offer liberation and redemption to its characters.

Traditional piety is even more evident in this film than in the previous two. Sunday-school-variety pictures of Jesus hang on the walls of the cramped Brown house, and the tyrannical father inveighs against sexuality to his children, yet the number of children in the household constantly increases. Christy notes rather late in the film that his mother bore twenty-two children in all, although "only" thirteen survived. Scenes of the father (Ray McAnally) rowdy in the pub and red faced with shame, anger, and drink when at home may at first strike the viewer as stereotypes of the loudmouthed but ineffectual Irish drunk, yet Mr. Brown does evolve into a more nuanced character through the course of the film. These scenes also serve to underscore the quiet resolve and enduring strength of Christy's mother, and in many ways the story is as much about her as it is about her more famous son. There is a trace of stereotyping even here—Irish literature and modern-day folklore are littered with sons who remain unnaturally attached to their "sainted" mothers, about whom they will not allow a single critical word to be spoken. *My Left Foot* carefully exploits this stereotype in its exploration of Christy's relationship with Mrs. Brown, in the process creating a rich and religiously significant portrait of mother and son.

Although many reviewers have written off the character of Mrs. Brown (Brenda Fricker) as either a saint or a doormat, the film clearly creates a character who is the archetype of woman as savior. Her centrality to the story is established almost immediately by the first dramatic sequence of the film, which involves the collapse of the very pregnant Mrs. Brown and the clever way that Christy, disabled and entirely mute at this point in the film, finds to call for help. The neighbors who discover the two of them misinterpret the episode and blame Christy for his mother's collapse, calling him a moron to his face, as if he does not understand what they are saying. One of the women clucks scoldingly, "God help her. He's a terrible cross to the poor woman." In one sense the rest of Christy's life is spent trying not to be a cross to his mother; early on, he diverts his father's attention during some of his worst rages and, much later, he gives her the advance money that he receives for the publication of his autobiography.

Mrs. Brown, however, is consistently portrayed as above any of these petty, earthly concerns for herself; far from considering Christy a cross to bear, she takes an obvious joy in his every accomplishment, beginning with the miraculous moment when Christy first manages to prove to his family that he is not mentally handicapped—he takes a piece of chalk between his toes and painstakingly, struggling with great force against every muscle in his body, he spells out the word "mother." She embodies motherly devotion and sacrifice over and over again, so that it does not at all strike the audience as hyperbole when she says to Christy during one of his deep struggles with despair, "You'll have me heart broken, Christy Brown. Sometimes I think you are my heart. Look, if I could give you my legs I'd gladly take yours." In a lesser movie these lines would be overkill, but within the integrity of this film they come across as a simple statement of fact.

Christy's life is spent not only trying to repay his mother for acts of kindness and generosity so large that they can never be properly recompensed, it is also spent in search of another person who can love him as completely and fiercely as she does. This proves in many ways a more difficult task than the overcoming of his physical disabilities. "Mother as savior" can be a sort of double-edged role, then, one that may place on the woman a certain amount of blame if her son is unable to find another woman who can live up to the standards she herself has set. There is a moment during his physical and speech therapy process when Mrs. Brown reveals her fear that, the more he progresses in his therapy, the greater chance she stands of losing him. Typically, she couches this fear in terms of her concern for him, saying, "There's something in that voice [his improved speaking voice] that disturbs me—there's too much hope in it."

Christy rather predictably falls in love with the doctor, Eileen Cole (Fiona Shaw), who works these therapeutic miracles on him, just as his mother had feared he might. When he learns that Dr. Shaw does not return his feelings, he turns on her and snarls the ultimate insult: "You're not my mother. Never forget that." He mocks her attempts to console him with the morsel of hope that they can continue to love each other platonically by shouting, "Fuck Plato. Fuck any love that's not 100 percent commitment." One hundred percent commitment is what Christy had from his mother, and he will not be satisfied with anything less. In the end it appears that he finds a satisfactory love in Mary, the woman he eventually marries; both nurse and lover, she is the perfect woman to devote herself to him. There is some hope, for feminist viewers of this film, that she may come to do so on her own terms. During one of their first interactions he becomes surly, demanding that she find a match for his cigarette, and she replies with a tart, "Don't think I'm your mother just 'cause I'm looking after you for the evening." Although his response is typically acerbic ("I don't need a fucking psychology lesson, I just need a fucking light."), he seems oddly mollified and even pleased by her assertions of independence.

Although Mrs. Brown is portrayed as taking comfort from her religious beliefs and rituals, the film itself displays a searing consciousness of the way religion can be used to demean or confine people. In a memorable sequence, Christy's mother finds a pornographic magazine in his "chariot" (a homemade wheelbarrow/chair). Not knowing that it was placed there by other children, she asks the priest to have a talk with Christy; he obliges by explaining what an eternity spent in the torments of hell might be like. Christy is understandably scared, even repulsed, by the man. In the next scene, the camera lingers on the flickering fires of votive candles during mass, and the smoke that altar candles make when they are being extinguished. Mrs. Brown is shown lighting a candle at a side sanctuary, Christy at her feet. She explains to him that on All Soul's Night it is possible to release a soul from purgatory by saying the appropriate prayers and lighting a votive candle. Christy makes a terrible fuss when he sees the priest blowing out candles as they are leaving, apparently afraid that his actions will jeopardize those same souls, leaving them trapped. As the priest hurriedly closes the door behind them, Mrs. Brown soothes her son by saying, "Don't worry, Christy—he won't blow out your candle. See, even God has to lock his house."

This scene effectively reveals the combinations of superstition and pragmatism, hope and fear, piety and prejudice, that make up the religious experience within Irish culture. It is a religious experience fed by folklore and ritual as much as by any set theology or doctrine, but this aspect of Irish Catholicism is not belittled by the movie. It is that peculiar mix of piety and pragmatism that makes an at-times unbearable life more than just bearable for Christy's mother. Were it not for religion, the moments of joy, of beauty, and of transcendence in Mrs. Brown's life would be few and far between indeed. Far from ridiculing her for her simplicity, the film saves its harshest judgment for the priest who stuck to his narrow theology and could find no way to give comfort to a suffering child: his face inhabits a painting of Christy's that looks remarkably like Edvard Munch's "The Scream," and the caption underneath reads simply, "Hell."

At one point in *My Left Foot*, an admirer asks Christy Brown, "How many kinds of painting are there, Christy?" and he replies with assurance, "There are only two kinds: religious . . . and the circus." If the same can be said of film, then I think it inescapable to conclude that all three of the films I have analyzed are indeed religious films. Each of them, in different ways, betrays suspicion toward symbols and expressions of institutionalized religion and its bulwark in Ireland, the Roman Catholic Church. But if the church is judged harshly by contemporary Irish films, personal devotion and spirituality are not.

Just as in the "elephant in at the altar" scene in *The Miracle*, the best moments in the films I have considered strip away what is false about institutionalized religion even as they point to the vital, universal human experience at the heart of the religious impulse. However much the church may be seen to be infringing upon the fullness of life for the characters in these films, theological debate or church reform are not issues that are of interest to them, or to the filmmakers. The protagonists will go on living and expressing their Catholicism as naturally as they breathe, even when they sometimes rebel against it. *The Dead* exhibits a truly religious sensibility in its scenes of a community gathering together at table to share bread and wine, along with their deepest desires and fears. *The Playboys* religiously reveals Tara's enjoyment of the sacramental reality of motherhood and indeed the whole realm of creation. *My Left Foot* demonstrates an enduring belief that every individual, however physically or emotionally misshapen, reflects the image of glory of God, and that the transcendent experience of grace can be found in the face of a loved one. These characters and these stories share, to use Andrew Greeley's phrase, a Catholic imagination; it is a heritage and a gift that no amount of oppression or colonization by the institutional church can stamp out.

# 14

# Cinematic Images of Irish Male Brutality and the Semiotics of Landscape in *The Field* and *Hear My Song*

Kerstin Ketteman

Through a solid financial backing that promotes commercially successful advertising and distribution campaigns, American and English produced films have traditionally dominated constructed cinematic images of Ireland and the Irish people. In general, the gaze of the colonizer has determined an Ireland that is mythologized as the land of rain and windswept emerald-green hills, usually near jagged cliffs surrounded by crashing waves of the wild (almost savage) sea. Despite its beauty the landscape is habitually shown to be untamable, harsh, and rural in a sense that differs markedly from the romantic way the English landscape is portrayed as a sweet calm misty rose garden: a realm of nature contained and orderly in its benevolent pastoral harmony. By contrast, it would almost seem as if Ireland has eluded the hand of the gardener who might transform and control its unmanageable terrain, calming the wind and water that are often shown to be raging, unharnessed, malevolent forces of nature. In this sense one could almost speak of an antipastoral vision that is imposed onto a landscape that resists the intrusive gardener/colonizer. Moreover, like most colonialist visions the imagery of landscape tends to focus on the rural, to the extent that it fixates Ireland as a slow-moving almost timeless place, negating the presence of urbanization, modern technology, and industrialism.

Landscape, particularly in the construction of native "otherness," is postulated as a reflection on the characteristics of the people, who by implication are unruly, hostile, treacherous, wild, and somehow primitive. Consistent with colonialist images of natives in general, the Irish are attributed with qualities that project an almost childish predisposition toward weakness, vice, violent temperaments, and a stubborn, sly lawlessness. Moreover, the would-be conqueror's tendency to presume an intellectual "lack" in the native (and the lower-class manual worker), combines with latent anti-Catholic sentiment to postulate an exaggeratedly pronounced anti-intellectualism in the general Irish public. The men are restrictively portrayed as fishermen, peasant farmers, pub owners or clergymen: enforcing the image of the patriarchal, hard-laboring, hard-drinking, fervently religious Irishman. Furthermore, the state of the land as it is portrayed invites "cultivation" and implies that the indigenous people have mismanaged their land, thereby forfeiting their rights to it. On another level, the establishment of stereotypes function to legitimize the presence of the colonizer as an emissary of a "higher civilization," and to convey how the land and the people conspire to resist what is ultimately for their own good.

My objective is to indicate how two films, *Hear My Song* and *The Field*, perhaps inadvertently replicate aspects of traditional colonialist imagery in their respective characterizations of Irish men as either patriarchal devouring monster or antiheroic rogue. Although these portrayals differ in basic orientation as malevolent or benevolent, these films, a comedy and a tragedy, incorporate similarities in characterization that imply a generalization of the Irish male as violent, domineering, impulsive, sly, and lawless. Thus, *Hear My Song* and *The Field* render two men who are diametrically opposed, yet strikingly similar.

Moreover, the Irish landscape is significantly used to facilitate violence, particularly in the use of cliffs and deep wells, as signs of the abyss. Thereby, the native, like the female, is once again postulated as possessing an instinctuality that promotes a communion with nature that is at once empowering, demonizing, and subtly dehumanizing. Furthermore, inscrutability, treachery, and diabolical power thereby become associated with the native who aligns with untamed nature as dual forces that conspire against the colonizer's self-image of entitlement to reign by supposed virtue of superiority. Thus, the fear and hostility of the colonizer is projected onto the colonized as a battle between an ostensibly objective rational intellect and the potentially subversive power of a supposedly nonrational consciousness.

*Hear My Song* concerns the trials of Mickey O'Neill (Adrian Dunbar), a young nightclub owner, in persuading the famous tenor Josef Locke to return to England for one final comeback performance. The fact that Locke fled England twenty-five years earlier, leaving behind his fiancée Miss Dairy Goodness, a sports car, and an irate tax assessor, complicates matters as there seems to be no statute of limitations re-

garding Mr. Locke's tax evasion. American actor Ned Beatty, in an un-
characteristic role, portrays Locke as a romantic rogue. The choice of
an actor whose physical appearance is not considered conventional
"leading man" material provides a showcase for Beatty's talent to
evoke the charismatic appeal of Locke the artist, whose voice is a
charm that works romantically, and to supply a sort of general natural
authority. Significantly, Locke is a master of escapes and elusiveness,
thereby becoming an Irish people's hero, to the extent that he embodies one of their own who has transcended and avoided the powers of
the British magistrate. In the scene depicting his dramatic escape, leap-
ing onto a boat that is moving away from the dock, a shot of a newspaper headline informs the viewer that the protagonist "ESCAPES UNFAIR
TAXES". Thus, Locke's evasion of paying taxes to the English state becomes a metaphor for the hope of a colonized people to rise above
their subjugated position, and to avoid the punitive, extortionary tactics of the colonizer.

Generally, *Hear My Song* carries out its basic premise as an anticolonialist film, focused on Josef Locke's triumph in the face of the re-
lentless tax assessor. Nevertheless, the film seems at times to
simultaneously rely on stereotypical presumptions of instinctiveness
and collusion with nature, which ultimately implies the residual gaze
of the colonizer in (re)constructing the Irishman as a sometimes noble
savage.

In a scene where Mickey and his friend have come to Ireland looking for Locke, Mickey stands on top of a green, windy, desolate hill-
side, and as the camera sweeps panoramically over the hills, an eerie
background music invites a sense of apprehension. Suddenly, Mickey
proclaims with a calm clairvoyant certainty, "This is the place. He's
here. I can feel it." Significantly, Mickey offers no deductive or observa-
tional reasoning for his feeling. At this point his friend urges Mickey to
get water from the stream at the foot of the hill, where he implausibly
encounters Josef Locke hunting with his Irish wolfhound. Though fate
and coincidence are routine, even necessary devices to enhance the
pace of cinematic plot, in this case the land seems to promote, even
momentarily, the sort of sixth sense that is at once supernatural and inherent in nature as oracle to fauna, female, and "uncivilized" man.

In a later scene after Mickey and Joe are acquainted, Joe brings
Mickey to an ancient building on the edge of the cliffs towering over
the raging sea. Thunderclouds gather ominously, and the background
noise of breakers crashing on the rocks implies a lurking danger. Inside
the structure Mickey asks, "I thought you were taking me for a drink,

what is this place?" To which Joe replies cryptically, "It used to be the edge of the known world, now the next parish is New York." Although Joe is ostensibly concerned about Mickey's motivations for seeking him out, the sinister undertone implies not only a hidden malevolence in the roguish bon vivant, but a sense of mystical spirituality associated with the stone tower as a religious house appropriately placed at the very "edge of the known world." Subtextually, the implication bespeaks an image, heightened in a rhetorical sense by its construction as an Irish self-image, of the Celtic nature as wild and "pagan" in an inherently negative, almost demonic type of pantheism. Joe leads Mickey outside, and the sound effects of waves and musical score crescendo as Joe suddenly lunges for Mickey and pins him down on the edge of the cliff, as the camera pans over the abyss of foamy sea and jagged rock below. As if by secret signal the local men appear behind Joe, their chief and leader. As Joe pushes Mickey nearer to death he demands to know the true reason why he has come to Tullamore. Terrified, Mickey screams his reply that he's "doin' it for the people" and as Joe, clearly dissatisfied, inches him over the edge he desperately cries out his true motivation to impress and win back an old girlfriend by persuading Joe to perform at his nightclub. At this point Joe pulls Mickey back to safety, but the audience is clearly convinced that he had every intention of dropping a potential foe into the abyss, with the local men of the village as witnesses and collaborators. Thus, not only Joe, but the locals have no qualms about deliberately using the local land and seascape as a facilitator of violence and murder. Furthermore, the convenient graveyard that washes away bodies and evidence seemingly confirms a secretive diabolical bond between the Irish man (since the local men are also included) and Irish nature. Moreover, the scene disturbingly elucidates not only the leadership of Joe and his hold on the loyal support of the locals, but a sense that this was slyly planned, to such efficiency in fact that it might be more than an isolated incident, perhaps even a traditional method of interrogation and disposal of intrusive enemies or "outsiders."

Joe continues his threats toward Mickey by saying: "In the old days the sailors didn't learn how to swim, it gave them more respect for the sea. . . . You think I trust you, Mickey? There's a well in the field, Mickey, nobody knows how deep it is, and if you're trying to pull a flanker on me, like others have done in the past, you'll end up at the bottom of it." Once more the threats implicate the land as complicit, dangerously offering an abyss that is taken advantage of by the men as an agency for terror and so-called perfect murders. Indeed, the reference to "others" from the past chillingly insinuates Joe's willingness and capacity to dispose of Mickey as he may have already disposed of others.

Interestingly, Mickey and his friend investigate the well, which is located in the middle of a field, precisely in order to find out how deep it is. At first a coin is thrown into it, and the two men, expecting to hear it drop are greeted by an eerie silence, after which the friend exclaims tensely, "I hate things like this." Their next attempt to plumb the depth involves a log hurled in by Mickey, saying, "Take that you great big gaping hole!" but once more the well remains silent. Agitated, one of the men cries, "Jesus Christ, I can't stand it," and lifts a second log attached by a long chain to a cow, sending it into the well. As the chain starts unraveling and pulling, the cow starts running toward the well, which prompts the men frantically to attempt to break the chain before the cow is drawn into the hole. Elegantly infusing a moment of dark humor into the mounting tension, they succeed in breaking the chain and finally hear the distant splash of the log dropping to the bottom of the well. Thus, Joe's threats and power are validated as the message is compounded and reiterated that the vision of a sinister unromantic Irish landscape offers a far more compelling weapon than the standard fare of guns and knives that neither conceal nor dispose of their victims.

Although *Hear My Song* reiterates some aspects of colonialist images that may at first glance appear to be in some way empowering, Joe is primarily shown as a benevolent character with an underlying capacity for sly stealth, and terrible violence, yet he is in a political context definitely shown as a transcendent, heroic figure. In this capacity nature is also shown as a positive agency: Joe returns to England for a final performance aware that the English police are waiting to arrest him after the show. As the curtain closes Joe finishes his encore number and police start closing in as the audience cheers. At this point Joe is drawn into the crowd as a woman gives him a rose, signifying the love of the people for a man who is more to them than a singer of old romantic love songs; he is an embodiment of the spirit that transforms the theme song *Hear My Song* from a love ballad into a popular anthem of the silenced, suppressed Irish nation. As Joe takes the rose the police become agitated, and by the clever use of both an American impostor to confuse police and a demolition crane, the figure of Joe is lifted over the crowd as he triumphantly ascends through the recently opened ceiling. Finally, as he is lifted through the ceiling above the cheering public, a flock of doves and pigeons ascends with him to signify the advent of freedom. Ultimately Joe metaphorically constitutes transcendence over confinement and constriction; nevertheless, as character and images of Ireland become ambivalent through residual stereotypes they fall subject to the gaze of the colonizer that is a veritable presence in the film.

Another film which incorporates similar images of the Irish male, particularly with regard to landscape is *The Field*. As a tragedy, this film differs markedly from *Hear My Song*, yet the main character, Bull (Richard Harris), is significantly like Joe. The story revolves around Bull as an impoverished tenant farmer who aspires for his son (Sean Bean) to own the field he has been cultivating since he was a young man. Clearly, Bull is a violent, extremely patriarchal figure who seems to have caused the death of his other son, thereby alienating his wife and remaining son, who nevertheless keep their "family secret" and continue living with him. Like Joe, Bull is a leader with a strong hold on the local men, almost a chief, but with a fanatic drive for land and power that maims and consumes those around him. Unfortunately, he refuses to recognize that his son has no interest in becoming a farmer, possessing instead some vague plans to emigrate to America. All the same, when his particular field is placed on the market Bull insists on his natural entitlement to purchase it for the ostensible benefit of his frustrated son. Interestingly, a young, handsome, relatively well-off Irish-American (Tom Berenger) has recently returned to Ireland. He is prepared to outbid Bull for the field, which he intends to develop commercially for a local business venture. Immediately a triangular conflict is constructed between Bull as warped monstrous patriarch, his reticent son, and the young, successful American who employs the industrial revolutionary rhetoric of capitalist "progress and development."

As the conflict heats up, and the American resists low-key pressure tactics to forfeit the land, Bull plans a physical confrontation between the two young men, assuming that his son will beat the intruder into submission. Significantly, the trio meets by a river, and as it becomes clear that his son will not emerge victorious, the enraged Bull smashes their heads together, and proceeds to hold the American's head under the water. After the American stubbornly insists on his right to purchase the field, Bull smashes his skull against a rock by the river, killing the young man with his repeated blows. Until this point the American has been portrayed as the calm, rational stoic who, in contrast to the crazed Bull and his surly son, has become an object of sympathy, perhaps even the sole heroic figure of the film. Although Bull immediately repents having used excessive force, he has become the villain: earlier, he was a murderer of his own child and now, he is the murderer of the returning immigrant, who is a metaphor for the hope of economic development.

Furthermore, the river and the rock once again supply the natural facilitators of violence and death. Water, so often symbolically associated with life and fertility, in this film takes on very sinister implications. The perpetual imagery of rain, mist, river, lake, and heaving surf creates the sense that something is being squelched or drowned.

To conceal the American's murder, Bull carries the body into his car and dumps the body in a nearby lake. Yet, the land is treacherous and prone to betrayal, particularly to those who claim to love it with the all-consumingly insane passion of Bull. In his attempts to focus his reticent son on the prospect of farming, Bull's speeches about the hardships of his life and a desire to acquire and cultivate the land, with an almost sensual joy in the labor and the feel of the soil, might allude to a sort of warped destructive passion that evolves from economic disenfranchisement: The more difficult land is to acquire, the more valuable it becomes; seemingly Bull is surrounded by it, spends his life laboring on it, yet it is always out of reach since it belongs to someone else.

Nevertheless, beyond the murdered Irish-American there are no local Irish characters to counterbalance or to mitigate the powerfully evil figure of Bull, and the pathetic figures of his followers. This imbalance implies a political subtext wherein it is important to bear in mind that this is an English-made film produced for English and American audiences, which offers an Irish-American as the sympathetic figure of a returning immigrant with ostensibly positive and innovative ambitions.

As Bull's son continues his passive resistance against his father, secretly spurning an intended bride for a young woman of low repute, the son intends to elope, leaving behind his oppressive father. His choice of woman is significant in that she is a "tinker," a vocation of wanderers, who take a fierce pride in their freedom from ties of land, conventions, laws, or any aspirations to social status. Moreover, in the constructed dichotomy between "tamed" and "untamed" women, the tinker's daughter is stereotypically cast as a beautiful, insolent girl, whose wild, red, wavy hair whirls seductively as she baits young men who decline (out of contempt or fear?) her invitations to "dance."

As a derrick recovers the body of the young American, Bull discovers that his son has left and that his dreams are in vain. In the final tragic scene he deliberately drives his cattle toward the edge of the cliff not realizing that his son is returning to say farewell to his father. As the son becomes trapped by the vicious stampede of the cattle he is forced to run with them over the edge of the abyss, rendering his father once more a monster who kills his children, and leaving Bull with the realization that he has caused the death of everything that he once valued in life. Thereby, the land becomes an instrument of death that cannot be trusted, as the finally completely insane Bull wanders through the wreckage on the beach and into the surf to meet his own death in the waves he slashes at with his cane.

Ultimately, although Joe is as much a hero as Bull is a tragic failure, the types of men in these films share certain specific qualities in that they are portrayed as domineering, treacherous men who specifically make use of and have a special communion with nature and the landscape. This is in my view furthermore postulated as a function of Irish ethnicity that is politically rooted in colonialist traditional images of native as "other." My aim was to focus on relatively recent cinematic images of the Irish male and the significance of landscape, particularly cliffs and wells, as signs of the abyss that function to facilitate violence and to promote an image of intense, in some cases supernatural collusion between man and nature. Finally, even a cursory look at English- and American-produced films about Ireland, for instance, *Ryan's Daughter,* of 1970, reveals not only a host of stereotypical archetypes, but a definite cinematic tradition that reconstructs this imagery, however inadvertently replicating colonial ideology.

# 15

# Synge on Film

Two *Playboys*

## Sanford Sternlicht

In 1907 Synge said: "On the stage one must have reality, and one must have joy." For Synge the essence of that reality and that joy resided in the words he "heard among the country people of Ireland . . . phrases I have heard from herds and fisherman along the coast from Kerry to Mayo, or from beggar women and ballad-singers nearer Dublin." The poetry inherent in the primal Celtic language could serve as the image-bearing, invocating medium that counteracted the flat and pallid slice of life that is realism or naturalism in drama. Perhaps Synge's intuitive genius was for combining the realism of Padraic Colum with the romanticism of Yeats. Any stage or film production of *The Playboy of the Western World* will be judged to a significant extent on its balance between the "reading" of the script, the projection of dialogue, and the verisimilitude of the mis en-scène.

Two film versions of *Playboy* are currently accessible: Brian Desmond Hurst's 1962 last commercial, big-screen release, and Alan Gibson's 1975 BBC-TV production. Both are color products. Both are respectful of the play text. The former is very much a movie, whereas the latter is clearly scripted for television values and advantages. It is interesting to compare the productions for their fidelity to the word and spirit of Synge, their evocation of time and place, their successes or failures as products of their respective media, and their entertainment value.

Hurst's *Playboy* is typical of that director's work. He was trained as a painter. He saw film as a series of carefully composed stills on the storyboard. There was always something distant and detached in his work on film. He was taken by "composition" like a formalist stage director. In particular he liked the portrait-posed two or three shot, "staged" with the front-open triangulation.

In his earlier attempt at adapting and "translating" a Synge drama for the screen, *Riders to the Sea* (1935), Hurst was acclaimed for the cinematic brilliance of the keening scene with the women crossing the rocky ground to Maurya's house. Like his *Playboy*, *Riders to the Sea* was filmed in the west of Ireland. With the sea nearby, Hurst could indulge his love for the extreme long shot, the slow pan, and the closed frame. Using "classic" plays as elemental material, Hurst could, and certainly did in *The Playboy of the Western World*, choose the objective point of view, the film dynamic seemingly most comfortable for an ex-painter, a storyboard director whose creativity is in the prevision rather than in the lens eye–inspired shot.

Of course, a film director with a stage play as his or her material must open it out. The fourth wall of the proscenium with its metonymical "beyond" must give way to a reification of space and time peripheral to the Aristotelian "action." Hurst chooses to "open" in reasonable places. For example, his first sequence has Christopher running and stumbling from frame right to left across field and strand, "escaping" into the Western World (a shot picked up almost exactly by Gibson in 1975). His next-to-last sequence has Christy walking off from the pub, his arm around the shoulders of his twice-wounded and now tamed father, as he leaves behind the challenge of the Western World. Picking up on Hurst's open out to fade, Gibson more effectively has Christy march straight ahead, also with back to camera as with Hurst, but with Old Mahon stumbling behind and trying to keep up. The action symbolizes the archetypal fate of fathers and the comedic triumph of the young. The signification is to establish Christy as conqueror of the Western World, now moving screen frame left to right and up to right corner infinity, returning triumphantly home, his father now *his* slave, his manhood finally achieved through violent brute strength and by cutting his emotional ties to Pegeen (alas), and thus arriving at a Pyrrhic victory over her and her sex in the eternal Irish war between women and men. Hurst cuts the second scene between the Widow Quin and Old Mahon in Synge's act 3 in order to open up the film to the joyous world of simple fun and good-natured competition of a West Country fair on the beach. Gibson cuts less and shows less, partly because he is working with a smaller budget, but also because as a television director he is aware of the small screen's reductive limitations in regard to the vast panorama.

Hurst overdoes the sequence. In trying to establish Christy as now possessed with the panache of a Celtic hero, he exaggerates and diminishes the verisimilitude he has in fact only barely established. Furthermore, he cannot resist overextending the sequence as his camera lovingly lingers on the folk "color": games, races, prizefighting, and so forth (Ridiculously, the horses of the race are fine, expensive, perfectly groomed Arabians; in the Gibson version they are, appropriately, shaggy ponies.). But Hurst always insists on the extreme long shot, the long shot, and a few medium shots. Hurst chooses to keep the audience at a distance even when he uses the open shot. It is as if he is a park ranger keeping tiresome, intrusive, potentially polluting visual tourists from getting too close to the wild fauna.

Hurst moves much of the end of act 3 out in front of the shebeen and in doing so loses the dramatically callous act of Pegeen's burning of Christy's leg, by which she symbolically burns the bridge of their love. The omission of this action eases the perfidy of Pegeen and keeps her fully likable, if foolish, but weakens the motivation for Christy's anger and sudden dislike for her and for women in general. The cut is a part of Hurst's unnecessary, uncalled for, but perhaps commercially dictated softening of the play, and like so much of the film, a seeming bow to tourist Ireland. Irish women portrayed for export may be strong-willed, and even strong-mouthed, but never violent.

Hurst's failures are several in his *Playboy* although, all in all, the film is pleasing. It is not easy to destroy Synge's *The Playboy of the Western World* as long as the audience plainly hear the dialogue. Hurst chooses something of a stage Irish over true regional dialect, in his desire for audience aural comprehension. Thus the "Irish" of the production is rather a bit of a potpourri.

Perhaps the most salient failure was to make the role of Pegeen into a star turn, although financial reasons may have been behind his casting of the thirty-nine-year-old Siobhán McKenna as Pegeen. Hurst had used McKenna before, in a small part in the 1946 film version of Daphne du Maurier's *Hungry Hill*. Now she was a full-fledged international star, but far too old to play a character described by Synge as "a wild-looking, but fine girl of about twenty." There is little of either passion or sex in her portrayal. She is petulant and fractious. It is as if she were not directed at all, but read her lines in a singsong, soft, nasal, squirrelly, and oddly cutesy attempt at western brogue.

In juxtaposition to McKenna, Garry Raymond as Christy is a great error. He is at least a decade younger than she. When he first appears he is spotless except for a single, carefully located smudge on his face. An artfully placed tear or two "symbolizes" his poverty, his cross-country flight, and his slavery to his father. Raymond is Hollywood handsome. He is tall and straight and always clean-shaven. In no way can one believe he is the archetypal loser, the biddable boy, the castrated son of the patriarch, who has failed in his attempt to defy, in La-canian terms, the law of the father, through the very aggression that enforces it.

Anyway, the courting scenes between Pegeen and Christy have the slightly noisome quality of incest. It is Hurst's style to use very few close-ups. Intimacy is portrayed generally in medium shots. Only in the proposal scene do we get a few close-ups, and they show the age differential. If the shot was saved for an effect of intimacy, it does not work well. Neither romance, passion, or sex crosses the screen.

Raymond is so strong that he cannot grow much in the part. He is misdirected and badly costumed. He is no broken, brutalized "Man with a Hoe." He is no victim of institutionalized and deeply resented patriarchal power. When he manipulates Shawn out of his fine duds and passes from the ragged to the dandiacal, the transition is weak-ened by the lack of extreme difference in apparel and appearance. But Raymond looks matinee-idol handsome in Shawn's clothes, which just happen to be exactly the right size for him. It is a musical comedy mo-ment, not a scene in a realistic drama.

Speaking of costumes: it is the costumer who should have been split with a loy. The barefoot Pegeen is richly dressed in a stylized Vic-torian costume, and she wears a bad red wig in a terribly dated sixties bouffant upsweep. As if in uniforms, the other women, including the widow, all wear essentially the same striped, neatly pressed, fine-fabric skirts. They are barefoot too and, having come across fields and over dusty paths, they have managed, apparently, to wash their feet before entering.

The casting of an overaged Pegeen led to another casting absur-dity. Her suitor, Shawn, played by Mícheal Ó Bríain, seems to be about fifty and skeletal, hardly Synge's "fat and fair young man" referred to in text and film as a "lad." Even for Ireland, land of superannuated suitors, it is a stretch.

Hurst sometimes seems not to have read his own screenplay, as, for example, when Pegeen says to the widow: "He's stretched out drowsy" when Widow Quin can plainly see him sitting on the bench eating and drinking. Apparently, Hurst was following the play text and certainly not listening as he watched the scene shape in rehearsal.

The film director does much better in casting the lesser roles, rely-ing on fine Irish actors for rich characterization and verbal texture. El-speth March as the Widow Quin is massive. And if she does not capture the pathetic desperation of Synge's widow, she does connive and intrigue wonderfully well. Of course, her conflict with Pegeen for possession of the "bloody" and therefore sexy available new male, which should be a battle of generations, turns out visually at least to be a struggle between a spinster and a widow of similar years.

The veteran actor Niall MacGinnis is sufficiently threatening and later appropriately submissive as Old Mahon. He and Raymond have a very good scene together, when Christy is hog-tied and on his belly, and twice-wounded Old Mahon crawls back in frame. They are in each other's faces like two reptiles spitting, or pit bulls crouching and straining to kill.

Grandest of all, however, is the Abbey's Liam Redmond as Pegeen's father, Michael James. He is the very essence of the publican who loves his product far too much. When he is on camera, he almost blows everyone else away. Hurst wisely edits him in for reaction shots.

Hurst is ham-fisted in his use of music despite the fact that, or because he employed the distinguished Irish musicologist Seán Ó Riada to compose and recreate on old instruments a nineteenth-century Irish sound. Ó Riada had achieved some early recognition for composing the music for two highly regarded Irish language films: *Mise Éire* (1959) and *Saoirse?* (1961) Hurst employed the musical group Ceoltóirí Cualann, a precursor of the Chieftains. However, the background mood music is pedestrianly employed, coming in at every expected moment. One can almost hear the Ampex click on in the sound editor's hand. On the one hand, with the exception of the games sequence, seldom does the music rise to provide a "dialogue" accompanying the scene. This *Playboy* music merely says "Irish color," "folk," or "love scene." It does not "articulate" the film. It is an entity standing, grandly perhaps, on its own. Is it a composition aimed at a soundtrack album? On the other hand, the film's music introduced traditional Irish music to an international audience for the first time, replacing pub music as representationally Irish.

Yet Hurst's *Playboy* will do for an introduction to Synge and is, in this critic's dangerous opinion, a better film about Old Ireland than *The Quiet Man* (1952) for showing on and about St. Patrick's Day in America. But Gibson's television *Playboy* has intimacy, integrity, grit, teeth, and bite, as well as a verisimilitude that would have been impossible to produce within the commercial requirements of the movie world of the 1960s in a film used in part for a star turn.

Gibson either understood that Synge's *Playboy* is a great, small play, or perhaps the limitations of the television medium and a low budget forced him to think small, claustrophobic, poor, mean-spirited, interior, and intimate, and to emphasize language. Extreme long shots, except for the opening sequence and a view of fisherman and their boats on the strand, are nonexistent. He wisely avoids matte shots, rear projections, or other inexpensive "opticals." Gibson must rely to a large extent on Synge's dialogue and his actors' projection for his poetry, not on sweeping pan shots of lovely west country scenery.

The basic and essential code of meaning in Gibson's product is the subjective dynamic: his point of view as a director is Pegeen's; the objectivist Hurst's is the lens's. Gibson is more fortunate or more astute than Hurst in his casting. Thus, he can rely heavily on the best television shot, the close-up, without destroying credibility. The young and lovely Sinéad Cusack is perfect in her role, creating a memorable Pegeen through a sensitive, seemingly intuitive characterization, and fine articulation of a carefully coached authentic dialect.

The thirty-five-year-old John Hurt is too old for Christy. There is nothing of the youth in him. But Hurt's acting ability, small stature and emaciated, bent body, and Gibson's good directing achieve credibility. When Hurt enters, he is appropriately "very tired and frightened and dirty." He shakes with terror. He looks like a drowned rat. He rightly never achieves the grandeur Raymond does. The real, wretched Christy leaks through brave words and Shawn's fine garments. But Hurt has room to build the character and he does so, while the audience, if not the Irish locals, always sees that he is a playboy emperor without clothes. The fact that he is not handsome or strong lends credence in a sardonic way to Pegeen's falling for his self-proclaimed reputation as a father-authority slayer, a role which after all is what the Irish had aspired to for four hundred years, thus supporting a major facet of Synge's satire.

The fine actor Donal McCann works well as suitor Shawn. He fits Synge's description, is the right age, and is properly chicken. Because of McCann's youth and health, little Hurt's dominance is a function of reputation, in contrast to the Hurst version, in which Raymond's and McKenna's bullying of Ó Bríain reads like senior citizen abuse.

Gibson's casting and direction of Pauline McCann as the Widow Quin provides a very different widow from the character built by Elspeth March and Hurst. The formidable March, and McCann—thin, somewhat haglike, and very shrewd and conspiratorial—both work as the widow, and each actor fits the dynamic of the particular film. However, the Gibson version has dimension, to be discussed below, that establishes a milieu, a political backdrop, that makes McCann's portrayal more integrated and more intellectually interesting than March's.

Kevin Flood's Old Mahon is very funny, much more so than MacGinnis's but so dumb as to be less credible. Joe Lynch, as Michael James, is effective enough, but no match for the scene-stealing Liam Redmond.

It is in translating the themes of Synge's *Playboy* that Gibson wins out over Hurst. Ironically, the BBC-TV version is more anti-British than the film in the way the characters snap off their antioccupier lines and in their initial automatic response to shelter a fellow Irishman from the Peelers. Later, they seem more craven for their early words, when they are anxious to save their own skins and avoid accessoryship in the second "death" of Old Mahon. Gibson's version has its Marxist elements. The poor people of the West, like Widow Quin, fear hunger. The gifts of food are generous indeed. The people have been abandoned by the powers in Dublin and London. Although there may be a priest around, he takes no interest in their secular life and worldly needs, and surely the teaching of morality has been skewered. The Mayoans are funny-sad because they have such needs—love, respect, courage, role models, freedom from fearful authority, food, recognition, knowledge of the world—and no way to meet them. Through Gibson, Synge is once again appropriately hard on the Irish. After all, Synge was not trying to bring planeloads to Shannon, but to point out to the people he loved their shortcomings, their distorted values and their vices.

Gibson also makes us feel for the plight of Irish women, widows and virgins, in want of husbands, a plight more poignant with Shawn as the seeming best of the local breed. The women of Mayo, foolish or not, built a man, and then drove him away, and Cusack's Pegeen knows exactly what she has done and grieves her great lost chance. Gibson has consciously moved Pegeen to the foreground. Hurst, despite the name star in the role, keeps Pegeen off center, as perhaps Synge intended, but Gibson's choice reads better today, for if *The Playboy of the Western World* is Christy's comedy of overcoming, it is Pegeen's tragic romance.

Both productions on film of *Playboy* offer entertainment satisfaction. Hurst offers slick, competent, commercial fare with good music and a star. He "showcases" Synge. He produces a prettified, nineteenth-century, "realistic" peasant painting. It is light work and intended that way. Gibson's *Playboy* assumes the director's responsibility to speak to his own time, while discovering what is archetypal in his source and material. I detect a subtle echo of a feminist agenda: when the women of Mayo laud and elevate Christy it is not necessarily because he has committed a "manly" deed, but also, or for them primarily, because he has, like the women, been an "other": exploited, used, commodified, disregarded; but unlike them he, their champion, has destroyed a father, the archetypal oppressor. In the end he doubly fails them: he was not the destroyer, and he becomes the oppressor.

# 16

## *The Quiet Man* Speaks

### James MacKillop

For many educated Irish-Americans, it is one of the plagues of March, right up there with green beer, plastic leprechauns, and Brendan Behan anecdotes. And it is ubiquitous, even two generations after its release. Video stores stock more copies each March than they do for *King Kong*, *Casablanca*, or *Citizen Kane*. With the advent of satellite dishes and advanced microwave transmission, many homeowners may receive *The Quiet Man* continuously from 10 March to 20 March.

Learned and critical disparagement accompany the film's sustained popularity. As early as 1953, Gate Theatre cofounder Hilton Edwards remonstrated, "I cannot for the life of me see that it has any relation to the Ireland I or anyone else can have seen or known." Falsity heads the litany of attributed sins; others habitually cited are sentimentalism, condescension, cliché and gimcrackery. The emerging generation of Irish filmmakers usually put distance between themselves and this Hollywood perennial. A commonplace in any interview with such young filmmakers is that they are striving to show us that Ireland is something other than what is seen in *The Quiet Man*. The film also suffers critical swipes from other contributors to this volume.

What our educated anxiety about *The Quiet Man* overlooks is that it is the single work of Irish or Irish-American literature that a citizen can be expected to know without having met the demand of some required reading list. The film continues to speak to audiences in both America and Ireland, where it has become popular at Christmastime. The people, to paraphrase Louis B. Mayer, are not wrong for liking what they do. Nor are they inattentive, callow, or unsophisticated. No less a personage than the late Princess Grace of Monaco, an Academy Award–winning actress and International Chairman of the Irish-American Cultural Institute, named *The Quiet Man* as her all time favorite film. Audiences listen. What do they hear?

*The Quiet Man* is one of the most personal of director John Ford's more than one hundred films. The idea to make the film had been in Ford's mind for sixteen years before he brought it to the screen. Although Ford was a mature man and a Hollywood institution, he had to argue, plead, and lie to Herbert J. Yates of Republic Studios to make it. Republic specialized in cheap second features, and *The Quiet Man*, at $1.75 million, was its most expensive film ever, and also its only film ever to premiere at Radio City Music Hall. But like all Hollywood productions, it was collaborative and united the efforts of many artists.

The script of the film is nominally based on a short story by Maurice Walsh that was first published in *The Saturday Evening Post*, the mass-circulation American weekly. Although subject to scant critical attention,[1] Walsh was a best-selling popular author in his day. Born in Ballydonoghue, County Kerry, not far from the literary town of Listowel, he spent most of his early professional life in the British civil service, chiefly as an excise officer in the Highlands of Scotland. He had sold over a million copies of his novels before "The Quiet Man" appeared in 1933, beginning a twenty-year-long association with the American magazine. Like many of Walsh's stories, "The Quiet Man" contains a number of autobiographical references. The sharp-tongued, red-headed heroine was based on Walsh's wife, Caroline, a Scottish woman met during his work in Banffshire. The story is set at Knockanore, site of the Walsh homestead, which, the reader is reminded, is seven miles from Listowel. In the film the village is called Innisfree, and the nearest railroad station, five miles away, is called Castletown. The location of the shooting was actually done around Cong, County Mayo, chosen not only for its scenic advantages and access to Connemara but also because it allowed the company to he housed in the nearby Ashford Castle hotel.

Walsh published two versions of the story. The *Saturday Evening Post* text runs a bit under 6,500 words, and the revised text in the collection *The Green Rushes* (1935) extends to about 9,500 words. In the original the title character was named Shawn Kelvin, his red-headed wife Ellen O'Grady, and her brother Big Liam O'Grady; in the revision they are Paddy Bawn Enright, Ellen Roe O'Danaher, and Red Will O'Danaher. The 1933 text has a rather spare setting, whereas the 1935 includes many references to local geography and contemporary events. Although many passages are substantially rewritten in the later version, the central events follow the same scenario. The 1935 text is to be preferred for several reasons, as Walsh's biographer Steve Matheson reminds us. Not only did Walsh chafe under the space limits of *The Saturday Evening Post*, but the later version employs the name of a lifelong family friend to whom the author wished to pay tribute, Paddy Bawn Enright.[2]

The story in either version differs from the script of the film in theme, tone, setting, narrative structure, and characterization. Walsh's action takes place during the Anglo-Irish War, about 1919 or 1920. The Quiet Man of the title, Paddy Bawn ["Fair Patrick"] Enright, looks nothing at all like John Wayne. He is a little below middle height and is referred to, at one point, as a runt. An actor from the golden days of Hollywood better suited to his physical appearance would have been James Cagney, but Paddy's mild manners are more like those of Pat O'Brien. He is Irish-born but has spent some time in America, from which he has returned. His quietness comes from a wish to retire from the industrial world he knew in Pittsburgh as well as from the turmoil in contemporary Ireland. He gardens and keeps a neat household. In the movie the Wayne character tends flowers, somewhat implausibly, but he is not especially reticent about speaking his mind, a contradiction with the title ignored by commentators. Paddy Bawn is a religious person who attends Mass regularly and says his beads.

Paddy Bawn's quietness is unruffled at the beginning of the story when he learns that Red Will O'Danaher has added the few acres of the Enright family croft to his own larger holdings. To the disappointment of the villagers, he buys back the family farm without complaint instead of asserting his rights and begins to work the land. After living alone for five years, he begins to think about a life's companion. Red Will offers the hand of his sister, Ellen Roe, without consulting her for her wishes. She is described as having short red hair and being past her first youth. The older brother does not, however, deliver Ellen Roe's dowry of £100 in part because he doubts the manhood of some one as diminutive and gentle as Paddy Bawn. Years pass, the couple produce a child, but still the dowry is not delivered. Because of the size difference between Paddy Bawn and Red Will, the villagers do not expect that the smaller man will fight for his wife's fortune, despite his having been a boxer in New York. Ellen Roe also doubts her husband's machismo and worries that their son will think his father a coward. Thus provoked, Paddy Bawn overcomes his passiveness and demands the £100 which he then throws into a fire. He and Will engage in a five-minute fistfight, which the smaller man, weighing forty pounds less, wins.

Notable among the villagers in the 1935 version is an IRA operative named Mickeen Oge Flynn. His age and size are not specified in the story, but he owns a touring car and transports his friends to see the contest between Paddy Bawn and Red Will. There is nothing in his meager characterization to anticipate the horse-driving shaughraun and turf accountant, Michaeleen Oge Flynn, played by Barry Fitzgerald.

Completely absent from the story are such important elements in the film as the tempestuous relationship between the male and female leads, the horse race, Catholic-Protestant tensions, awareness of class differences, and American and Irish misperceptions of one another.

Although many hands helped to expand the narrative from the story to screenplay, John Ford led and shaped the effort. Ford bought the rights to "The Quiet Man" in 1936, shortly after the story appeared in *The Green Rushes* and Ford had achieved critical and commercial success with an earlier Irish labor of the heart, *The Informer.* Over the years Ford had made several unsuccessful attempts to interest producers in the project, and saw his best chance in 1950 after the completion of his so-called Cavalry Trilogy, the last film of which, *Rio Grande,* was made by Herbert J. Yates's Republic Films. Ford pleaded, complained, and threatened. He took Yates to the west of Ireland and pointed to a thatched, white-washed cottage and wept, "That's the house where I was born."[3] Although any studio biography could have told Yates that Ford was born in Cape Elizabeth, Maine, he relented.

Ford contracted Welsh writer Richard Llewellyn, author of *How Green Was My Valley,* to turn the story into a novella. Copies of that version of the story are not available, but we have the testimony of Dan Ford, John's grandson, that it made much of the setting in the Black and Tan War.[4] When Ford and his longtime collaborator, writer Frank S. Nugent, used the Llewellyn draft as the basis of their filmscript they jettisoned most of the references to war outside the village, although a number of IRA men still appear in tams and jodhpurs. Costumes send mixed signals about the time of the filmscript, many of the women dressed in the netherpresent of 1951–52, the men dressed to fit a time perhaps thirty years earlier. The choice of the archaic but freshly painted passenger cars, shown in the early scene at the train station, signals a dating before 1930. Although Nugent is given sole credit for the script, he acknowledged in a letter to Lindsay Anderson that Ford worked on every step of the writing, contributing many lines of dialogue, notably the one most often quoted from the film.[5] Michaeleen Oge, departing from the stone bridge, remarks, "It's a fine soft night so I think I'll go and talk a little treason with me comrades."

Nugent, incidentally, wrote the script of the only other Maurice Walsh story to be filmed. The undistinguished *Trouble in the Glen* (directed by Herbert Wilcox, 1953) is set in Scotland and is memorable mostly for having Forrest Tucker pretend to speak Scottish Gaelic and for putting Orson Welles in kilts.

Part of Ford's contribution was to make good on his prevarication to Yates. Bit by bit the story began to take on more of his personal stamp. The title character was given height and weight to accommodate John Wayne, an actor associated with Ford as early as *Hangman's House* (1928), another Irish film made in Hollywood. More importantly the character's name was changed to Sean Thornton. The Christian name "Sean" is not only the Irish version of "John" but it was the name under which the youthful John Ford was known. The family name "Thornton" is taken from Ford's relatives who had fought in the Irish revolution. Ford's actual family name, "Feeney," is ascribed to Will Danaher's diminutive retainer, played in the film by Jack Mac-Gowran. And the location shooting around Cong and the Ashford Castle allowed some footage to be taken in County Galway, from whence Ford's mother and father had emigrated, and where there were, indeed, thatched cottages in which many of his ancestors had been born.

The most significant change Ford wrought in the story taken from Walsh is to have the Quiet Man, now Sean Thornton, be an American arriving in Ireland as a stranger rather than being an Irishman returned from America. And the village he seeks has taken the name of "Innisfree," an evocation of the longing for the magic of the west of Ireland once felt by a very different kind of cosmopolitan.

Quite apart from Sean Thornton's befuddling encounters with quaint and irritating Irish customs, the America he left is a continuing unseen presence in the narrative. Only an American finds any humor in Michaeleen Oge's assumption that every American city is in Massachusetts. Even more telling is the extraordinary long take of a pub named "Cohan's," a common enough surname in Ireland, that is humorous only to an American mass audience of a generation ago who might be expected to think the name was "Cohen." Ford overstates the point further by having Michaeleen Oge come in from the side of the frame and explain that "we pronounce the name 'Ko-HAN.' " Along with this unseen presence the film is populated with faces from other Ford films, the famous "stock company" of Wayne, Ward Bond, Victor McLaglen, John Ford's brother Francis, and so on. These American allusions in casting extend into some very minor roles; the walk-on part of Father Paul's mother is played by Mae Marsh, star of D. W. Griffith's silent epics *Birth of a Nation* and *Intolerance*.

Sean has not merely emigrated to Ireland but he has retreated from the United States and is on pilgrimage to his ancestral home. We shall learn later that he suffers anxiety from having killed an opponent in a boxing ring (a theme unanticipated in the Walsh story), and he says he wishes to flee the satanic mills of Pittsburgh that are so hot "a man forgets his fear of hell." Sean has a heroic past to recover as his grandfather, the patriotic old Sean Thornton, who died in a penal colony in Australia. Further, young Sean's mother, who died when he was twelve, begged him to return to the family smallholding at the idyllically named "White O'Morn." When buying the property from the Anglo-Irish Widow Tillane (Mildred Natwick), Sean avers that it sounds like heaven to him. How different Sean's calling from that given Gabriel Conroy by Miss Ivors. How different his journey from that of the old woman in Frank O'Connor's "Long Road to Ummera."

The initial vision of Ireland in *The Quiet Man* is based on an American pastoralism unimagined by Maurice Walsh. Ford's many westerns, notably those set in Arizona's Monument Valley, have much in common with Ford's vision of Ireland. The Mayo and Galway of the film are feudal variants of the American dream of the Edenic garden, a land without poverty, inflation, bigotry, intolerance, injustice, crime, or very expensive real estate. Ford signals this transit to Eden early in the narrative when Michaeleen Oge's trap passes under the viaduct carrying the train back to urban Ireland. Shortly after, Sean and Michaeleen Oge encounter a rather pre-Raphaelite tableau in which the barefoot Danaher girl (the O' was dropped from the Walsh text) is seen driving sheep across a meadow. Sean asks, "Is this real?" Michaeleen Oge answers, "No, it's a mirage, brought on by your terrible thirst." When such sequences were shown in the rushes to producer Herbert J. Yates, he gasped, "But everything's all green," a remark that was often repeated in derision before the filming was done.[6]

Ford's Innisfree has no radios and few telephones. The only automobile belongs to a Church of Ireland bishop and appears to be of World War I vintage. The horse is still common in both transportation and agriculture, and Mary Kate advises Sean to use horses on the farm instead of smelly tractors. Red Will Danaher's farm equipment is a kind that disappeared from American agriculture a generation previously.

Although there's no questioning the authenticity of the locales, different scenes are rife with solecisms. The gardening Sean Thornton digs with the wrong foot, for example. How could a middle-aged man in a pub in 1920 remember Fenians being sent to Australia in 1867? The cast speak a medley of accents, more than could be found in any large Irish town. And who but an American would fail to notice that Victor McLaglen, born in Tunbridge Wells, England, is Irish in family name only.

Though Sean Thornton may be an innocent abroad, like so many Americans before, he seeks to improve the natives he finds. Objecting to Michaeleen Oge's supervision of his courtship, he opines that "if this were the States I'd just blow my horn in front of the girl's house and she'd come runnin'." And despite Mary Kate's repeated attempts to explain that the payment of her dowry ensures her identity and independence, guaranteeing that she will not merely be a servant in a man's house, he persists in seeing the custom as both mercenary and archaic. Unlike the Quiet Man of Walsh's story who is too reticent to ask for the dowry, Sean Thornton refuses to accept the importance of a strange tradition.

Although Sean's attitude probably seems a bit obtuse to observers today, it undoubtedly expressed the values of many in an American audience in 1952. In those last years of the Truman administration, seven years after the triumphs of V E and V-J days, with unparalleled world dominance in commerce and technology, American self-confidence was at an all-time high and American introspection was at a low ebb. American society had begun the building of suburbia, a process that would withdraw people from older, ethnic, immigrant communities and resettle them according to their ability to make mortgage payments. In an American urban environment, the custom of requiring a dowry in a woman's family, when her husband does not require it, would be a tiresome impediment on the path to pluralism. Sean Thornton seems to feel, as Douglas MacArthur did in Japan, that if only the world would adopt American ways, we could all get along more easily.

Sean's Americanism completely changes the meaning of the climactic episode of both Walsh's story and Ford's film, that of Will's handing over of his sister's "fortune" and the dispatch of the money to the flames. In Walsh's story Paddy Bawn has found his gumption and answered his wife's call that he assert his manhood. In the film Sean drags his wife five miles from the railroad station at Castletown before presenting Will with the option of either delivering the dowry or taking his sister back. When Sean accepts and then destroys the money, he puts the question of the dowry out of his life. He does not accept Irish custom; he obliterates it. Sean's wife then marches off, satisfied that her need has been filled, indifferent to the ensuing brawl between her husband and her brother, promising to be a dutiful woman of the house. Could we expect that any daughter of Sean Thornton and his wife would want to have a dowry?

For many reasons we look at the episode differently today, not the least of which has been the repeated failure to "Americanize" different corners of the world. More importantly, we hear Mary Kate Danaher's plaintive voice when she argues that her dowry would allow her to retain the identity of her family and would keep her from being a servant, sentiments not found in Walsh's story. On the one hand, any number of Irish-Americans have told me with some embarrassment that women in Ireland are not required to have dowries to get married; they seem to share Sean Thornton's perception that the necessity for a dowry is a kind of bondage. On the other hand, dowries certainly were commonplace when Maurice Walsh was a young man; he was twenty-one in 1900. Furthermore, several feminist commentators have accepted the implicit thesis of the filmscript. Molly Haskell in *From Reverence to Rape: The Treatment of Women in the Movies*,[7] praises *The Quiet Man*'s insight into a woman's need for a sense of self, continuity, and property. Brandon French puts a picture of a defiant Maureen O'Hara on the cover of *On the Verge of Revolt: Women in American Films of the Fifties*,[8] implying that *The Quiet Man* is the key feminist-awakening film of the decade.

The resonances of the wife's characterization reach backward in time as well as forward. As we have considered, the wife in the original story was based on the author's wife, a tart-tongued redhead, as described by Walsh's friend and fellow Listowel writer, Bryan Mac-Mahon.[9] When Maureen O'Hara was cast to play her, the wife's role gained new dimensions that the script alone cannot explain. Although only thirty-one when the film was shot, O'Hara (born Maureen Fitz-Simons in suburban Dublin) had been a familiar presence in Hollywood for more than ten years. In her previous film, *Rio Grande,* also directed by John Ford for Republic, she played a Southern wife in post–Civil War America whose values were in conflict with those of her Yankee husband, John Wayne. In both films the antagonism between wife and husband is cultural and sexual, with the O'Hara character representing the older, more agrarian values.

In the Walsh story the wife's name is Ellen Roe, but in the film she is Mary Kate. Source materials on John Ford do not suggest any autobiographical allusions here, but reasons for the name change are not hard to find. The "Mary" half of the name is explained by Sean Thornton's repeated assertions that she is a saint or a goddess, and a virgin at that. The "Kate" half is a transparent allusion to the title character in *The Taming of the Shrew*. Like Katherina, Mary Kate is on the far side of youth as well as being a spitfire. Like Petruchio, Sean is undeterred by the rebuffs of his loved one. And like Petruchio also, Sean humiliates his shrew, this time by dragging her five miles, a journey which causes her to lose a shoe as well as her dignity. Along the route a red-shawled old lady offers Sean a stick with which to beat his wife.

Unlike that of Petruchio and Katherina, or of Paddy Bawn and Ellen Roe of the Walsh story, the love of Sean and Mary Kate is invested with a curious G-rated sensuality. Indeed, *The Quiet Man* contains some of the most obsessive sexuality ever to be found in a Hollywood product classed as a "family movie." Steven Spielberg exploits Sean Thornton's furious ardor to witty effect in an extensive quotation from *The Quiet Man* in *E.T. The Extra Terrestrial* (1982). More important than the discussion of who is sleeping with whom and when, the locked doors and broken beds, and so forth, is the persistence of water imagery in the film. When Sean first tries to speak with Mary Kate, he puts his hand in the holy water font and obliges her to take water from his palm. Michaeleen Oge correctly calls this provocation "pattyfingers." Later, during their courtship, Sean and Mary Kate break free from Michaeleen Oge's chaperoning and ride a tandem bicycle to the edge of a small stream. While Sean and the camera modestly avert their eyes, Mary Kate takes off her shoes and stockings so that she might wade the stream with naked feet. Sean understands the invitation and charges across the rivulet. When Sean is united with the barefoot Mary Kate he doffs his incongruous bowler, an emblem of Irish decorum and restraint. A little later, framed in the doorway of a monastic ruin, the lovers embrace during a rainstorm, their clothes clinging to their bodies in the closest thing to a nude scene that the conventions of the early 1950s would allow. At the end of the film when the dowry has been paid and burned, and the shrew has been tamed, the two lovers cross stepping stones in a small stream to White O'Morn. As they step Sean drops a stick, presumably the one given to him to beat his wife by the red-shawled woman.

Ford's film assumes that the concord of husband, wife, and brother-in-law should be reflected throughout the village of Innisfree. We are invited to believe that Irish religious and class differences can melt away. Such an assumption is based on the assertion that the Irish have short memories and care very little about their history. The Anglo-Irish Widow Tillane has to remind Sean and the audience that her family

has been in Ireland for five hundred years. Michaeleen Oge passes a
ruin and says it is the ancestral home of the ancient Flynns, taken from
them by the . . . [he hesitates] . . . the druids, as if he were unaware of
the cultural and political identity of the residents of the great house,
and he an IRA man. The aristocratic Widow Tillane and the rising
Catholic bourgeois Will Danaher divide the economic power of the village between them, an arbitrary hegemony that no one challenges. The
Widow, however, is justly outraged at Will's announcement of their be-
trothal without his having asked her intentions. What seems less plausible is that she accepts him at the end. Put in American terms that
Ford should have understood, the Widow Tillane is a Compson
whereas Danaher is a Snopes. The union is one that few marriage
counselors would bless.

Ford and his scriptwriters had an even more difficult time with religious questions, none of which are foreshadowed in Walsh's story.
The role of the parish priest, Father Peter Lonergan, was given to Ward
Bond, an actor who had figured prominently in Ford's other films. Initially the role appears to be expanded as Father Lonergan narrates the
early parts of the film, but as the action progresses he becomes less and
less visible or audible. Eventually, without any notice, he is dropped as
the narrator, and we see activities that he knows nothing about and
which must be explained to him. Although he promises a 7:00 A.M.
Mass in memory of Sean's mother and expects Sean to attend, he does
not interfere much with the lives of the villagers. He does cross Will
Danaher, however, who threatens to join the Church of Ireland in retal-
iation; to which Father Lonergan retorts, "If they'd have you." When
Mary Kate shares her anguish at her unconsummated marriage we
learn that Father Lonergan is an Irish speaker. The priest spends most
of his time trying to catch a great salmon, but the wisdom of Fionn mac
Cumhaill is denied him.

The clergyman who figures larger in the action is the Church of Ireland Reverend Playfair, who is a former boxer like Sean and who reveals the secret of his guilty past. Sean addresses him affectionately as
"Padre." Taking this role was Arthur Shields, an Abbey Theatre veteran long associated with John Ford, often seen as a clergyman, notably as the fire-breathing Calvinist in *Drums Along the Mohawk*.
Reverend Playfair lives with his wife in a comfortable home presumably built when all Irishmen had to support the Established Church.
The script implies heartfelt regret that he has become an economic
anachronism in contemporary Ireland, heading a parish with only

three families. Thus the happy ecumenicism at the end of the film has the Catholic villagers, led by Father Lonergan, impersonate a nonexistent Church of Ireland parish so that Reverend Playfair might be allowed to stay in Edenic Innisfree.

The only character not addressed here directly is also the most interesting one, Michaeleen Oge Flynn, as played by Barry Fitzgerald. One must add immediately that "Barry Fitzgerald" was in fact a life-long role created by William Joseph Shields, Arthur's older brother. While the Barry Fitzgerald persona draws much from Irish literature, taking from Charles Lever, Samuel Lover, Dion Boucicault,[10] Somerville and Ross, and Sean O'Casey, in whose plays the actor first distinguished himself, Barry Fitzgerald did not always play "Barry Fitzgerald." French director René Clair, for example, chose him to play a well-born, devious judge in *And Then There Were None* (1945), an adaptation of Agatha Christie's *Ten Little Indians*. If many Irish-Americans remember Barry Fitzgerald as a drunken blarney-talking layabout, they do not recall his performance in *The Quiet Man*. Indeed, I am confident that if Barry Fitzgerald had played only this one role in the movies, it would be remembered as a minor jewel, much as Abbey player F. J. McCormick's role in *Odd Man Out* is. One of the most attractive aspects of his characterization is the pithiness of dialogue. At the opening sequence he leads Sean Thornton away from the station without uttering a word. Later, when Sean praises the liberality of American courting customs as against the regressive restraint of Irish ones, Michaeleen dismisses the presumption in two well-delivered words, "American? . . . prohibition." He also delivers the best line in the entire film. On the morning after the Thornton wedding night he visits the bedroom of the couple and sees the broken bed, assuming that things had worked out quite differently from what we know they have. After a long take he turns to the camera and utters the words, "Impetuous . . . Homeric."

None of the above should be seen as evidence to argue that *The Quiet Man* is an undervalued masterpiece. There are too many cinematic and thematic solecisms for that. Instead, I am content in saying that the film is not the piece of trash that I myself thought it was in the years I avoided seeing it out of expected embarrassment. The real significance of the film is not its considerable if flawed artistry but rather the dialogue it makes with its audience. To some it may appear that *The Quiet Man* is the ultimate expression in a tourist's vision of Ireland, and, indeed, the film probably does relate to the Irish tourist industry in somewhat the same way *Uncle Tom's Cabin* relates to abolitionism. Except that Sean Thornton is not a tourist: he is a settler. He returns to Ireland to recreate himself.

The most lasting thing *The Quiet Man* has to say is to announce the beginning of third-generation-return literature. The first generation was characterized by sentimental immigrant memories, which survive in such songs as "Galway Bay" and "Did Your Mother Come from Ireland?" The second generation was assimilationist and ethnically anonymous. Think of such writers as Eugene O'Neill, F. Scott Fitzgerald, and Philip Barry. In second-generation movies the Jimmy Cagney and Pat O'Brien characters have Irish names but they usually do not think of themselves as Irish. The third generation seeks out an Ireland lost from family memory.

As mentioned earlier, Grace Kelly always described *The Quiet Man* as her favorite film. She was the half-German daughter of a prosperous Philadelphia contractor and the niece of an assimilated Irish-American playwright, George Kelly. She saw the film when she was twenty-four and appearing in its chief rival at the Academy Awards ceremony, *High Noon*. Was it because of her family's heritage or because of *The Quiet Man* that she devoted so much of her postacting career to Irish culture?

If the conception of Ireland in *The Quiet Man* is a kind of Gaelic Cockaigne or Hibernian Erewhon, at least it was constructed with images of the country that still may be found. The stone bridge on the Galway-Clifden Road, the grounds of the Ashford Castle, even the Cong town square with Cohan's Pub may be photographed again and reinterpreted. Put another way, Ford's Innisfree provides the traveler with artifacts to focus quest, even if they are not quite objective correlatives of diasporic dreaming. In contrast, Yeats's Innisfree, conceived from London and wholly innocent of the social and political turmoil of the 1890s, has vanished if indeed it ever existed. Sligo's Lough Gill, containing that Innisfree (Ir. *heathery island*), is today lined with posh summer homes where a hut built of wattles would be unlikely to meet zoning-code restrictions.

The third-generation return to Ireland signaled by *The Quiet Man* has led at an even larger fourth-generation migration, our own. Dublin now ranks ahead of Rome as an American airline destination. Tourists, those despised trenchermen of commodified culture, now contribute the second largest economic sector of the once "most distressful nation." Once arrived, they have more to do than kiss the Blarney Stone. In 1998 there were thirty-six summer schools devoted to Irish literature and culture, beginning with Yeats, Synge, and Irish language instruction. Irish studies, a term that barely existed in 1952, now flourish in American universities and colleges; more than 430 institutions of higher learning now provide instruction on Irish subjects. The American Conference for Irish Studies, founded in 1962, now boasts 1,500 members, substantially more than The North American Conference for British Studies.

In the end, *The Quiet Man* may have contributed more to the emerging Irish film culture than is usually acknowledged. An instance of this contribution appeared during a recent tour of the Irish Film Centre on Eustace Street in Dublin. On sale in the Centre shop, next to a cafe that dispenses cappuccino as well as Guinness, was a poster for "John Ford's Timeless Masterpiece, *The Quiet Man*," a souvenir from a recent revival. On the wall of the Irish Film Archive adjacent to the IFC is a plaque honoring *The Quiet Man*. The archive is the culmination of decades of effort on the part of many historian and critics, most notably the late Liam O'Leary, but it was completed with a bequest from the United States. Confessedly, I tried to bait my tour guide that a tribute to Hollywood kitsch did not belong in such a citadel of aestheticism. The young male guide, clad in street-apache black leather topped with a shock of Berliozian curly red hair, allowed not so much as a smile. "Without *The Quiet Man*," he allowed, "we probably wouldn't be here."

# 17

## Selected Filmography of Irish And Irish-Related Feature Films

Anthony Kirby and James MacKillop

An "Irish film" is here defined as (a) one made in Ireland, with (b) an Irish director, (c) produced or backed by an Irish company, and (d) based on a text by an Irish writer, or a compelling minority of those four elements. John Ford's *Rising of the Moon* (1958), adapting three short works by Irish writers and produced at Ardmore Studios, is here classed as "Irish"; Ford's *The Quiet Man* (1952), shot largely in Ireland for Republic Pictures, is here "Irish Related." Neil Jordan's *Angel* (1982) is "Irish"; his *Mona Lisa* (1986), set in London, is "Irish Related." In cases of ambiguity, for example, the British-produced *Cal* (1984), the listing favors "Irish" over "Irish Related." The majority of international films incidentally shot in Ireland, for example, John Boorman's *Zardoz* (1974), or Tom Donovan's *Lovespell* (1979), are ignored, but those where an Irish context may be inferred, for example, Robert Altman's *Images* (1972), are noted. Ignored also are films of the Irish diaspora, such as Donald Crombie's *The Irishman* (Australia, 1978) or Edward Burns's *The Brothers McMullen* (USA, 1995), and many silent features.

A "feature film" may be a fictional narrative or a documentary, regardless of whether it was produced for distribution in a cinema house or for television. Some short films by noteworthy directors have been included here, but no attempt was made to list all short films, many of them fugitive, especially when they were produced for educational, governmental, or religious markets, or for industrial promotion.

Additional listings may be found in Matthew Stevens's 140–page *Directory of Irish and Irish-Related Films* (Trowbridge, UK: Flicks Books; Urbana: University of Illinois Press, 1989) and Kevin Rockett's 751–page *Irish Filmography* (Dublin: Red Mountain, 1996).

## Abbreviations

| | |
|---|---|
| aka | also known as, alternate title |
| BBC | British Broadcasting Corporation; cf. Channel 4. |
| b/w | black and white |
| C | cast |
| Channel 4 | British arts television |
| col | color |
| D | director |
| dist. | distributed |
| docu | documentary or nonfiction film |
| m | minutes |
| M | music composed or arranged by |
| Narr | narrated by |
| Ph | photographer, cinematographer |
| RTE | Radio Telefis Éireann, i.e., Irish television |
| Prod | produced by, i.e., producing company |
| W | writer, scenarist |
| W/D | writer/director |

## Irish Films

*After Midnight* (1990), 90m, col.
W/D: Shani S. Grewal. Ph: Jack Conroy. M: Mickey Gallagher. C: Saeed Jaffrey, Hayley Mills, Ian Drury, Dhirendra, Vladek Sheybal, Maurice O'Donoghue, Pat Laffan. Co-prod: Channel 4.

*After '68* (1993), 25m
W/D: Stephen Burke. Ph: Donal Gilligan. M: Maurice McGrath. C: Deirdre Molloy, Ger Ryan, Fidelma Murphy, Dermott Martin. Co-prod: RTE.

*Age of de Valera, The* (1983), 5 parts, 26m each, col, docu.
D: Peter Feeney. W: Gearoid Ó Tuathaigh. Ph: Ken Murphy. Prod: RTE.

*AIDS: A Priest's Testament* (1988), 52m, col, docu.
D: Conor McAnally. W: Conor McAnally, Fr. Bernard Lynch. Ph: Sean Corcoran. Narr: Fr. Bernard Lynch. Prod: Radharc Films.

*Ailsa* (1994), 78m, col.
D: Paddy Breathnach. W: Joe O'Connor, adapting his novel of the same title. Ph: Cian de Buitléar. M: Dario Marinelli. C: Brendan Doyle, An-

drea Irvine, Juliette Gruber, Gary Lydon, Darragh Kelly. Co-prod: RTE, France, Germany.

*Aimsir Padraig.* See *In the Days of St. Patrick.*

*Aiséirghe* (1942), 30m, b/w, docu, silent.
W/D, Ph: Liam O'Leary.

*All Things Bright and Beautiful* (1994), 90m, col.
W/D: Barry Devlin. Ph: Declan Quinn. M: Jim Lockhart. C: Ciaran Fitzgerald, Gabrielle Reidy, Gabriel Byrne, Kevin McNally, Tom Wilkinson, Lorraine Pilkington. Co-prod: BBC Northern Ireland, RTE (Distinguish from the unrelated UK film [1979] of the same title).

*Amongst Women* (1998), col.
D: Tom Cairns, Colin Tucker. W: Adrian Hodges, adapted the John Mc-Gahern novel of the same title. Ph: Sue Gibson, Ian Foster. C: Tony Doyle, Ger Ryan, Susan Lynch, Anne-Marie Duff, Geraldine O'Rawe, Damien McAdam, Eamonn Owens, Ciaran Owens, Brian F. O'Byrne, Bosco Hogan, Darragh Conboy, Ronan Leahy, Neili Conroy, Aoife Moriarty, Pauline Lynch. Prod: RTE/BBC.

*An,* Irish definite, see next word of title.

*Angel* (1982), 92m, col; U.S. title *Danny Boy.*
W/D: Neil Jordan. Ph: Chris Menges. M: Keith Donald, Paddy Meegan, Giuseppe Verdi. C: Stephen Rea, Honor Heffernan, Veronica Quilligan, Alan Devlin, Peter Caffrey, Marie Kean, Ray McAnally, Donal McCann. Co-prod: UK.

*Angela Mooney Does Again* (1997), 90m, col.
Tommy McArdle. W: Tommy McArdle, John McArdle. C: Mia Farrow, Brendan Gleeson, Patrick Bergin, Alan Devine, Lisa O'Reilly.

*Anne Devlin* (1984), 124m, col.
W/D: Pat Murphy. Ph: Thaddeus O'Sullivan. M: Robert Boyle. C: Bríd Brennan, Bosco Hogan, Des McAleer, Gillian Hackett, Ian McElhinny, David Kelly, Niall O'Brien, Chris O'Neill.

*Another Island.* See *Oilean Eile.*

*At a Dublin Inn* (1950), 80m, b/w, aka *Stranger at My Door.*
D: Brendan J. Stafford, Desmond Leslie. W: Desmond Leslie. M: Leslie Bridgewater. C: Valentine Dyall, Joseph O'Connor, Agnes Bernelle, Maire O'Neill.

*At The Cinema Palace: Liam O'Leary* (1983), 53m, col, docu.
W/D: Donald Taylor Black. Ph: Sean Corcoran. M: Bill Whelan. C: Liam O'Leary, Michael Powell, Lindsay Anderson, Cyril Cusack, Kevin Brownlow, Denis Forman, Sean MacBride.

*Atlantean* (1984), 3 parts, each 53m, col, docu.
W/D: Bob Quinn. Ph: Seamus Deasy, Sean Corcoran, Thaddeus O'Sullivan, Joe Comerford, Nick O'Neill, Abdelhadi Tazi. M: Roger Doyle. Narr: Alan Stanford.

*Attracta* (1983), 55m, col.
D: Kieran Hickey. W: William Trevor, based on his short story of the same title. Ph: Sean Corcoran. C: Wendy Hiller, Kate Thompson, Joe McPartland, John Kavanagh, Kate Flynn, Deirdre Donnelly, Cathleen Delaney.

*Ballroom of Romance, The* (1982), 52m, col.
D: Pat O'Connor. W: William Trevor, based on his short story of the same title. Ph: Nat Crosby. C: Brenda Fricker, John Kavanagh, Cyril Cusack, Anita Reeves, Mick Lally, Niall Toibín. Prod: BBC-TV.

*Bargain Shop, The* (1992), 57m, col.
W/D: Johnny Gogan. Ph: Declan Quinn. M: Cathal Coughlan. C: Emer McCourt, Garrett Keogh, Stuart Graham, Ruth McCabe, Brendan Gleeson. Co-prod: RTE, Germany.

*Basket Full of Wallpaper* (1998), 100m, col.
D: Joe Lee. W: Robert J. Quinn. Ph: James Mather. C: Paul Humphries, Togo Igawa, John Cronin, Tom Lawlor, Anne Kent, Aongus Óg McAnally, David Finn, Diare McRoais.

*Best Man, The* (1983), 85m, col.
W/D: Joe Mahon. Ph: Terry McDonald. M: Eamon Friel. C: Seamus Ball, Máiréad Mullan, Denis McGowan, Jean Flagherty, Mickey McGowan.

*Between the Line* (1977), 30m, col, docu.
W/D: Ph: John T. Davis.

*Big Birthday, The* (1959), 77m, b/w, aka *Broth of a Boy*
D: George Pollock. W: Patrick Kirwan, Blanaid Irvine, adapting the stage play of the same title by Hugh Leonard. Ph: Walter J. Harvey. M: Stanley Black. C: Barry Fitzgerald, June Thornburn, Tony Wright, Harry Brogan, Eddie Golden, Marie Kean.

*Bishop's Story* (1994), 83m, a reediting of *Budawanny* (1987), col and b/w, partly silent.
W/D: Bob Quinn, based on the novel *Súil le Breith [Lovers]*, by Pádraic Standúin. Ph: Seamus Deasy. M: Roger Doyle. C: Donal McCann, Maggie Fegan, Tomas Ó Flaithearta, Peadar Lamb, Freda Gillen, Ray McBride, Seán Ó Colsdealbha.

*Blarney* (1938), 66m, b/w.
D: Harry O'Donovan. W: Harry O'Donovan, Jimmy O'Dea. Ph: Harry O'Donovan. C: Jimmy O'Dea, Ken Warrington, Julie Suedo, Noel Purcell, Rodney Malcolmson, Hazel Hughes, Myrette Morven.

*Bogwoman* (1997), 84m, col.
W/D: Tom Collins. Ph: Peter Robertson. M: Fiachra Trench. C: Rachel Dowling, Peter Mullan, Darren McHugh, Maria McDermottroe, Noelle Brown, Sean McGinley.

*Boom Babies* (1986), 34m, col.
W/D: Siobhán Twomey. Ph: Nicholas O'Neill. M: John and Neil McGrory. C: John Ryan, Aisling Toibín, Andrew Connolly.

*Boy from Mercury, The* (1996), 88m, col.
W/D: Martin Duffy. Ph: Seamus Deasy. C: James Hickey, Rita Tushingham, Hugh O'Conor, Joanne Marie Gerard, Tom Courtenay, Sean Flanagan.

*Boyd's Shop* (1960), 55m, b/w.
D: Henry Cass. W: Philip Howard, adapting the stage play of the same title by St. John Ervine. M: Stanley Black. C: Eileen Crowe, Geoffrey Golden, Aideen O'Kelly, Vincent Dowling, Aiden Crenwell.

*Boys and Men* (1996), 40m, col.
D: Sean Hinds. W: Brian Lally. C: Conor Mullen, Patrick Leech. Released only in 16mm and video.

*Boxer, The* (1997), 95m, col.
D: Jim Sheridan. W: Jim Sheridan and Terry George. C: Daniel Day-Lewis, Emily Watson, Gerard McSorley, Brian Cox.

*Brendan Behan's Dublin* (1966), 29m, col, docu.
D: Norman Cohen. W: Carolyn Swift. Ph: Robert Monks. M: The Dubliners. Narr: Ray McAnally.

*Broken Harvest* (1995), 97/110m, col.
D: Maurice O'Callaghan. W: Maurice O'Callaghan, Kate O'Callaghan, adapting the short story "The Shilling," by Maurice O'Callaghan. Ph: Jack Conroy. M: Patrick Cassidy. C: Darren McHugh, Colin Lane, Marian Quinn, Niall O'Brien, Joe Jeffers, Joy Florish.

**Broth of a Boy. See *The Big Birthday*.**

*Budawanny* (1987). See *The Bishop's Story* (1994).

*Butcher Boy, The* (1997), 106/147m, col.
D: Neil Jordan. W: Neil Jordan and Patrick McCabe, adapting Patrick McCabe's novel of the same title. Ph: Adrian Biddle. C: Eamonn Owens, Alan Boyle, Fiona Shaw, Andrew Fullarton, Stephen Rea, Ian Hart, Aisling O'Sullivan, Sinéad O'Connor.

*By Accident* (1930), 60m, b/w, silent.
W/D: J.N.G. Davidson. C: C. Clarke-Clifford, Olive Purcell, Mary Manning, Paul Farrell.

*Cal* (1984), 102m, col.
D: Pat O'Connor. W: Bernard MacLaverty, from his novel of the same title. Ph: Jerzy Zielinski. M: Mark Knopfler. C: Helen Mirren, John Lynch, Ray McAnally, Donal McCann, John Kavanagh, Tom Hickey. Prod: UK.

*Cancer* (1976), 63m, col.
D: Deirdre Friel. W: Eugene McCabe. Ph: Stuart Hetherington. C: J. G. Devlin, Louis Rolston.

*Caoineadh Airt Uí Laoire/Lament for Art O'Leary* (1975), 56m, col.
W/D: Bob Quinn. Ph: Joe Comerford. M: M. Finn. C: Séan Bán Breathnach, Eibhlín Nic Dhonncha, John Arden. Irish language dialogue.

*Caught in a Free State* (1983), 56m, col.
D: Peter Ormrod. W: Brian Lynch. Ph: Eugene McVeigh. M: Seoirse Bodley. C: Gotz Burger, Benno Hoffman, Peter Jankowsky, John Kavanagh, Barry McGovern, Niall Toibín. Prod: RTE and BBC-Channel 4.

*Child's Voice, A* (1978), 30m, col.
D: Kieran Hickey. W: David Thomson. Ph: Sean Corcoran. Narr: Valentine Dyall. C: T. P. McKenna, Stephen Brennan, R. D. Smith, June Tobin.

*Christy Ring* (1963), 23m, col, docu.
D: Louis Marcus. Ph: Vincent Corcoran.

*Circle of Friends* (1995), 110m, col.
D: Pat O'Connor. W: Andrew Davies, adapting the novel of the same title by Maeve Binchy. Ph: Kenneth MacMillan. M: Michael Kamen. C: Minnie Driver, Chris O'Donnell, Geraldine O'Rawe, Saffron Burrows, Alan Cumming, Colin Firth, John Kavanagh, Ruth McCabe.

*Clash of the Ash* (1987), 53m, col.
W/D: Fergus Tighe. Ph: Declan Quinn. C: William Heffernan, Vincent Murphy, Gina Moxley, Alan Devlin.

*Cloch* (1975), 26m, col.
W/D, Ph: Bob Quinn. M: Roger Doyle. C: James McKenna.

*Colleen Bawn, The* (1920), 90m, b/w, silent; aka *Willie Reilly and His Colleen Bawn.*
D: John MacDonagh. W: Dr. D. Moriarty, after the novel by the same title by William Carleton. C: Brian Macgowan, Frances Alexander, George Nesbit, Jim Plant, John MacDonagh. Prod: the Film Company of Ireland. (Distinguish from the Irish-related *Colleen Bawn* (1911).)

*Comely Maidens* (1995), 35m, col, docu.
D: Hillary Dully, Fintan Connolly.

*Commitments, The* (1991), 117m, col.
D: Alan Parker. W: Dick Clement, Ian Le Frenais, and Roddy Doyle, after Doyle's novel of the same title. Ph: Gale Tattersall. M: Wilson Pickett, Otis Redding, etc. C: Robert Arkins, Michael Aherne, Angeline Ball, Maria Doyle, Dave Finnegan, Bronagh Gallagher, Félim Gormley, Glen Hansard, Dick Massey, Johnny Murphy, Kenneth McCluskey, Andrew Strong, Colm Meaney. Prod: UK television.

*Connemara and Its Ponies* (1971), 28m, col, docu.
D, Ph: David Shaw-Smith. W, Narr: Michael Killanan. M: Donal Lunny, Drowsey Maggie.

*Country Girls, The* (1983), 103m, col.
D: Desmond Davis. W: Edna O'Brien, from her novel of the same title. Ph: Denis Lewiston. M: Francis Shaw. C: Maeve Germaine, Jill Doyle, John Olohan, Anna Manahan, Sam Neill, John Kavanagh, Niall Toibín. Prod: UK.

*Courier, The* (1987), 85m, col.
D: Joe Lee, Frank Deasy. W: Frank Deasy. Ph: Gabriel Beristain. M: Declan MacManus (aka Elvis Costello), etc. C: Gabriel Byrne, Ian Bannen, Patrick Bergin, Cait O'Riordan, Padraig O'Loinsigh, Andrew Connolly, Michelle Houlden, Mary Ryan. Prod: UK.

*Criminal Affairs* (1997), 94m, col.
D: Jeremiah Cullinane. W: Charles Picket. C: James Marshall, Louis Mandylor, Renee Allman, Luke Heyden, Maria Tecce, Bill Murphy.

*Criminal Conversation* (1980), 60m, col.
D: Kieran Hickey. W: Kieran Hickey and Philip Davison based on the short story of the same title by Philip Davison. Ph: Sean Corcoran. C: Emmet Bergin, Deirdre Donnelly, Leslie Lalor, Peter Caffrey. Prod: BAC Films.

*Cruiskeen Lawn* (1924), b/w, silent.
D: John MacDonagh. C: Jimmy O'Dea, Tom Moran, Kathleen Armstrong, Berrett MacDonnell, Chris Sylvester, Fred Jeffs.

*Cry of the Innocent* (1980), 105m, col.
D: Michael O'Herlihy. W: Sidney Michaels, adapting the novel of the same title by Frederick Forsyth. C: Rod Taylor, Joanna Pettet, Nigel Davenport, Cyril Cusack, Walter Gotell, Alexander Knox. Prod: Ireland; dist. on TV in North America.

*Crying Game, The* (1992), 112m, col.
W/D: Neil Jordan. M: Anne Duncan. C: Stephen Rea, Jaye Davidson, Miranda Richardson, Forest Whitaker, Jim Broadbent, Ralph Brown, Adrian Dunbar.

*Cycle of Violence* (1998), 90m, col.
D: Henry Herbert. W: Colin Bateman. C: Gerard Mooney, Maria Lennon, Paula McFetridge, Des Cave, Edna Oates, Conteth Hill, Doreen Keogh, Alan McKee, John Keegan, Peter Ballance.

*Da* (1988), 96m, col.
D: Matt Clark. W: Hugh Leonard, after his stageplay of the same title. Ph: Alar Kivilo. M: Elmer Bernstein. C: Barnard Hughes, Martin Sheen, William Hickey, Karl Hayden, Doreen Hepburn, Hugh O'Conor, Ingrid Craigie. Co-prod: USA.

*Dancing at Lughnasa* (1998), 120m, col.
D: Pat O'Connor. W: Brian Friel, Frank McGuinness, adapting Friel's stageplay of the same title. C: Meryl Streep, Bríd Brennan, Kathy Burke, Sophie Thompson, Catherine McCormack, Darrell Johnson, Michael Gambon, Rhys Ifans, Lorcan Cranitch, James Gavigan, Peter Gowan, Dawn Bradfield, Marie Cullen, John Kavanagh, Kate O'Toole, Gareth Stewart.

*Danny Boy.* See *Angel.*

*Daughters of the Troubles: Belfast Stories* (1997), 60m, col, docu.
D: Marcia Rock. W: Jack Holland. Narr: Anjelica Huston.

*Dawn, The* (1936), 87m, b/w.
D: Tom Cooper. W: Tom Cooper and Dr. D. A. Moriarty. Ph: James B. S. Lawler. M: Pat Crawley's Dance Band. C: Tom Cooper, Brian O'Sullivan, Eileen Davis, Donal O'Cahill, Jerry O'Mahony, Bill Murphy, Marion O'Connell, Jack Scully, John McCarthy, Hubert Martin, Dodo Hurley, Oliver Mason, John Cooper, Paddy Looney, Nora Burke, Mary Meagher, T. M. O'Sullivan, Tommy Cooper.

*December Bride* (1990), 90m, col.
D: Thaddeus O'Sullivan. W: David Rudkin, based on the novel of the same title by Sam Hanna Bell. Ph: Bruno de Keyser. M: Jurgen Kneiper. C: Saskia Reeves, Donal McCann, Ciaran Hinds, Patrick Malahide, Brenda Bruce, Michael McKnight, Dervla Kirwan, Geoffrey Golden, Cathleen Delaney, Peter Capaldi. Prod: UK.

*Desecration* (1981), 52m, col.
D: Neville Presho. W: Breandán Ó hEithir, Declan Burke-Kennedy. Ph: Godfrey Graham. M: Jolyon Jackson. C: Tom Hickey, Johnny Murphy, Eamon Keane, Frank McDonald.

*Devil's Rock* (1938), 55m, b/w.
D: Germain G. Burger, Richard Hayward. W: Victor Haddick. Ph: Germain G. Burger. C: Charles Fagan, Geraldine Mitchel, Richard Hayward, Terence Grainger.

*Diary of a Madman* (1991), 77/83m, col.
D: Ronan O'Leary. W: Tim McDonnell, adapting the stage play of the same title by Nicolai Gogol. Ph: Walter Lasally. C: Tim McDonnell, Siobhán Miley, Deirdre O'Connell, Conor Mullen. Co-prod: RTE.

*Disappearance of Finbar, The* (1996), 100m, col.
D: Sue Clayton. W: Dermot Bolger, Sue Clayton, adapting the novel *The Disappearance of Rory Brophy,* by Carl Lombard. Ph: Eduardo Serra. M: Davy Spillane. C: Luke Griffin, Lorraine Pilkington, Jonathan Rhys-Myers, Sean McGinley, Laura Brennan, Fanny Risberg, Sif Ruud.

*Double Carpet* (1998), 120m/55m, col.
W/D: Mark Kilroy. Ph: James Mather. C: Tom Hickey, Darragh Kelly, Garrett Keogh, Damien McAdam, Johnny Murphy, Bernie Downs, Pauline Downs, Pauline Hutton, Nick Nolan, Oliver Maguire, Anto Nolan, Jack Lynch. Prod: RTE.

*Down the Corner* (1977), 60m, col.
D: Joe Comerford. W: Noel McFarlane, after his novel of the same title. Ph: Adam Barker-Mill. M: Liam Weldon, Roger Doyle. C: Joe Keenan, Kevin Doyle, Declan Cronin, Christy Keogh.

*Draíocht [Magic]* (1996), 50/52m, col.
D: Áine O'Connor. W: Gabriel Byrne. C: Gabriel Byrne, James Murphy, Charlotte Brady, Frank O'Sullivan. Irish language soundtrack.

*Driftwood* (1995), 90/100/112m, col.
D: Ronan O'Leary, W: Ronan O'Leary, Richard Waring. C: James Spader, Anne Brochet, Barry McGovern, Anna Massey, Kevin McHugh, Ger Ryan, Aiden Grennell.

*Drinking Crude* (1997), 85m, col.
W/D: Owen McPolin. Ph: Ossie McLean M: Bill Corkey. C: Andrew Scott, James Quarton, Eva Birthistle, Colin Farrell, Maria Hayden, Sarah Pilkington, Darren Monks, Natalie Stringer, James Hornby.

*Dublin Mystic, The.* See *Misteach Baile Átha Cliath.*

*Dusk 'til Dawn* (1997), 60m, b/w, docu.
W/D: Sinéad O'Brien.

*Dust on the Bible* (1989), 52m, col, docu.
D: John T. Davis. Ph: John T. Davis. C: Martin Donnelly. Narr: Damian Gorman. Prod: BBC Channel 4.

*Eamon de Valera* (1975), 58m, b/w, docu.
D: George Morrison. W: George Morrison, Robert Kee. Narr: Robert Kee.

*Eamon de Valera: Portrait of a Statesman* (1968), 30m, b/w and col, docu.
D: George Fleischmann. W: Peter O'Reilly. Ph: George Fleischmann.

*Early Bird* (1936), 71m, b/w.
W/D: Donovan Pedelty, adapting the stageplay of the same title by J. McGregor Douglas. C: Richard Hayward, Jimmy Mageean, Charlotte Tedlie, Myrtle Adams.

*Eat the Peach* (1986), 95m, col.
D: Peter Ormrod. W: John Kelleher, Peter Ormrod. Ph: Arthur Wooster. M: Donal Lunny. C: Stephen Brennan, Eamon Morrissey, Catherine Byrne, Niall Toibín, Joe Lynch, Takashi Kawahara, Pat Kenny.

*Eh Joe* (1986), 38m, col.
D: Alan Gilsenan. W: Samuel Beckett. Ph: Peter Butler. C: Tom Hickey, Siobhán McKenna (voice only).

*Eileen Aroon.* See *The Islandman.*

*Eliminator, The* (1996), 83m, col.
W/D: Enda Hughes. C: Barry Wallace, Michael Hughes, Mik Duffy.

*End of the World Man, The* (1985), 82m, col.
D: Bill Miskelly. W: Marie Jackson. Ph: Seamus Deasy. M: John Anderson. C: John Hewitt, Leanne O'Malley, Claire Weir, Maureen Dow, Michael Knowles. A children's feature.

*Exposure* (1978), 48m, col.
D: Kieran Hickey. W: Kieran Hickey, Philip Davison. Ph: Sean Corcoran. M: Ludwig van Beethoven. C: Catherine Schell, T. P. McKenna, Bosco Hogan, Niall O'Brien. Prod: BAC Films.

*Falling for a Dancer* (1998), col.
D: Richard Standeven. W: Deirdre Purcell. Ph: Kevin Rowley, Geoff Glover. C: Elizabeth Dermot Walsh, Liam Cunningham, Elinor Methven, Dermot Crowley, Maurice O'Donoghue, Marcella Plunkett, Maeve Kearney, Colin Farrell, Ian McGuirk, Angela Newman, Karen Collins, Derry Power, Oliver Maguire, Anne-Marie Cotter, Joe Stockdale, Claire Cullinane.

*Family* (1994), 4 parts, 52m each, col.
D: Michael Winterbottom. W: Roddy Doyle. Ph: Andrew Eaton. C: Sean McGinley, Ger Ryan, Neili Conroy, Barry Ward. Prod: RTE/BBC.

*Family* (1995), 90m, col.
A feature-length version of the miniseries, cited above.

*Fanatic Heart* (1995), 87m, col, aka *Nothing Personal.*
D: Thaddeus O'Sullivan. W: Daniel Morin, Thaddeus O'Sullivan, adapting Daniel Morin's novel *All Our Fault.* Ph: Dick Pope. M: Philip Appleby. C: Ian Hart, John Lynch, James Frain, Gerard McSorley, Gary Lydon, Ruaidhrí Conroy, Jennifer Courtney, Michael Gambon, Maria Doyle Kennedy, Ciaran Fitzgerald. Co-prod: Channel 4.

*Fantasist, The* (1986), 98m, col.
W/D: Robin Hardy, adapting the novel *Goosefoot,* by Patrick McGinley. Ph: Frank Gell. M: Stanislas Syrewicz. C: Moira Harris, Christopher Cazenove, Timothy Bottoms, John Kavanagh, Mick Lally, Bairbre Ní Chaoimh.

*Fear of the Dark* (1986), 53m, col.
D: Tony Barry. W: Robert Wynne-Simmons. Ph: Breffni Byrne. M: Tim Doherty. C: Hugh O'Conor, Aisling Toibín, Owen O'Gorman, Donal O'Kelly.

*Field, The* (1990), 107/110m, col.
D: Jim Sheridan. W: Jim Sheridan, adapting the stageplay of the same title by John B. Keane. Ph: Jim Sheridan. M: Elmer Bernstein. C:

Richard Harris, John Hurt, Sean Bean, Tom Berenger, Brenda Fricker, Frances Tomelty, Malachy McCourt, John Cowley, Sean McGinley, Jenny Conroy. Co-prod: UK.

*Fifth Province, The* (1997), 89m, col.
D: Frank Stapleton. W: Frank Stapleton and Nina Fitzpatrick. C: Brian F. O'Byrne, Ian Richardson, Anthony Higgins, Lia Williams.

*50,000 Secret Journeys* (1994), 30m, col, docu.
D: Hillary Dully.

*Fleadh Ceoil/Folk Music Festival* (1967), 23m, b/w, docu.
D: Louis Marcus. W: Breandán Ó hEithir. Ph: Robert Monks. Narr: Chris Curran.

*Fools of Fortune* (1990), 109m, col.
D: Pat O'Connor. W: Michael Hirst, adapting the novel of the same title by William Trevor. Ph: Jerzy Zielinski. M: Hans Zimmer. C: Iain Glen, Mary Elizabeth Mastrantonio, Julie Christie, Michael Kitchen, Sean McClory, Frankie McCafferty, Niamh Cusack, John Kavanagh, Mick Lally, Ronnie Masterson, Rosaleen Linehan. Prod: UK.

*Force of Duty* (1992), 81m, col.
D: Pat O'Connor. W: Bill Morrison and Chris Ryder. Ph: Eric Gillespie. M: John Keane. C: Donal McCann, Adrian Dunbar, Patrick Malahide, Ingrid Craigie. Prod: BBC-TV Belfast.

*Frankie Starlight* (1995), 101m, col.
D: Michael Lindsay-Hogg. W: Chet Raymo and Ronan O'Leary, adapting Chet Raymo's novel, *The Dork of Cork*. Ph: Paul Laufer. M: Elmer Bernstein. C: Anne Parillaud, Matt Dillon, Gabriel Byrne, Rudi Davies, Corban Walker, Georgina Cates, Alan Pentony, Niall Toibín. Prod: RTE, Channel 4, Canal + (France).

*Freedom.* See *Saoirse?*

*Further Gesture* (1995/1997), 98m, col.
D: Robert Dornhelm. W: Ronan Bennett. C: Stephen Rea, Rosanna Pastor, Alfred Molina, Maria Doyle Kennedy, Brendan Gleeson, Sean McGinley, Jorge Sanz. Co-prod: Germany, UK; first broadcast on television.

*Goban Saor, An* (1995), 52m, col.
D: Liadh Ní Riada. W: Nuala Ní Dhomhnaill. C: Eamonn Kelly, Macdara Ó Fathatha, Mairín Ní Shuilleabhain. Irish language soundtrack.

*Gold in the Streets* (1997), 98m, col.
D: Elizabeth Gill. W: Janet Noble, Noel Pearson, adapting Janet Noble's stage play of the same title. Ph: Jack Conroy. M: Kila. C: Karl Geary, Jim Belushi, Tom Hickey, Jared Harris, Aiden Gillen, Ian Hart, Louise Lombard, Lorraine Pilkington, Andrea Irvine. Co-prod: UK.

*Goodbye to the Hill. See Paddy.*

*Graceville* (1996), col., docu.
D: Bob Quinn. W: Seosamh Ó Cuiag, Bob Quinn.

*Guests of the Nation* (1935), 50m, b/w, silent.
D: Denis Johnston. W: Denis Johnston, Frank O'Connor, Mary Manning, adapting Frank O'Connor's short story of the same title. C: Barry Fitzgerald, Cyril Cusack, Shelagh Richards, Fred Johnson, Denis O'Dea, Hilton Edwards, Frank O'Connor.

*Guiltrip* (1995), 88m, col.
W/D: Gerard Stembridge. Ph: Eugene O'Connor. M: Brendan Power. C: Andrew Connolly, Jasmine Russell, Peter Hanly, Michelle Houlden, Pauline McLynn, Frankie McCafferty, Mikel Murfi. Prod: Ireland/France/Italy/Spain.

*Hanging Gale, The* (1995), 4 parts, 52m each, col.
D: Diarmuid Lawrence. W: Allan Cubitt. Ph: Rex Maidment. M: Shaun Davey. C: Joe McGann, Mark McGann, Paul McGann, Stephen McGann, Michael Kitchen, Fiona Victory, Gerard McSorley, Tina Kellegher, Sean McGinley, Birdy Sweeney, Joe Pilkington, Ciaran Fitzgerald, Ciara Marley, Dylan O'Connell, Barry Barnes, Marie Ní Ghráinne, Tom Hickey.

*Harp of My Country* (1986), 76m, col, docu.
D: P. J. Barron. W: Tim Pat Coogan. Ph: Gerrard MacArthur. C: Niall Murray, Suzanne Rhattigan, James Barkley.

*Heart on the Line* (1990), 61m, col, docu.
D: John T. Davis. Ph: David Barker, John T. Davis. Prod: Channel 4.

*Hebrew Lesson* (1972), 32m, col.
W/D: Wolf Mankiewicz. Ph: Gunther Wulff. C: Milo O'Shea, Patrick Dawson, Harry Towb, Alun Owen.

*Hello Stranger* (1992), 61m, col.
D: Ronan O'Leary. W: Truman Capote, adapting his own short story of the same title. Ph: Cedric Culliton. M: Frank McNamara. C: Daniel J. Travanti, Tim McDonnell, O. Z. Whitehead, Jan Widger. Co-prod: RTE.

*Heritage of Ireland, The* (1978), 6 parts, each 50m, col, docu.
D: Louis Marcus. Ph: Robert Monks. M: Seán Ó Riada.

*High Boot Benny* (1993), 83m, col.
W/D: Joe Comerford. Ph: Donal Gilligan. M: Gaye McIntyre. C: Frances Tomelty, Alan Devlin, Mark O'Shea, Fiona Nicholas. Prod: RTE, Channel 4, Spain, France.

*Hip to the Tip—Atlantic: The Independent Years* (1993), 104m, col, docu.
D: John T. Davis, Uri Fruchtmann. Ph: John T. Davis. Prod: Channel 4.

*Hobo* (1991), 90m, col, docu.
D: John T. Davis. Ph: John T. Davis, David Barker. Prod: BBC-TV.

*Holigans* (1998), col.
D: Paul Tickell. W: James Mather. Ph: Benito Stragio. C: Darren Healy, Jeff O'Toole, Vivian Verveen, Mark Dunn, Mary Murray, Angela Harding, Stuart Dunn, Frank Coughlin.

*Home Is the Hero* (1959), 80m, b/w.
D: Fielder Cook. W: Henry Keating, after the stage play of the same title by Walter Macken. Ph: Stanley Pavey. M: Bruce Montgomery. C: Walter Macken, Eileen Crowe, Arthur Kennedy, Joan O'Hara, Maire O'Donnell.

*Hoodwinked* (1997), 60m, col, docu.
D: Trish McAdam.

*How to Cheat on the Leaving Certificate* (1997), 80m, b/w.
D: Graham Jones. W: Graham Jones, Tadhg O'Higgins, Aislinn O'Loughlin. C: Aileen O'Connor, Garret Baker, John Wright, Tara Ford, Alison Coffey, Philip Bredin.

*Hush-a-Bye-Baby* (1990), 72/78m, col.
D: Margo Harkin. W: Margo Harkin, Stephanie English. Ph: Breffni Byrne. M: Sinéad O'Connor. C: Emer McCourt, Michael Liebman, Cathy Casey, Julie Marie Reynolds, Sinéad O'Connor. Prod: Derry Film/Video Collective, Channel 4, RTE.

*I Am Ireland.* See *Mise Éire.*

*I Can't, I Can't . . .* (1969), 99m, col, aka *Wedding Night.*
D: Piers Haggard. W: Robert I. Holt, Lee Dunne, from a story by Robert I. Holt. Ph: Ray Sturgess. M: Cyril Ornadel. C: Dennis Waterman, Tessa Wyatt, Alexandra Bastedo, Eddie Byrne, Patrick Laffan, Martin Dempsey.

*I Went Down* (1997), col.
D: Paddy Breathnach. W: Conor McPherson. Ph: Cian de Buitléar. C: Brendan Gleeson, Peter MacDonald, Peter Caffrey, Tony Doyle.

*In the Days of St. Patrick/Aimsir Padraig* (1920), 6 reels, silent, b/w, Gaelic title cards.
D: Norman Whitten. Ph: J. Gordon Lewis. C: Vernon Whitten, Gilbert Green, Ira Allen, Alice Cardinall, Dermot McCarthy, Alice Keating, Herbert Mayne.

*In the Name of the Father* (1993), 127m, col.
D: Jim Sheridan. W: Jim Sheridan and Terry George, based on the book by Jerry Conlon, *Proved Innocent.* Ph: Peter Biziou. M: Trevor Jones. C: Daniel Day-Lewis, Pete Postlethwaite, Emma Thompson, Mark Sheppard, Britta Smith, John Lynch, Corin Redgrave, Beatie Edney, Daniel Massey.

*Informant, The* (1997), 105m, col.
D: Jim McBride. W: Nicholas Meyer, adapting the novel *Field of Blood,* by Gerald Seymour. Ph: Alfonso Beato. M: The Pogues. C: Timothy Dalton, Cary Elwes, Anthony Brophy, Maria Lennon, John Kavanagh, Sean McGinley, Frankie McCafferty, Stuart Graham, Gary Lydon, Simone Bendix, Paul Hickey. Co-prod: USA.

*Into the West* (1993), 90/102m, col.
D: Mike Newell. W: Jim Sheridan, after the short story by Michael Pierce. Ph: Tom Sigel. M: John McDonnell. C: Ciaran Fitzgerald, Ru-

aidhrí Conroy, Gabriel Byrne, Colm Meaney, Ellen Barkin, David Kelly, Johnny Murphy, John Kavanagh, Pauline Delaney, Brendan Gleeson.

*Irish and Proud of It* (1936), 72m, b/w.
D: Donovan Pedelty. W: David Evans, Donovan Pedelty, after the story by Dorothea Donn Byrne. C: Richard Hayward, Dinah Sheridan, Gwen Gill, George Pembroke.

*Irish Cinema: Ourselves Alone* (1996), 51m, col, docu.
D: Donald Taylor Black. W: Kevin Rockett.

*Irish Destiny* (1925), 73/93m, b/w, silent.
D: George Dewhurst. W: Dr. Isaac J. Eppel. Ph: Joe Rosenthal. C: Brian Macgowan, Frances MacNamara, Patrick (Paddy Dunne) Cullinane, Tom Flood, Cathal McGarvey.

*Is There No One Who Understands Me?/The World of James Joyce* (c. 1985), 120m, col, docu.
D: Seán Ó Mórdha. W: Colbert Kearney. Ph: Peter Dorney. M: Seoirse Bodley. Narr: T. P. McKenna. Voice of James Joyce: John Kavanagh. Readers: Barry McGovern, Seamus Forde. Other voices: Martin Dempsey, Marie Hastings, Frank Kelly, Andreas O'Gallchoir, Maureen Toal. Prod: RTE; consultant: Richard Ellmann.

*Islandman, The* (1939), 48/64m, b/w, aka *West of Kerry, Eileen Aroon.*
W/D: Patrick Keenan Heale, adapting a story by Donal Cahill. Ph: Victor Taylor. M: Horace Sheldon. C: Cecil Ford, Eileen Curran, Brian O'Sullivan, Gabriel Fallon, Delia Murphy.

*It's Handy When People Don't Die* (1980), 100m, col.
D: Tom McArdle. W: John McArdle, after his short story of the same title. Ph: Ciaran Tanham. M: Mícheál Ó Súilleabháin. C: Garrett Keogh, Brendan Cauldwell, Bob Carlyle, Catherine Gibson, Barbara McNamara.

*James Joyce's Women* (1983), 91m, col.
D: Michael Pearce. W: Fionnula Flanagan. Ph: John Metcalfe. C: Fionnula Flanagan, Chris O'Neill, Timothy O'Grady, Tony Lyons, Maureen Potter. Prod: USA and Ireland.

*Joe My Friend* (1996), 95/101m, col, aka *My Friend Joe*
D: Chris Bould. W: David Howard, Declan Hughes, adapting Peter Pohl's novel, *Janne, Min Van.* Ph: Michael Faust. M: Ronan Hardiman.

C: John Cleere, Schuyler Fisk, Stanley Townsend, Pauline McLynn, Stephen McHattie. Co-prod: Germany.

*John, Love* (1983), 34m, col.
D: John T. Davis. Ph: Sue Gibson. C: Nuala Hayes, Niall O'Brien, Tony Hyland, Carmel Callan, Danny Cummins, Martin Dempsey. Prod: UK commercial TV.

*Jonathan Swift* (1967), 30m, b/w, docu.
D: Kieran Hickey. W: David Thomson. Ph: Theo Hogers. Narr: Cyril Cusack, Alan Badel, Patrick Magee, Siobhán McKenna.

*Joyriders* (1988), 96m, col.
D: Aisling Walsh. W: Andy Smith. Ph: Gabriel Beristain. M: Tony Britten. C: Patricia Kerrigan, Andrew Connolly, Billie Whitelaw, John Kavanagh, David Kelly, Deirdre Donoghue, Tracy Peacock.

*Just in Time* (1998), 52m, col.
D: John Carney, Tom Hall. W: John Carney. C: Gerard McSorley, Frances Barber, Michael McElhatton.

*Kickhams, The* (1992), 55m, col, docu.
W/D: Brendan J. Byrne. C: Raymond Mooney, Ciaran Murphy, Mick Mallon. Co-prod: Italy, UK.

*Kinkisha, The* (1977), 65m, col.
D: Tom McArdle. W: John McArdle. Ph: Ciaran Tanham. M: Mícheál Ó Súilleabháin. C: Barbara McNamara, John McArdle, Catherine Gibson, David Byrne.

*Knocknagow* (1918), 60m, b/w, silent.
W/D: Fred O'Donovan, based on the novel of the same title by Charles J. Kickham. Ph: William Moser. C: Brian Magowan, Kathleen Murphy, J. M. Carre, Alice Keating, Charles Power, Dermot O'Dowd, Cyril Cusack.

*Korea* (1995), 75/90m, col.
D: Cathal Black. W: Joe O'Byrne and John D'Alton, after the short story of the same title by John McGahern. Ph: Nic Morris. M: Stephen McKean. C: Donal Donnelly, Andrew Scott, Fiona Molony, Vass Anderson, Eileen Ward.

*Lamb* (1985), 110m, col.
D: Colin Gregg. W: Bernard MacLaverty, after his novel of the same title. Ph: Mike McGarfath. M: Van Morrison. C: Liam Neeson, Harry Towb, Hugh O'Conor, Frances Tomelty, Ian Bannen, Ronan Wilmot.

*Lament for Art O'Leary.* See *Caoineadh Airt Uí Laoire.*

*Land of Her Fathers* (1924), b/w, silent.
W/D: John Hurley, based on the short story of the same title by Dorothea Donn Byrne. C: Micheál MacLiammóir, Frank Hugh O'Donnell, Phyllis O'Hara, Barry Fitzgerald, Tom Moran, F. J. McCormick, Maureen Dalaney.

*Lapsed Catholics* (1987), 52m, col.
W/D: Barry Devlin. C: Patrick Bergin, Gerard McSorley, Joe Sorvino, Gina Moxley.

*Larry* (1959), 27m, b/w.
D: Robert Dawson, Shelagh Richards. W: Seamus Byrne, adapting the short story "My Oedipus Complex," by Frank O'Connor. Ph: Bestick Williams. M: Paddy Bawn Ó Broin. C: Geoffrey Golden, Neasa Ní Anracháin, John Cowley.

*Last Bus Home* (1997), 93m, col.
D: Johnny Gogan. W: Paul Donovan. Ph: James Mather. M: Cathal Coughlan. C: Annie Ryan, Brian O'Byrne, John Cronin, Barry Comerford, Anthony Brophy, Gemma Craven.

*Last of the High Kings* (1996), 95m, col, aka *Summer Fling.*
D: David Keating. W: Gabriel Byrne, David Keating, adapting the novel of the same title by Ferdia MacAnna. C: Catherine O'Hara, Gabriel Byrne, Jared Leto, Christina Ricci, Stephen Rea, Colm Meaney, Renee Weldon, Lorraine Pilkington, Emily Mortimer, Karl Hayden, Jason Barry.

*Lies My Father Told Me* (1960), 60m, b/w.
D: Don Chaffey. W: Ted Allan, adapting his original story of the same title. Ph: Gerald Gibbs. M: Wilfred Joseph. C: Harry Brogan, Betsy Blair, Edward Golden, Rita O'Dea. (Distinguish from the Canadian-made feature of the same title [1975], also based on the Ted Allan story.)

*Light of Other Days, The* (197?), 50m, b/w, docu.
D: Kieran Hickey. W: Des Hickey. Ph: Sean Corcoran. M: John Beckett.
Narr: Colin Blakely, Marie Kean. Prod: BAC Films.

*Living Flame, The.* See *Tine Bheo, An.*

*Long Way Home, The* (1995), 45m, col.
D: Paddy Breathnach. W: Joseph O'Connor. C: Niall O'Brien, Phelim
Drew, Anne Kent, Frankie McCafferty, Vinny Murphy.

*Luck of the Irish, The* (1935), 80m, b/w.
D: Donovan Pedelty. W: Colonel Victor Haddick, adapting his novel of
the same title. C: Richard Hayward, Kay Walsh, Niall MacGinnis, J. R.
Magecan, R. H. MacCanless.

*Maeve* (1981), 110m, col.
D: Pat Murphy, John Davies. W: Pat Murphy. Ph: Robert Smith. M:
Molly Brambeld and the Country Four, etc. C: Mary Jackson, Bríd
Brennan, Mark Mulholland, Trudy Kelly, John Keegan, Nuala McCann.

*Magic.* See *Draíocht.*

*Man of No Importance, A* (1994), 99m, col.
D: Suri Krishnamma. W: Barry Devlin. Ph: Jonathan Cavendish. C: Al-
bert Finney, Brenda Fricker, Michael Gambon, Tara Fitzgerald, Rufus
Sewell, Patrick Malahide, David Kelly, Anna Manahan. Co-prod: UK.

*Meteor* (1998), 120m, col.
W/D: Joe O'Byrne. Ph: Paul Sarossy. C: Brenda Fricker, Alfred Molina,
Mike Myers, John Kavanagh, Dervla Kirwan, Ian Costello, Gavin
Dowdell, Natasha Corcoran, Fiona Galscott, Stephen Lynch, Derek
Reid, Dawn Bradfield, Mick Nolan, Pat McGrath, Jamie McCormac,
Catherine Byrne.

*Michael Collins* (1996), 135m, col.
W/D: Neil Jordan. Ph: Chris Menges. C: Liam Neeson, Stephen Rea,
Julia Roberts, Alan Rickman, Aidan Quinn, Ian Hart, Charles Dance,
Brendan Gleeson. Co-prod: USA.

*Miracle, The* (1991), 96m, col.
W/D: Neil Jordan. C: Beverly D'Angelo, Donal McCann, Niall Byrne,
Lorraine Pilkington, J. G. Devlin, Christopher Casson, Shane Con-
naughton, Mary Coughlan.

*Mise Éire [I Am Ireland]* (1959), 90m, b/w, docu.
D: George Morrison. W: George Morrison, Seán MacReamoinn. Ph: Vincent Corcoran, with archival footage. M: Seán Ó Riada. Narr: Liam Budhaéir, Padraig Ó Raghallaigh, Andreas Ó Gallchóir. Irish language soundtrack. Prod: Gael Linn.

*Misteach Baile Átha Cliath/The Dublin Mystic* (1995), 35m, col.
D: Paul Duane. W: Seamus Mac Annaide, Paul Duane, adapting a short story by Mac Annaide. Ph: Fiona Keane. C: Kevin Reynolds, Mick Lally, Catríona Ní Mhurchu. Mostly Irish sound track. Prod: RTE, BBC-Northern Ireland.

*Memories in Focus* (1995), 6 parts, 60m each, b/w, docu.
D: Peter Canning. W: Niall Toibín. Ph: Robert Monks, with archival footage. Narr: Niall Toibín. Prod: RTE.

*Moon on My Back, The* (1996), 40m, col, docu.
D: Jonathan White.

*Moondance* (1994), 92m, col.
D: Dagmar Hertz. W: Burt Weinshanker, Mark Watters, adapting the novel *The White Hare*, by Francis Stuart. Ph: Steven Bernstein. M: Van Morrison. C: Ruaidhrí Conroy, Ian Shaw, Julia Brendler, Marianne Faithfull, Brendan Grace, Jasmine Russell. Co-prod: Germany/UK.

*More Than a Sacrifice* (1996), 51m, col, docu.
D: Tommy Collins.

*Mother Ireland* (1988), 52m, col, docu.
D: Anne Crilly. M: Maura Starkie. Prod: Derry Film & Video Workshop, Channel 4.

*Moving Myths* (1989), 52m, col, docu.
D: Cahal McLaughlin.

*Murder in Eden* (1994)
Adapts Patrick McGinley's *Bog Mail*. Prod: RTE.

*My Hands Are Clay* (1948), 60/62m, b/w.
D: Lionel Tomlinson. W: Paul Trippe. Ph: Patrick McCrossan. C: Robert Dawson, Bernadette Leahy, Shelagh Richards, Cecil Brock.

*My Left Foot* (1989), 103m, col.
D: Jim Sheridan. W: Jim Sheridan, Shane Connaughton, adapting Christy Brown's autobiography of the same title and (uncredited) auobiographical fiction, *Down All the Days*. Ph: Jack Conroy. M: Elmer Bernstein. C: Daniel Day-Lewis, Brenda Fricker, Ray McAnally, Hugh O'Conor, Fiona Shaw, Alison Whelan, Ruth McCabe, Adrian Dunbar, Cyril Cusack, Kirsten Sheridan. Prod: Ferndale Films.

*My Friend Joe*. See *Joe My Friend*.

*Navigatio—Atlantean 2* (1998), 60m, col, docu.
W/D: Bob Quinn.

*Nephew, The* (1997), 107m, col.
D: Eugene Brady. W: Jacqueline O'Neill, Sean P. Steele. M: Stephen McKeon. C: Donal McCann, Pierce Brosnan, Sinéad Cusack, Aislin McGuckin, Niall Toibín, Hill Harper.

*New Gates Wide Open*. See *Osclaíonn Geata Nua Leathan*.

*Night in Tunisia* (1983), 52m, col.
D: Pat O'Connor. W: Neil Jordan, adapting his short story of the same title. Ph: Peter Dorney. C: Michael (Mick) Lally, Ciaran Burns, Jill Doyle, Jim Culleton. Prod: RTE.

*Nothing Personal*. See *Fanatic Heart*.

*November Afternoon* (1996), 82m, b/w.
W/D: John Carney, Tom Hall. C: Michael McElhatton, Jayne Snow, Tristan Gribben.

*Oidhche Sheanchais [Storyteller's Night]* (1935), c.20m, b/w, docu.
D: Robert Flaherty. W: Irish Department of Education. Irish language soundtrack.

*Oilean Eile/Another Island* (1985), 135m, col, docu.
W/D: Muiris Mac Conghaill. Ph: Breffni Byrne. M: Gerard Victory. Irish language soundtrack. Prod: RTE.

*tOileanach a dFhill*. See *tOileanach a dFhill, An*, under *T*.

*On a Paving Stone Mounted* (1978), 96m, b/w.
W/D: Thaddeus O'Sullivan. Ph: Thaddeus O'Sullivan. M: Christy Moore. C: J. M. O'Neill, Maureen Toal, Arthur O'Sullivan, John Mur-

phy, Annabel Leventon, Stephen Rea, Miriam Margoyles, Mannix Flynn, Gabriel Byrne. Prod: UK and Ireland.

*On the Road to God Knows Where* (1988), 51m, col, docu.
W/D: Alan Gilsenan.

*One Day Time* (1982), 30m, col, docu.
D: Joe Lee. W: Joe Lee, Frank Deasy. Ph: John Malachy Coleman, Joe Mulholland. M: Resisdance, John McMenamin. C: Gregg Gough, Siobhán McCluskey, Vincent McCabe, Garrett Keogh, Helen Roche. Prod: Cityvision.

*One Nighters, The* (1963), 48m, b/w, docu.
W/D: Peter Collinson. Ph: Robert Monks. M: The Royal Showband. Narr: Frank Hall.

*One of Ourselves* (1983), 50m, col.
D: Pat O'Connor. W: William Trevor, based on his short story of the same title. Ph: Kenneth MacMillan. M: Trevor Jones. C: Cyril Cusack, Niall Toibín, Frances Quinn, Stephen Mason, Bill Paterson.

*O'Neill of the Glen* (1916), 3 reels, b/w, silent.
D: J. M. Kerrigan. W: W. J. Lysaght, adapting the short story of the same title by M. T. Pender. C: J. M. Kerrigan, Fred O'Donovan, J. M. Carre, Nora Clancy, Brian Magowan.

*Oscar Wilde: Spendthrift of Genius* (1986), 58m, col, docu.
D: Seán Ó Mórdha. W: Richard Ellmann. Ph: Cedric Culliton. M: Alan Seavers. Narr: Denys Hawthorne. Voices of: Alan Stanford, Barbara Brennan, Seamus Forde.

*Osclaíonn Geata Nua Leathan* [*New Gates Wide Open*] (1998), 55m, col, docu.
W/D: Peter Carr. Ph: Seamus Deasy, Tony Coldwell, Andy Carchrae. M: Peadar Ó Riada.

*Our Boys* (1980), 42m, b/w, docu.
D: Cathal Black. W: Dermot Healy. Ph: Thaddeus O'Sullivan, M: Bill Summerville-Large. C: Michael Lally, Vincent McCabe, Archie O'Sullivan, Seamus Ellis, Noel O'Donovan. Prod: RTE.

*Out of Time* (1987), 53m, col.
D: Robert Wynne-Simmons. W: Ronald Frame. Ph: Thaddeus O'Sulli-
van. M: Roger Doyle. C: Sian Phillips, Phyllis Logan, Kate Thompson,
Oliver Maguire. Prod: Strongbow Films.

*Outcasts, The* (1982), 100/113m, col.
D: Robert Wynne-Simmons. Ph: Seamus Corcoran. M: Stephen Cooney.
C: Mick Lally, Mary Ryan, Cyril Cusack, Brenda Scallon, Don Foley.
Co-prod: UK.

*Paddy* (1969), 97m, col, aka *Goodbye to the Hill.*
D: Daniel Haller. W: Lee Dunne, based on his novel *Goodbye to the Hill.*
Ph: Daniel Lacambre. C: Des Cave, Milo O'Shea, Dearbhla Molloy,
Maureen Toal, Judy Cornwell, Donal Le Blanc, Peggy Cass.

*Pigs* (1984), 79m, col.
D: Cathal Black. W: Jimmy Brennan. Ph: Thaddeus O'Sullivan. M:
Roger Doyle. C: Jimmy Brennan (also narr.), George Shane, Maurice
O'Donoghue, Liam Halligan, Kwesi Kay, Joan Harpur.

*Playboy of the Western World* (1962), 100m, col.
W: Brian Desmond Hurst. W: Brian Desmond Hurst, adapting John
Millington Synge's stageplay of the same title. Ph: Geoffrey Unsworth.
M: Seán Ó Riada. C: Gary Raymond, Siobhán McKenna, Elspeth
March, Mícheál Ó Bríain, Liam Redmond, Niall MacGinnis.

*Playboy of the Western World* (1975), 110m, col.
W/D Alan Gibson, adapting the stageplay of the same title by John
Millington Synge. Ph: Peter Sargent. C: John Hurt, Sinéad Cusack,
Donal McCann, Pauline Delaney, Joe Lynch, Kevin Flood, James Caf-
frey, John Malloy, Eileen Murphy, Eve Bolton. Prod: BBC-TV.

*Playboys, The* (1992), 110m, col.
D: Gillies MacKinnon. W: Shane Connaughton, based on his short
story of the same title. C: Aidan Quinn, Robin Wright, Albert Finney,
Niamh Cusack, Alan Devlin, Milo O'Shea, Ian McElhinney, Niall
Buggy, Adrian Dunbar, Shane Connaughton. Co-prod: UK.

*Poacher's Daughter, The* (1958, 1960), 74m, b/w, aka *Sally's Irish
    Rogue.*
D: George Pollock. W: Patrick Kirwan, Blanaid Irvine, adapting the
stageplay *The New Gossoon*, by George Shiels. Ph: Stanley Pavey. M:

Ivor Slaney. C: Julie Harris, Tim Seeley, Harry Brogan, Marie Kean, Bríd Lynch, Noel Magee.

*Poitín/Poteen* (1978), 65m, col.
D: Bob Quinn. W: Colm Bairéad, Bob Quinn, adapting Bairéad's short story. Ph: Seamus Deasy. C: Niall Toibín, Donal McCann, Cyril Cusack, Máiréad Ní Conghaile. Irish language soundtrack.

*Power in the Blood* (1989), 76m, col, docu.
W/D: John T. Davis. Ph: David Barker. Prod: BBC-TV.

*Professor Tim* (1957), 57m, b/w.
D: Henry Cass. W: Robert S. Baker, adapting the stageplay of the same title by George Shiels. Ph: Walter J. Harvey. M: Stanley Black. C: Ray McAnally, Maire O'Donnell, Seamus Kavanaugh, Marie Kean.

*Promise of Barty O'Brien, The* (1951), 49m, b/w.
D: George Freedland. W: Sean O'Faolain. Ph: Brendan Stafford. C: Eric Doyle, Harry Brogan, Eileen Crowe.

*Protex Hurrah* (1980), 75m, col, docu.
W/D: John T. Davis. Ph: John T. Davis, Byron Lovelace. Part of punk rock trilogy, with *Self-Conscious over You* and *Shellshock Rock*.

*Purple Taxi, The* (1977), 120m, col, aka *Un Taxi Mauve.*
D: Yves Boisset. W: Michel Déon, Yves Boisset, adapting the novel of the same title by Michel Déon. Ph: Tonino Delli Colli. M: Philippe Sarde, Franz Schubert. C: Fred Astaire, Charlotte Rampling, Peter Ustinov, Philippe Noiret, Agostina Belli, Edward Albert. Co-prod: France/Italy.

*Reefer and the Model* (1987), 93m, col.
D: Joe Comerford. W: Joe Comerford, Eoghan Harris. Ph: Breffni Byrne. M: Johnny Duhan. C: Ian McElhinney, Carol Scanlan, Sean Lawlor, Ray McBride, Eve Watkinson. Co-prod: UK.

*Remembering Jimmy O'Dea* (1985), 52m, col, docu.
W/D: Donald Taylor. Ph: Sean Corcoran. C: Maureen Potter, Ursula Doyle, Rita O'Dea, Noel Purcell, James Plunkett, Connie Ryan, John Jordan.

*Resurrection Man* (1998)
D: Marc Evans. Adapting the novel of the same title by Eoin McNamee.

*Return of the Islander.* See *tOileanach a dFhill, An.*

*Return to Glennascaul* (1951), 22m, b/w.
W/D: Hilton Edwards. Ph: George Fleischmann. M: Hans Gunther Stumpf. C: Orson Welles, Michael Laurence, Helena Hughes, Shelagh Richards.

*Return to the Island* (1963), 27m, col, docu.
D: George Fleischmann. W: Reg Coast. Prod: Ireland, UK, West Germany.

*Revival-Pearse's Concept of Ireland* (1980), 74m, col, docu.
D: Louis Marcus. Ph: Robert Monks, John Kavanagh. Narr: Andy O'Mahoney.

*Riders to the Sea* (1935), 40m, b/w.
W/D: Brian Desmond Hurst, adapting John Millington Synge's stageplay of the same title. Ph: Eugen Schüfftan. C: Ria Mooney, Denis Johnston, Kevin Guthrie, Sara Allgood, Shelagh Richards.

*Riders to the Sea* (1987), 46m, col.
W/D: Ronan O'Leary, adapting the John Millington Synge's stageplay of the same title. Ph: Wolfgang Suschitzky. M: Ian Llande, Michael Hewer. C: Geraldine Page, Amanda Plummer, Barry McGovern, John O'Hara, Mícheal Ó Bríain, Sachi Parker.

*Rising of the Moon, The* (1957), 81m, b/w, aka *Three Leaves of the Shamrock.*
D: John Ford. W: Frank Nugent, adapting Frank O'Connor's short story, "Majesty of the Law," Malcolm J. McHugh's stageplay *A Minute's Wait,* and Lady Augusta Gregory's stageplay, *1921.* Ph: Robert Lasker. M: Eamonn O'Gallagher. Narr: Tyrone Power. C: Noel Purcell, Cyril Cusack, Jack MacGowran, Jimmy O'Dea, Donal Donnelly, Maureen Delaney, Maureen Connell, Eileen Crowe, Martin Thornton, Mauren Potter. Prod: Ireland/USA.

*River of Sound, A: The Changing Course of Irish Traditional Music.*
    (1995), 4 parts, 40m each, col, docu.
D: Philip King. W: Mícheál Ó Súilleabháin, Nuala O'Connor. Ph: Seamus Deasy. M: Brian Masterson.

*Rockingham Shoot, The* (1987), 60m, col.
D: Kieran Hickey. W: John McGahern, adapting his short story of the same title. Ph: Philip Dawson. M: W. A. Mozart. C: Bosco Hogan, Niall Toibín, Tony Rohr, Marie Kean, Oliver Maguire. Prod: BBC-Northern Ireland.

*Rocky Road to Dublin* (1968), 52/75m, b/w, docu.
W/D: Peter Lennon. Ph: Raoul Coutard, Georges Liron. M: The Dubliners, Luke Kelly. C: Sean O'Faolain, Conor Cruise O'Brien. John Huston, Douglas Gageby, Jim Fitzgerald. Co-prod: France.

*Route 66* (1985), 104m, col, docu.
W/D: John T. Davis. Ph: Peter Grenhalgh. Prod: Central TV, Iona Productions.

*Run of the Country* (1995), 100m, col.
D: Peter Yates. W: Shane Connaughton, adapting his novel of the same title. Ph: Mike Southon. M: Cynthia Millar. C: Albert Finney, Matt Keeslar, Victoria Smurfit, Anthony Brophy, Dearbhla Molloy, Carole Nimmons, David Kelly. Prod: UK.

*Sally's Irish Rogue*. See *The Poacher's Daughter*.

*Sam Thompson: Voice of Many Men* (1986), 53m, col, docu.
W/D: Donald Taylor Black. Ph: Thaddeus O'Sullivan. M: Bill Whelan. C: Stephen Rea.

*Samuel Beckett, Silence to Silence* (1984), 80m, col, docu.
D: Seán Ó Mórdha. W: Richard Ellmann, Declan Kiberd. Ph: Peter Dorney. M: Franz Schubert. C: Billie Whitelaw, Jack MacGowran, Patrick Magee, David Warrilow.

*Saoirse? [Freedom]*. (1961), 90m, docu.
D: George Morrison. W: George Morrison, Seán MacReamoinn. Ph: Vincent Corcoran and archival footage. M: Seán Ó Riada. Narr: Liam Budhlaéir, Pádraig Ó Raghallaigh, Aindreas Ó Gallchóir.

*Scar, The* (1987), 53m, col.
D: Robert Wynne-Simmons. W: Robert Wynne-Simmons, Tom Gallacher, adapting the novel of the same title by A. V. Mellor. Ph: Thaddeus O'Sullivan. M: Stephen Cooney. C: Ken Colley, Gerard McSorley, Olwen Fouere, David Heap. Prod: UK/Ireland.

*Schooner, The* (1983), 53m, col.
D. Bill Miskelly. W: Marie Jackson, adapting the short story of the same title by Michael McLaverty. Ph: Seamus Deasy. M: Van Morrison. C: Lucie Jamieson, Michael Gormley, Johnny Marley, Ann Hasson, Barry Lynch.

*Sean Keating—The Pilgrim Soul* (1996), 54m, col, docu.
D: David Keating. W: Justin Keating. Narr: Justin Keating.

*Second of June, A* (1984), 40m, col.
D: Francis Stapleton. W: Francis Stapleton, Fergus Manifold. Ph: Nick O'Neill. M: Roger Doyle. C: Lisa Birthistle, Dermot King, Mary Stokes, Derek Molloy.

*Self-Conscious over You* (1981), 40m, col, docu.
W/D: John T. Davis. Ph: David Barker. Prod: BBC-Northern Ireland. Part of punk rock trilogy with *Protex Hurrah* and *Shellshock Rock.*

*Sheila* (1985), 23m, col.
W/D: Alan Gilsenan. Ph: Peter Butler. C: Anne Enright, Jean Trench.

*Shellshock Rock* (1978), 52m, col, docu.
W/D: John T. Davis. Ph: John T. Davis, Alwyn James, Tommy McConville. Part of punk rock trilogy with *Protex Hurrah* and *Self-Conscious over you.*

*Short Story: Irish Cinema, 1945–1958* (1985), 62m, b/w and col.
W/D: Kieran Hickey. Ph: Archival footage. Narr: Bosco Hogan.

*Siege* (1976), 28m, col.
D: Deirdre Friel. W: Eugene McCabe. Ph: Stuart Hetherington. Prod: RTE.

*Snakes and Ladders* (1996), 92m, col.
W/D: Trish McAdam. Ph: Dietrich Lohmann. M: Pierce Turner. C: Pam Boyd, Paudge Behan, Sean Hughes, Gina Moxley, Cathy White, Rosaleen Linehan. Co-prod: Germany.

*Some Mother's Son* (1996), 90/112m, col.
D: Terry George. W: Jim Sheridan Ph: Geoffrey Simpson. C: Helen Mirren, Fionnula Flanagan, John Lynch, David O'Hara, Aiden Gillen, Tom Hollander, Tim Woodward, Gerard McSorley.

*Some Say Chance* (1934), c. 45m, b/w, silent.
W/D: Michael Farrell. C: Austin Meldon, Eileen Ashe, Margot Bigland, Florence Macmillan, B. Callows.

*Sometime City* (1986), 37m, col.
D: Joe Lee, Frank Deasy. W: Frank Deasy. Ph: Seamus Deasy M: Michael Holohan. C: Michele Houldon, David O'Meara, David Nolan, Mary Ryan, Jo Savino. Prod: Cityvision.

*Sons of Derry* (1993), 58m, col, docu.
D: Marcia Rock.

*Spaghetti Slow* (1996), 96m, col.
D: Valerio Jalongo. W: Valerio Jalongo, Barry Devlin, Lucinda Coxon. Ph: Cian de Buitléar. C: Giulio di Mauro, Niamh O'Byrne, Brendan Gleeson, Ivano Marescotti, Gary Fitzpatrick, Frankie McCafferty.

*Steel Chest, Nail in the Book, and the Barking Dog* (1986), 53m, col, docu.
W/D: David Hammond. Ph: David Barker. M: John Anderson.

*Storyteller's Night.* See *Oidhche Sheanchais.*

*Stranger at My Door.* See *At a Dublin Inn.*

*Strumpet City* (1979), 7 parts, 52m each, col.
D: Tony Barry. W: Hugh Leonard, after the novel of the same title by James Plunkett. M: Proinnsias Ó Duinn. C: Cyril Cusack, Frank Grimes, David Kelly, Donal McCann, Angela Harding, Bryan Murray, Denys Hawthorne, Brendan Cauldwell, Ronnie Walsh, Daphne Carroll, Marin D. O'Sullivan, Vincent McCabe, Ruth Hagerty, Gerard O'Brien, Eileen Murphy, Seamus Forde, Peter Kerrigan, Donal Farmer, Don Foley, Patricia Martin, Peter O'Toole, Peter Ustinov.

*Summer Fling.* See *Last of the High Kings.*

*Summer Ghost, A* (1987), 53m, col.
D: Robert Wynne-Simmons. W: M. J. Fitzgerald. Ph: Thaddeus O'Sullivan. M: John Buckley. C: Susan Bradley, Dearbhla Molloy, Brian McGrath, Alison McKenna. Prod: Ireland/UK.

*Sun, The Moon, and the Stars, The* (1996), 90m, col.
W/D: Geraldine Creed. Ph: Ciaran Tanham. C: Gina Moxley, Jason Donovan, Elaine Cassidy, Aisling Corcoran, Angie Dickinson, David Murray, Vinnie Murphy.

*Sunset Heights* (1998), 90m, col.
D: Colum Villa. W: Paula Mulroe. Ph: Roger Bonnici. C: Jim Norton, Toby Stephens, James Cosmo, Patrick O'Kane, Joe Rea, Peter Ballance, Michael Liebman, Emer McCourt, B. J. Hogg, Seamus Ball, Marcella O'Riordan, Don Baker, Christian Burgess, Brenda Winter, Gordon Fulton, Hannah Carnegie, Delores McNally, Laine Megaw.

*Sweet Inniscarra* (1934), 72m, b/w.
W/D: Emmett Moore. Ph: Emmett Moore. C: Sean Rogers, Mae Ryan.

*Taxi Mauve, Un.* See *Purple Taxi, The.*

*This Is the Sea* (1997), 102/118m, col.
W/D: Mary McGuckian. Ph: Des Whelan. M: Mike Scott, The Waterboys, Brian Kennedy. C: Samantha Morton, Ross McDade, Richard Harris, Gabriel Byrne, John Lynch, Ian McElhinney, Dearbhla Molloy.

*This Other Eden* (1959), 80m, b/w.
D: Muriel Box. W: Patrick Kirwan, Blanaid Irvine, adapting the stageplay of the same title by Louis D'Alton. Ph: Gerald Gibbs. M: W. Lambert Williamson. C: Leslie Phillips, Niall MacGinnis, Harry Brogan, Paul Farrell, Geoffrey Golden, Audrey Dalton, Milo O'Shea, Norman Rodway.

*Three Leaves of the Shamrock.* See *The Rising of the Moon.*

*Tine Bheo, An/The Living Flame* (1966), 45m, col, docu.
D: Louis Marcus. W: Breandán Ó hEithir. Ph. Robert Monks. M: Seán Ó Riada. C: Narr: Eoin Ó Súilleabháin, Chris Curran, Seamus Forde, Vincent Dowling, Howard Marion Crowford.

*To the Western World* (1982), 32m, col, docu.
W/D, Narr: Margy Kinmonth. Ph: Ivan Strasburg. M: Richard Harvey. C: Niall Toibín, Patrick Laffan, Tom Hickey, Brendan Cauldwell.

*tOileanach a dFhill, An/Return of the Islander.* (1970), 25m, col.
W/D: James Mulkerns. Ph: Val Ennis, Alan Blowey. M: Noel Kelehan. Narr: Richard Harris. Michael Connely, Máire Burke.

*Transfer* (1975), 30m, col, docu.
W/D: John T. Davis. Ph: John T. Davis, Dick Sinclair.

*Traveller* (1981), 80m, col.
D: Joe Comerford. W: Neil Jordan. Ph: Thaddeus O'Sullivan. M: Davy Spillane. C: Judy Donovan, Davy Spillane, Alan Devlin, Marian Richardson, Johnny Choil Mhadhc, Paddy Donovan. Co-prod. UK

*Treaty, The* (1992), 104m, col.
D: Jonathan Lewis. W: Brian Phelan. M: Mícheál Ó Súilleabháin. C: Brendan Gleeson, Patrick Condren, Ian Bannen, Julien Fellowes, Malcolm Douglas, Dave Duffy, Joshua Losey, Richard Michaels, Liam Callaghan, Anne Byrne, Tim Wylton, Barry McGovern, John Warner, Wesley Murphy, Alan Stanford, Alan Barry, David Carey, Bosco Hogan, Ronan Wilmot, Tony Doyle, Brian McGrath, Tom Lawlor, Anna Manahan, Peadar Lamb, Ann Thornton, Owen Rowe, Tom Hickey, Rachel Dowling, Barry Cassin, Pat Laffan, Christopher Casson.

*Trojan Eddie* (1996), 105m, col.
D: Gillies MacKinnon. W: Billy Roche. Ph: John de Borman. C: Stephen Rea, Richard Harris, Stuart Townsend, Aislin McGuckin, Brendan Gleeson, Sean McGinley, Angeline Ball, Angela O'Driscoll, Bríd Brennan. Co-prod: UK.

*Truth about Claire, The* (1990), 150m, col.
D: Gerry Stembridge

*Uncle Jack, The* (1995), 76/80m, col, docu.
D: John T. Davis. W: John T. Davis, Sé Merry Doyle.

*Uncle Nick* (1938), 60m, b/w.
W/D: Tom Cooper. Ph: Tom Cooper. M: Dunne & Locke. C: Jerry O'Mahony, Bonzer Horgan, John Cranitch, Valentine Vousden.

*Undercurrent* (1995), 85m, col.
D: Brian O'Flaherty. C: Stanley Townsend, Owen Row, Tina Kellegher, Orla Charlton, Ali White.

*Van, The* (1996), 90m, col.
D: Stephen Frears. W: Roddy Doyle, adapting his novel of the same title. Ph: Oliver Stapleton. C: Colm Meaney, Donal O'Kelly, Ger Ryan,

Caroline Rothwell, Brendan O'Carroll, Stuart Dunne, Jack Lynch, Neili Conroy, Ruaidhrí Conroy.

*Very Unlucky Leprechaun, A* (1998), 91m, col.
D: Brian Kelly. W: Craig J. Nevius. C: Warwick Davis, Tim Matheson, Lisa Thornhill, Nick Nolan, Una Crawford, Jimmy Keough, Danielle Lombardi, Stephanie Lombardi.

*Voice of Ireland, The* (1932), 49m, b/w.
D/W: Colonel Victor Haddick. M: Richard Hayward, Victor Haddick, Barney O'Hara.

*W. B. Yeats—A Tribute* (1950), 27m, b/w, docu.
D: George Fleischmann. W: John D. Sheridan. Ph: George Fleischmann. M: Eamonn Ó Gallchobhair. Cyril Cusack, Siobhán McKenna, Micheál MacLiammóir.

*Wedding Night.* See *I Can't, I Can't . . .*

*Week in the Life of Martin Cluxton, A* (1971), 70m, col.
D: Brian MacLochlainn. W: Caoimhín Ó Marcaigh, Brian MacLochlainn. Ph: Stuart Hetherington. C: Laurie Morton, Bill Foley, Dearbhla Molloy, Jimmy Bartley, Derek King. Prod: RTE.

*West of Kerry.* See *The Islandman.*

*When Love Came to Gavin Burke* (1917), 6 reels, b/w, silent.
W/D: Fred O'Donovan. C: Fred O'Donovan, Nora Clancy, Stephen Gould, Brian Magowan, Valentine Roberts.

*Willie Reilly and His Colleen Bawn* (1920). See *Colleen Bawn.*

*Withdrawal* (1982), 27m, b/w.
D: Joe Comerford. W: Jimmy Brennan, adapting David Chapman's novel of the same title. M: Roger Doyle. C: Mark Quinn, Marian O'Loughlin. Narr: Jimmy Brennan.

*Woman Who Married Clark Gable, The* (1985), 28m, b/w.
D: Thaddeus O'Sullivan. W: Andrew Pattman, adapting the short story of the same title by Sean O'Faolain. Ph: Jack Conroy. M: John Buckley. C: Bob Hoskins, Brenda Fricker, Eamonn Kelly, Peter Caffrey. Co-prod: UK.

*Words upon the Windowpane* (1994), 90/100m, col.
W/D: Mary McGuckian, adapting the stage play of same title by William Butler Yeats. Ph: Des Whelan. M: Niall Byrne. C: Geraldine Chaplin, Geraldine James, Ian Richardson, John Lynch, Gerard McSorley, Donal Donnelly, Gemma Craven, Bríd Brennan, Jim Sheridan, Hugh O'Conor.

*World of James Joyce, The.* See *Is There One Who Understands Me?*

*Year of the French, The* (1982), 6 parts, 52m each, col.
D: Michael Garvey. W: Eugene McCabe, Pierre Lary, adapting the novel of the same title by Thomas Flanagan. Ph: Ken Murphy. M: Paddy Moloney. C: Jeremy Clyde, Oliver Cotton, Jean-Claude Drouot, Keith Buckley, Philip Hurdwood, Niall O'Brien, Robert Stephens, Nuala Hayes, Alan Devlin, Veronica Duffy, Dan Foley, Mick Lally, Fintan McKeown, Brian Murray. Prod: RTE/French television.

## Irish-Related Films

*Acceptable Levels* (1983/1984), UK, 100/103m, col, docu.
D: John Davies. W: Gordon Hann, Kate McManus, Elin Hare, John Davies, Robert Smith, Alastair Herron. Ph: Robert Smith. M: Nick Garvey.

*Adventuress, The* (1945/1946), UK, 114m [US prints 98m], col, aka *I See a Dark Stranger.*
D: Frank Launder. W: Frank Launder, Sidney Gilliat, Wolfgang Wilhelm. Ph: Wilkie Cooper. M: William Alwyn. C: Deborah Kerr, Trevor Howard, Raymond Huntley, Norman Shelley, Michael Howard, Brenda Bruce, Liam Redmond, Brefni O'Rourke, Harry Webster.

*Arrah-na-Pogue* (1911), USA, 3 reels, 3000', b/w, silent.
D: Sidney Olcott. W: Gene Gauntier, adapting the stageplay of the same title by Dion Boucicault. C: Jack Clark, Gene Gauntier, Sidney Olcott, Agnes Mapes, Arthur Donaldson, Robert Vignola.

*Ascendancy* (1982), UK, 85m, col, aka *Ascendancy: Belfast 1920.*
D: Edward Bennett. W: Edward Bennett, Nigel Gearing. Ph: Clive Tickner. M: Ronnie Leahy. C: Julie Covington, Ian Charleson, John Phillips, Susan Engel, Philip Locke.

*At Swim-Two-Birds* (1997), Austria, 87m, col.
W/D: Kurt Palm, adapting the novel of the same title by Flann O'Brien. C: Andreas Sobik, Renato Uz, Johannes Friesinger, Andreas Karner.

*Barry Lyndon* (1975), UK, 187m, col.
W/D: Stanley Kubrick, adapting the novel of the same title by W. M. Thackeray. Ph: John Alcott. M: Leonard Rosenman, The Chieftains. C: Ryan O'Neal, Marisa Berenson, Patrick Magee, Steven Berkoff, Hardy Kruger, Guy Hamilton, Murray Melvin, Frank Middlemass, Andre Morell, Leonard Rossiter, Marie Kean. Narr: Michael Horden.

*Beloved Enemy* (1936), USA, 86m, b/w.
D: H. C. Potter. W: John Balderson, Rose Franken, William Brown Meloney, David Hart. Ph: Gregg Toland. M: Alfred Newman. C: Brian Aherne, Merle Oberon, Karen Morley, Henry Stephenson, Jerome Cowan, David Niven, Donald Crisp.

*Boy Soldier* (1986), UK/Wales, 100m, col, aka *Milwr Byehan.*
W/D: Karl Francis. Ph: Roger Pugh Evans. M: Graham Williams. C: Richard Lynch, Emer Gillespie, Bernard Hill, James Donnelly, Dafydd Hywel. Welsh soundtrack, English subtitle. Prod: Welsh Channel 4.

*Brylcreem Boys, The* (1996), 102m, col.
D: Terence Ryan. W: Terence Ryan, Jamie Brown, Susan Murrall. C: Bill Campbell, William McNamara, Angus MacFadyen, John Gordon Sinclair, Gabriel Byrne, Jean Butler.

*Captain Boycott* (1947), UK, 93m, b/w.
D: Frank Launder. W: Wolfgang Wilhelm, Frank Launder, Paul Vincent Carroll, Patrick Campbell, adapting the novel of the same title by Philip Rooney. Ph: Wilkie Cooper. M: William Alwyn. C: Stewart Granger, Kathleen Ryan, Alastair Sim, Robert Donat, Mervyn Johns, Cecil Parker, Noel Purcell, Niall MacGinnis.

*Captain Lightfoot* (1955), USA, 91m, col.
D: Douglas Sirk. W: W. R. Burnett, Oscar Brodney. Ph: Irving Glassberg. M: Joseph Gershenson. C: Rock Hudson, Barbara Rush, Jeff Morrow, Finlay Currie, Kathleen Ryan, Denis O'Dea.

*Catholics* (1973), USA, 78m, col, aka *The Conflict.*
D: Jack Gold. W: Brian Moore, adapting his novel of the same title. C: Trevor Howard, Martin Sheen, Raf Vallone, Cyril Cusack, Andrew Keir, Godfrey Quigley, Michael Gambon, Leon Vitale.

*Cause of Ireland, The* (1983), UK, 107m, col, docu.
D: Chris Reeves. W: Geoffrey Bell. Ph: David Glyn, Steve Sprung. Narr: Anne Lamont.

*Coilin and Platonida* (1976), UK/Germany, col.
W/D: James Scott, adapting the novels *Kotin the Provider* and *Platonida*, by L. S. Leskov. Ph: Adam Barker-Mill, Joe Comerford. C: Marion Joyce, Seán Bán Breathnach, Katrina Joyce, Bairbre Bolustrum, Bairbre Ní Dhonncha. Part silent; English and German titles.

*Colleen Bawn, The* (1911), USA, 3 reels, b/w, silent.
D: Sidney Olcott. W: Gene Gauntier, adapting the stageplay of the same title by Dion Boucicault. C: Sidney Olcott, Gene Gauntier, Jack Clark, Robert G. Vignola, J. P. McGowan, George H. Fisher. (Distinguish from the Irish-made *The Colleen Bawn* [1920].)

*Company of Wolves, The* (1984), UK, 95m, col.
D: Neil Jordan. W: Neil Jordan, Angela Carter, adapting short stories by Angela Carter. Ph: Bryan Loftus. M: George Fenton. C: Sarah Patterson, Angela Lansbury, David Warner, Micha Bergese, Stephen Rea, Graham Crowden, Brian Glover, Tusse Silberg.

*Conflict, The.* See *Catholics.*

*Curious Journey* (1979), UK, 50m, col, docu.
D: Gareth Wynne Jones. W: Kenneth Griffiths. Ph: Gareth Owen, Mike Reynolds. M: The Chieftains.

*Darby O'Gill and the Little People* (1959), USA, 90m, col.
D: Robert Stevenson. W: Lawrence Edward Watkin, adapting stories by H. T. Kavanagh. C: Albert Sharpe, Jimmy O'Dea, Sean Connery, Janet Munro, Kieron Moore, Estelle Winwood, Walter Fitzgerald, Jack MacGowran, J. G. Devlin.

*Dawning, The* (1988), UK, 97m, col.
D: Robert Knights. W: Moira Williams, adapting the novel *The Old Jest*, by Jennifer Johnston. Ph: Adrian Biddle. M: Simon May. C: Anthony

Hopkins, Jean Simmons, Trevor Howard, Hugh Grant, Rebecca Pidgeon, Tara MacGowran.

*Dead, The* (1987), UK, USA, West Germany, 83/85m, col.
D: John Huston. W: Tony Huston, adapting the short story of the same title by James Joyce. C: Anjelica Huston, Donal McCann, Dan O'Herlihy, Donal Donnelly, Rachael Dowling, Cathleen Delaney, Helena Carroll, Ingrid Craigie, Marie Kean, Marie McDermottroe, Sean McClory.

*Dementia 13* (1963), USA/Ireland, 91m, b/w, aka *The Haunted and the Hunted.*
W/D: Francis Ford Coppola. Ph: Charles Hannawalt. M: Ronald Stein. C: William Campbell, Luana Anders, Bart Patton, Patrick Magee, Mary Mitchell, Eithne Dunne.

*Echoes* (1988), UK, 4 parts, 52m each, col.
D: Barbara Rennie. W: Barbara Rennie, Julia Jones, Donald Churchill, adapting the novel by the same title by Maeve Binchy. Ph: Vitold Stok. M: Richard Holms, Tony Britten. C: Barbara Brenna, John Cowley, Dermot Crowley, Sharon Devlin, Alison Doody, Barnie Downs, Eleanor Feely, Robert Hines, Stephen Holland, Geraldine James, John Kavanagh, Vincent Murphy, Niall O'Brien, Aisling Toibín.

*Every Picture Tells a Story* (1984), UK, 85m, col.
D: James Scott. W: Shane Connaughton. Ph: Adam Barker-Mill. M: Michael Storey. C: Phyllis Logan, Alex Norton, Leonard O'Malley, John Dochtery, Mark Airlie, Paul Wilson, Willie Joss.

*Excalibur* (1981), USA, 140m, col.
D: John Boorman. W: John Boorman, Rospo Pallenberg. Ph: Alex Thompson. M: Trevor Jones. C: Nigel Terry, Helen Mirren, Nicol Williamson, Nicholas Clay, Cherie Lunghi, Corin Redgrave, Paul Geoffrey, Patrick Stewart, Gabriel Byrne, Liam Neeson.

*Far and Away* (1992), USA, 140m, col.
D: Ron Howard. W: Ron Howard, Bob Dolman. Ph: Mikael Saloman. M: John Williams, Paddy Moloney, Enya. C: Tom Cruise, Nicole Kidman, Thomas Gibson, Robert Prosky, Barbara Babcock, Colm Meaney, Eileen Pollock, Michelle Johnson, Cyril Cusack, Clint Howard, Rance Howard, Niall Toibín.

*Fighting O'Flynn, The* (1949), USA, 94m, b/w.
D: Arthur Pierson. W: Douglas Fairbanks, Jr., Robert Thoeren, adapting the novel *The O'Flynn,* by Justin Huntly McCarthy. Ph: Arthur Edeson. M: Frank Skinner. C: Douglas Fairbanks, Jr., Helena Carter, Richard Greene, Patricia Medina, Arthur Shields, J. M. Kerrigan.

*Fighting Prince of Donegal, The* (1966), UK, 104m, col.
D: Michael O'Herlihy. W: Robert Westerby, adapting a novel by Robert T. Reilly. Ph: Arthur Ibbetson. M: George Bruns. C: Peter McEnery, Susan Hampshire, Tom Adams, Gordon Jackson, Donal McCann, Andrew Keir, Maurice Roeves.

*Film (A Screen Play by Samuel Beckett)* (1965), UK, 24m, b/w.
D: Alan Schneider. W: Samuel Beckett. Ph: Boris Kaufman. C: Buster Keaton, Nell Harrison, James Karen, Susan Reed.

*Film (A Screen Play By Samuel Beckett)* (1979), UK, 26m, col.
D: David Rayner. W: Samuel Beckett. Ph: Mike Tomlinson. M: Franz Schubert. C: Max Wall, Patricia Hayes, Richard Golden.

*Finnegans Wake.* See *Passages from James Joyce's* **Finnegans Wake.**

*Flight of the Doves* (1971), UK/USA, 105m, col.
W/D: Ralph Nelson, adapting a novel by Walter Macken. Ph: Harry Waxman. M: Roy Budd. C: Ron Moody, Dorothy McGuire, Helen Raye, Dana, Jack Wild, Stanley Holloway, Niall Toibín, William Rushton.

*Four Days in July* (1984), UK, 95m, col.
W/D: Mike Leigh. Ph: Remi Adefarasin. M: Rachel Portman. C: Bríd Brennan, Des McAleer, Paula Hamilton, Charles Lawson, Stephen Rea, Shane Connaughton. Prod: BBC-TV.

*Fun Loving.* See *Quackser Fortune Has a Cousin in the Bronx.*

*Gentle Gunman, The* (1952), UK, 88m, b/w.
D: Basil Deardon. W: Roger MacDougall. Ph: Gordon Dines. M: John Greenwood. C: John Mills, Dirk Bogarde, Elizabeth Sellars, Barbara Mullen, Eddie Byrne, Joseph Tomelty, Gilbert Harding, Robert Beatty, Liam Redmond, Jack MacGowran.

*Ginger Man, The* (1994), USA/Germany/Ireland, col.
D: Peter Medals. W. J. P. Donleavy, adapting his novel of the same title. C: Aidan Quinn, Philip Dunleavy, Anjelica Huston.

*Girl with Green Eyes* (1962, 1964), UK, 91m, b/w, aka *The Lonely Girl.*
D: Desmond Davis. W: Edna O'Brien, adapting her novel. Ph: Manny
Wynn. M: John Addison. C: Rita Tushingham, Peter Finch, Lynn Red-
grave, T. P. McKenna, Julian Glover, Marie Kean.

*Guns in the Heather* (1968), UK, 90m, col.
D: Robert Butler. W: Herman Groves, adapting a novel by Lockart
Amerman. Ph: Michael Reed. M: Buddy Baker. C: Glenn Corbett, Al-
fred Burke, Kurt Russell, Patricia Dawson, Niall Toibín.

*Hangman's House* (1928), USA, 6518', b/w, silent.
D: John Ford. W: Marian Orth, Willard Mack, adapting the novel of the
same title by Donn Byrne. Ph: George Schneiderman. C: Victor McLaglen, June Collyer, Larry Kent, Earle Fox.

*Hang Up Your Brightest Colors* (1972), UK, 90m, b/w and col, docu.
W/D: Kenneth Griffith.

*Happy Ever After* (1954), UK, 87m, col.
D: Mario Zampi. W: Jack Davies, Michael Pertwee, L.A.G. Strong. Ph:
Stan Pavey. M: Stanley Black. C: David Niven, Barry Fitzgerald,
Yvonne De Carlo, Joseph Tomelty, Eddie Byrne, Liam Redmond.

*Hard Way, The* (1979), UK, 88m, col.
D: Michael Dryhurst. C: Patrick McGoohan, Lee Van Cleef, Donal Mc-
Cann, Edna O'Brien. (Distinguish from two unrelated US films of the
same title, 1942 and 1991.)

*Haunted and the Hunted, The.* See *Dementia 13.*

*Hear My Song* (1991), UK, 104m, col.
D: Peter Chelsom. W: Peter Chelsom, Adrian Dunbar, adapting a story
by Peter Chelsom. Ph: Sue Gibson. M: John Altman. C: Adrian Dunbar,
Shirley Anne Field, Tara Fitzgerald, Ned Beatty, David McCallum,
William Hookins, Harold Berens, James Nesbit.

*Hennessy* (1975), UK, 104m, col.
D: Don Sharp. W: John Gay, adapting a story by Richard Johnson. Ph:
Ernest Stewart. M: John Scott. C: Rod Steiger, Richard Johnson, Lee
Remick, Trevor Howard, Eric Porter, Peter Egan.

*Hidden Agenda* (1990), UK, 108m, col.
D: Ken Loach. W: Jim Allen. Ph: Clive Tickner. M: Stewart Copeland. C: Frances McDormand, Brian Cox, Mai Zetterling, Maurice Roeves, Michelle Fairley, Jim Norton, Brad Dourif, Ian McElhinney, Patrick Kavanagh, John McDonnell.

*High Spirits* (1988), USA, 97m, col.
W/D: Neil Jordan. Ph: Alex Thomson. M: George Fenton. C: Steve Guttenberg, Daryl Hannah, Peter O'Toole, Beverly D'Angelo, Jennifer Tilly, Liam Neeson, Ray McAnally, Peter Gallagher, Donal McCann, Connie Booth, Liz Smith.

*Hostage* (1984), UK, 40m, col.
W/D: Aisling Walsh. Ph: Denis Crossman. M: Steve Marshall. C: Veronica Quilligan, Alan Devlin, Fintan McKeown, Seumus Healy.

*How Many Miles to Babylon* (1982), UK, 90m, col.
D: Moira Armstrong. W: Derek Mahon, adapting the novel of the same title by Jennifer Johnston. Ph: John Hooper. M: Geoffrey Burgon. C: Daniel Day-Lewis, Christopher Firbank, Barry Foster, Sian Phillips, Alan MacNaughton, David Gwillam, Patrick Hannaway, Kevin Moore, Frank Williams, Philip Fox. Prod: BBC-TV.

*Hungry Hill* (1946), UK, 92m, b/w.
D: Brian Desmond Hurst. W: Daphne du Maurier, adapting her novel of the same title. Ph: Desmond Dickinson. C: Margaret Lockwood, Dennis Price, Cecil Parker, Michael Denison, F. J. McCormick, Dermot Walsh, Jean Simmons, Eileen Herlie, Siobhán McKenna, Eileen Crowe, Dan O'Herlihy.

*I See a Dark Stranger.* See *The Adventuress.*

*I Was Happy Here.* See *Time Lost and Time Remembered.*

*Images* (1972), UK/USA, 101m, col.
W/D: Robert Altman, adapting the story "In Search of the Unicorn," by Susannah York. Ph: Vilmos Zsigmond. M: John Williams. C: Susannah York, Rene Auberjonois, Marcel Bozzuffi, Hugh Millais, Cathryn Harrison, John Morley.

*Informer, The* (1929), UK, 83m, b/w, silent.
D: Arthur Robison. W: Benn W. Levy, Rolfe E. Vanlo, adapting the novel of the same title by Liam O'Flaherty. Ph: Werner Brandes,

T. Sparkuhl. C: Lars Hanson, Lya de Putti, Warwick Ward, Carl Harbord.

*Informer, The* (1935), USA, 91m, b/w.
D: John Ford. W: Dudley Nichols, adapting Liam O'Flaherty's novel. Ph. Joseph H. August. M: Max Steiner. C: Victor McLaglen, Heather Angel, Margot Grahame, Preston Foster, J. M. Kerrigan, Una O'Connor.

*Investigation, The: Inside a Terrorist Bombing* (1990), UK/Ireland, 115m, col.
D: Mike Beckham. W: Rob Ritchie, based on report of Peter Mullen (M.P., Labor). C: John Hurt, Martin Shaw, Roger Allam, Donal McCann, Niall Toibín, Peter Gowan. Prod: BBC-TV.

*Ireland: Behind the Wire* (1974), UK, 110m, b/w, docu.
Prod: Berwick Street Collective.

*Ireland: The Silent Voices* (1983), 80m, col, docu.
D: Rod Stoneman.

*Irish R. M. The* (1989), 104m, col.
D: Robert Chetwyn. W: Rosemary Anne Sisson, adapting the novels by Edith Somerville and Martin Ross. M: Nick Bicat. C: Peter Bowles, Bryan Murray, Doran Goodwin, Lise-Anne McLaughlin, Anna Manahan, Brendan Conroy, Faith Brook, Marie Kean, Joe Lynch, Donald Pickering, Beryl Reid, Niall Toibín, Tim Woodward. Adapted from the Ulster television series, 1982.

*Irish R. M., The* (1982) Six-hour version of above entry.
Made for Ulster-TV.

*Jack B. Yeats: Assembled Memories, 1871–1957* (1980), UK, 37m, col.
W/D, Ph: Thaddeus O'Sullivan. M: John Tams, Graeme Taylor. C: Bosco Hogan, Sebastian Shaw.

*Jacqueline* (1956), UK, 93m, b/w.
D: Roy Baker. W: Patrick Kirwan, Liam O'Flaherty. Ph: Geoffrey Unsworth. M: Cedric Thorpe Davie. C: John Gregson, Kathleen Ryan, Jacqueline Ryan, Noel Purcell, Cyril Cusack, Marie Kean, Liam Redmond, Maureen Delaney.

*James Joyce's* **Finnegans Wake.** See *Passages from James Joyce's* **Finnegans Wake.**

*John Huston and the Dubliners* (1987), USA, 55m, col, docu.
D: Lilyan Sievernich. Ph: Lisa Rinzler. M: Alex North. John Huston and the cast of *The Dead*.

*Johnny Nobody* (1960), UK, 88m, b/w.
D: Nigel Patrick. W: Patrick Kirwan, adapting a story by Albert Z. Carr. Ph: Ted More. M: Ron Goodwin. C: Nigel Patrick, Aldo Ray, Yvonne Mitchell, William Bendix, Cyril Cusack, Niall MacGinnis, Noel Purcell, Jimmy O'Dea.

*Juno and the Paycock* (1930), UK, 85m, b/w.
D: Alfred Hitchcock. W: Alfred Hitchcock, Alma Reville, adapting the stageplay of the same title by Sean O'Casey. Ph: Jack Cox. C: Sara Allgood, Edward Chapman, Marie O'Neill, Sidney Morgan, John Laurie, Dennis Wyndham, John Longden, Kathleen O'Regan, Barry Fitzgerald.

*Key, The* (1934), USA, 69m and 74m, b/w.
D: Michael Curtiz. W: Laird Doyle, based on the stageplay by R. Gore Brown and J. L. Hardy. Ph: Ernest Haller. M: Mort Dixon, Alice Wurbel. C: Edna Best, William Powell, Colin Clive, Maxine Doyle, Donald Crisp, Hobart Cavanagh, Halliwell Hobbs, Phil Regan, Arthur Treacher, Arthur Aylesworth, Dawn O'Day, Gertrude Short, Henry O'Neill, J. M. Kerrigan.

*Lamb* (1985), UK, 110m, col.
D: Colin Gregg. W: Bernard MacLaverty, adapting his novel of the same title. Ph: Mike Garfath. M: Van Morrison. C: Liam Neeson, Hugh O'Conor, Ian Bannen, Harry Towb, Frances Tomelty, Ronan Wilmot, Dudley Sutton.

*Langrishe, Go Down* (c. 1985), 110m, col.
W: Harold Pinter, adapting the novel of the same title by Aidan Higgins. C: Jeremy Irons. Prod: UK television.

*Last Hunger Strike, The: Ireland, 1981* (1982), USA, 60m, col, docu.
D: Tami Gold-Ahern.

*Leap of Faith, A* (1996), USA, 87m, col, docu.
W/D: Tricia Regan, Jenifer McShane. Narr: Liam Neeson.

*Lily of Killarney* (1934), UK, 88m, b/w.
D: Maurice Elvey. W: H. Fowler, adapting the stageplay *The Colleen Bawn* by Dion Boucicault. C: John Garrick, Gina Malo, Stanley Holloway, Dorothy Boyd, Leslie Perrins.

*Lonely Girl, The.* See *Girl with Green Eyes.*

*Lonely Passion of Judith Herne, The* (1987) UK, 116m, col.
D: Jack Clayton. W: Peter Nelson, adapting the novel of the same title by Brian Moore. C: Maggie Smith, Bob Hoskins, Wendy Hiller, Marie Kean, Prunella Scales, Ian McNeice, Alan Devlin, Rudi Davies.

*Lost Belongings* (1986), 6 parts, 52m each, col.
D: Tony Bicat. W: Stewart Parker. Ph: Gabriel Beristain. C: Catherine Byrne, Harry Towb, Struan Ridger, Oengus Macnamara, Colum Convey, Gerard O'Hare, Sharon Holm, Bruce Payne, Stephen Rea. Prod: Thames-TV.

*Luck of Ginger Coffey, The* (1964), Canada/USA, 100m, b/w.
D: Irvin Kershner. W: Brian Moore, adapting his novel of the same title. Ph: Manny Winn. M: Bernardo Segall. C: Robert Shaw, Mary Ure, Liam Redmond, Tom Harvey, Libby McClintock, Leo Layden.

*McCourts of Limerick, The* (1997), 60m, USA, docu.
D: Conor McCourt.

*Man of Aran* (1934), USA/UK, 76m, b/w, docu.
D/Ph: Robert Flaherty. W: Robert and Frances Flaherty. M: John Greenwood. C: Colman "Tiger" King, Maggie Dirane, Michael Dillane.

*Matchmaker, The* (1997), USA/UK/Ireland 96m, col.
D: Mark Joffe. W: Karen Janszen, Louis Nowra, Graham Linehan, based on a story by Greg Dinner. Ph: Ellery Ryan. M: John Altman. C: Janeane Garafalo, David O'Hara, Jay O. Sanders, Dennis Leary, Milo O'Shea, Saffron Burrows, Rosaleen Linehan, Paul Hickey, Maria Doyle Kennedy, Jimmy Keogh.

*Mein Leben für Ireland/My Life for Ireland* (1941), 90m, Germany, b/w.
D: Max W. Kimmich. W: Toni Huppertz. Ph: Richard Angst. M: Alois Melichar. C: Anna Dammann, René Deltgen, Eugen Klöpfer, Paul Wegener, Werner Hinz.

*Michael.* See *The Outsider.*

*Milwyr Byehan.* See *Boy Soldier.*

*Mona Lisa* (1986), UK, 104m, col.
D: Neil Jordan. W: Neil Jordan, David Leland. Ph: Roger Pratt. M: Michael Kamen. C: Bob Hoskins, Cathy Tyson, Michael Caine, Robbie Coltrane, Clarke Peters, Kate Hardie, Zoe Nathenson, Sammi Davis.

*Mountains O'Mourne* (1938), UK, 85m, b/w.
D: Harry Hughes. W: Gerald Brosnan, adapting a story by Daisy L. Fielding. C: Niall MacGinnis, Rene Ray, Jerry Verno, Betty Ann Davies.

*My Irish Molly* (1938), UK, 69m, b/w.
D: Alex Bryce. W: Alex Bryce, Ian Walker, W. G. Fay. Ph: Ernest Palmer. C: Binkie Stuart, Maureen O'Hara, Tom Burke, Philip Reed.

*My Life for Ireland.* See *Mein Leben für Irland.*

*Naming the Names* (1986), UK, 86m, col.
D: Stuart Burge. W: Anne Devlin. Ph: Michael Williams. M: Simon Rogers. C: Sylvestra le Touzel, Mick Ford, James Ellis, Michael Maloney, Eileen Way. Prod: BBC-TV.

*Night Fighters.* See *A Terrible Beauty.*

*No Resting Place* (1951), UK, 77m, b/w.
D: Paul Rotha. W: Paul Rotha, Colin Lesslie, Michael Orram, adapting a novel by Ian Naill. Ph: Wolfgang Suschitsky. M: William Alwyn. C: Michael Gough, Noel Purcell, Jack MacGowran, Eithne Dunne, Brian O'Higgins.

*No Surrender* (1985), UK, 104m, col.
D: Peter Smith. W: Alan Blaisdale. Ph: Mick Coulter. M: Daryl Runswick. C: Michael Angelis, Ray McAnally, Avis Bunnage, Bernard Hill, Joanne Whalley, James Ellis, Mark Mulholland, Michael Ripper, Elvis Costello.

*Nous étions tous les noms d'arbres.* See *The Writing on the Wall.*

*Odd Man Out* (1947), UK, 115m, b/w.
D: Carol Reed. W: F. L. Green, R. C. Sheriff, after the novel by F. L. Green. Ph: Robert Krasker. M: William Alwyn. C: James Mason, Robert

Newton, F. J. McCormick, Cyril Cusack, Kathleen Ryan, Dan O'Herlihy, Denis O'Dea, Robert Beatty, Maureen Delaney, Joseph Tomelty, William Hartnell, Fay Compton.

*On a Paving Stone Mounted* (1978), UK, 96m, b/w, docu.
W/D, Ph: Thaddeus O'Sullivan. M: Christy Moore. C: Annabel Leventon, Stephen Rea, Miriam Margoyles, Mannix Flynn, Gabriel Byrne.

*Ourselves Alone* (1936), UK, 70m, b/w, aka *River of Unrest.*
D: Walter Summers, Brian Desmond Hurst. W: Dudley Leslie, Marjorie Jeans, Denis Johnston, adapting a short story by Dudley Sturrock, Noel Scott. Ph: Walter Harvey, Bryan Langley. C: John Lodge, John Loder, Antoinette Cellier, Niall MacGinnis, Maire O'Neill.

*Out of Ireland* (1994), USA, 120m, col, docu.
D: Paul Wagner. W: Paul Wagner, Kerby Miller. Ph: Erich Rolland. M: Mick Moloney. Narr: Kelly McGillis. Voices of: Aidan Quinn, Barry Barnes, Joe Gallagher, Liam Neeson, Pat Laffan, Gabriel Byrne, Tina Kellegher, Brenda Fricker, Des Braydon, Martin Dempsey, Stephen Kennedy.

*Outsider, The* (1979), Netherlands, 128m, col, aka *Michael.*
W/D: Tony Luraschi, adapting a short story by Colin Leinster. Ph: Ricardo Aronovitch. M: Ken Thorne, Matt Molloy. C: Craig Wasson, Sterling Hayden, Patricia Quinn, Niall O'Brien, T. P. McKenna, Niall Toibín, Ray McAnally, Bosco Hogan, Elizabeth Begley, Frank Grimes.

*Paddy the Next Best Thing* (1923), UK, 7200', b/w, silent.
D: Graham Cutts. W: Herbert Wilcox, Eliot Stannard, adapting the novel and stageplay of Gertrude Page. Ph: Rene Guisart. C: Mae Marsh, Darby Foster, Lilian Douglas, George K. Arthur.

*Paddy the Next Best Thing* (1933), USA, 75m, b/w.
D: Harry Lachman. W: Edwin Burke, adapting the novel and stageplay of Gertrude Page. Ph: John Seitz. C: Janet Gaynor, Warner Baxter, Walter Connolly, Harvey Stephens, Margaret Lindsay.

*Parnell* (1937), USA, 115m, b/w.
D: John M. Stahl. W: John Van Druten, S. N. Behrman, adapting the stageplay of the same title by Elsie T. Schauffler. Ph: Karl Freund. M: William Axt. C: Clark Gable, Myrna Loy, Edmund Gwynn, Edna May Oliver, Alan Marshall, Donald Crisp, Billie Burke, Donald Meek.

*Parnell and the Englishwoman* (1992), UK, 6 parts, 52m each, col.
D: John Bruce. W: Hugh Leonard, adapting his novel of the same title.
Ph: Keith Schofield. M: Jim Parker, James Galway. C: Trevor Eve,
Francesca Annis, David Robb, Robert Lang, T. P. McKenna, John Savi-
dent, Sheila Ruskin, Liam de Static, Jack Walsh, James Curran, Stanley
Townsend, Dermod Moore, Emer McCourt, Geoffrey Toone, Anne
Queensberry.

*Passages from James Joyce's* **Finnegans Wake** (1965), USA, 97m, b/w.
D: Mary Ellen Bute. W: Mary Ellen Bute, Mary Manning, adapting the
novel of the same title by James Joyce. Ph: Ted Nemeth. M: Elliott Ka-
plan. C: Martin J. Kelly, Jane Reilly, Peter Haskell, Page Johnson, John
V. Kelleher, Roy Flanagan.

*Patriot Game, The* (1978), France, 97m, b/w, docu.
W/D: Arthur MacCaig. Ph: Arthur MacCaig, Théo Robichet. M:
Horselips. Narr: Winnie Marshall.

*Patriot Games* (1992), USA, 116m, col.
D: Phillip Noyce. W: Donald Stewart, Peter Iliff, Steven Zallian after
the novel of the same title by Tom Clancy. C: Harrison Ford, Anne
Archer, Patrick Bergin, Sean Bean, James Fox, Thora Birch, Richard
Harris, James Earl Jones, Samuel L. Jackson, Polly Walker.

*People of Ireland* (1987), UK, 95m, b/w, docu.
Prod: Cinema Action.

*Philadelphia, Here I Come* (1975), USA, UK, 95m, col.
D: John Quested. W: Brian Friel, adapting his stage play of the same
title. C: Donal McCann, Des Cave, Siobhán McKenna, Eamonn Kelly,
Fidelma Murphy, Liam Redmond.

*Pint of Plain, A* (1972), UK, 40m, b/w, docu.
W/D: Thaddeus O'Sullivan, Derrick O'Connor. Ph: Dick Perrin. C:
Tony Haygarth, Tony Rohr, Toby Salaman, Anthony Trent.

*Plough and the Stars, The* (1936), USA, 72m, b/w.
D: John Ford. W: Dudley Nichols, adapting the stageplay of the same
title by Sean O'Casey. Ph: Joseph August. M: Roy Webb. C: Barbara
Stanwyck, Preston Foster, Barry Fitzgerald, Denis O'Dea, J. M. Kerri-
gan, F. J. McCormick, Eileen Crowe, Arthur Shields, Bonita Granville,
Una O'Connor.

*Portrait of the Artist as a Young Man, A* (1977), UK, 92m, col.
D: Joseph Strick. W: Judith Rascoe, adapting the novel of the same title by James Joyce. Ph: Stuart Hetherington. M: Stanley Myers. C: Bosco Hogan, T. P. McKenna, John Gielgud, Rosaleen Linehan, Maureen Potter, Niall Buggy, Brian Murray.

*Prayer for the Dying, A* (1987), UK, 108m, col.
D: Mike Hodges. W: Edmund Ward, Martin Lynch, adapting the novel of the same title by Jack Higgins. Ph: Mike Garfarth. C: Mickey Rourke, Alan Bates, Bob Hoskins, Sammi Davis, Christopher Fulford, Liam Neeson, Alison Doody.

*Le Puritain* (1937), France, 87m, b/w, French dialogue.
W/D: Jeff Musso, adapting a short story by Liam O'Flaherty. Ph: C. Courant. M: J. Dollin, Jeff Musso. C: Jean-Louis Barrault, Viviane Romance, Pierre Fresnay, Mady Berry, Jean Tisier.

*Quackser Fortune Has a Cousin in the Bronx* (1970), USA, 90m, col, aka *Fun Loving*.
D: Waris Hussein. W: Gabriel Walsh. Ph: Gil Taylor. M: Michael Dress. C: Gene Wilder, Margot Kidder, Eileen Colgan, Seamus Forde.

*Quare Fellow, The* (1962), UK, 90m, b/w.
W/D: Arthur Dreifuss, adapting the stage play of the same title by Brendan Behan. Ph: Peter Hennessey. M: Alexander Faris. C: Patrick McGoohan, Sylvia Sims, Walter Macken, Dermot Kelly, T. P. McKenna, Hilton Edwards, Jack Cunningham.

*Quiet Day in Belfast, A* (1974), Canada, 92m, col.
D: Milad Bessada. W: Andrew Angus Dalrymple, based on his stage-play of the same title. C: Margot Kidder, Barry Foster.

*Quiet Man, The* (1952), USA, 129m, col.
D: John Ford. W: Frank Nugent, adapting the short story of the same title by Maurice Walsh. Ph: Winton C. Hoch, Archie Stout. M: Victor Young. C: John Wayne, Maureen O'Hara, Barry Fitzgerald, Victor McLaglen, Mildred Natwick, Arthur Shields, Ward Bond, Francis Ford, Sean McClory, Jack MacGowran, Ken Curtis.

*Rebellion* (1963), UK, 58m, b/w, docu.
D: George Morrison. W/Narr: Robert Kee. Ph: George Morrison.

*Reflections* (1984), UK, 100m, col.
D: Kevin Billington. W: John Banville, adapting his novel, *The Newton Letter.* Ph: Mike Molloy. M: Rachel Portman. C: Gabriel Byrne, Harriet Walter, Donal McCann, Fionnula Flanagan.

*Railway Station Man, The* (1992), USA/UK, 102m, col.
D: Michael Whyte. W: Shelagh Delaney, adapting the novel of the same title by Jennifer Johnston. M: Richard Hartley. C: Julie Christie, Donald Sutherland, John Lynch, Frank MacCusker, Mark Tandy, Niall Cusack, Ingrid Craigie, Peadar Lamb. Prod: Turner Network Television/BBC-TV.

*Real Charlotte, The* (1991), UK, 240m, col.
D: Tony Barry. W: Bernard MacLaverty, adapting the novel of the same title by Somerville and Ross. Ph: Jack Conroy. M: Paul Corbett, Michael Casey. C: Jeananne Crowley, Patrick Bergin, Joanna Roth. Prod: Granada Television.

*River of Unrest.* See *Ourselves Alone.*

*Rooney* (1958), UK, 88m, b/w.
D: George Pollock. W: Patrick Kirwan, adapting a novel by Catherine Cookson. Ph: Christopher Challis. M: Philip Green. C: John Gregson, Barry Fitzgerald, Eddie Byrne, Philip O'Flynn, Noel Purcell, Miare Kean, Jack MacGowran, Liam Redmond.

*Ryan's Daughter* (1970), UK, 206m, col.
D: David Lean. W: Robert Bolt. Ph: Freddie Young. M: Maurice Jarré. C: Sarah Miles, Robert Mitchum, Christopher Jones, John Mills, Trevor Howard, Leo McKern, Niall Toibín, Barry Foster, Marie Kean.

*Saints and Sinners* (1948), UK, 85m, b/w.
D: Leslie Arliss. W: Paul Vincent Carroll, Leslie Arliss. Ph: Osmond H. Borradaile. M: Philip Green. C: Kieron Moore, Sheila Manahan, Christine Norden, Michael Dolan, Maire O'Neill, Liam Redmond, Noel Purcell.

*Secret of Roan Inish* (1994), USA, 103m, col.
W/D: John Sayles, adapting the novel *The Secret of Ron Mor Skerry*; by Rosalie Frye. Ph: Haskell Wexler. C: Jeni Courtney, Eileen Colgan, Mick Lally, John Lynch, Richard Sheridan.

*Sense of Loss, A* (1972), Switzerland/USA, 132m, b/w and col, docu. W/D: Marcel Ophuls. Ph: Simon Edelstein. M: Melanie, traditional, etc. C: Bernadette Devlin, Ian Paisley, Terence O'Neill, Conor Cruise O'Brien.

*Sglyfaeth* (1986), UK [Wales], 98m, col. D: Gareth Wynn Jones. W: H. Pritchard Jones.

*Shadows on Our Skin* (1980), UK, 80m, col. D: Jim O'Brien. W: Derek Mahon, adapting the novel of the same title by Jennifer Johnston. C: Macrae Clarke. Prod: BBC-TV.

*Shake Hands with the Devil* (1959), UK/USA, 110m, b/w. D: Michael Anderson. W: Ivan Goff, Ben Roberts, adapting the novel by Rearden Connor. Ph: Erwin Hollier. M: William Alwyn. C: James Cagney, Dana Wynter, Glynis Johns, Cyril Cusack, Don Murray, Michael Redgrave, Sybil Thorndike, Noel Purcell, Niall MacGinnis, Richard Harris, Ray McAnally.

*She Didn't Say No* (1958), UK, 97m, col. D: Cyril Frankel. W: T. J. Morrison, Una Troy, adapting the novel of Una Troy. Ph: Gilbert Taylor. M: Tristram Cary. C: Niall MacGinnis, Jack MacGowran, Eileen Herlie, Patrick McAlinney, Joan O'Hara, Hilton Edwards, Ray McAnally.

*Snapper, The* (1993), UK, 90m, col. D: Stephen Frears. W: Roddy Doyle, based on his novel of the same title. Ph: Oliver Stapleton. C: Colm Meaney, Tina Kellegher, Colm O'Byrne, Ruth McCabe, Eanna Macliam, Ciara Duffy, Joanne Gerard, Peter Rowen, Fionnula Murphy, Karen Woodley, Pat Laffan, Brendon Gleeson. Prod: BBC-TV.

*Song O' My Heart* (1930), USA, 91m, b/w. D: Frank Borzage. W: Tom Barry, J. J. McCarthy. Ph: Chester Lyons, Al Brick. C: John McCormack, Maureen O'Sullivan, John Garrick, J. M. Kerrigan, Alice Joyce.

*Taffin* (1988), UK, 96m, col. D: Francis Megahy. W: David Ambrose, adapting a novel by Lyndon Mallett. Ph: Paul Beeson. M: Stanley Myers, Hans Zimmer. C: Pierce Brosnan, Ray McAnally, Alison Doody, Jeremy Child, Patrick Bergin, Dearbhla Molloy, Jim Bartley, Alan Stanford.

*Terrible Beauty, A* (1960), UK, 90m, b/w, aka *Night Fighters.*
D: Tay Garnett. W: Robert Wright Campbell, adapting the novel by Arthur J. Roth. M: Cedric Thorpe Davie. C: Robert Mitchum, Anne Heywood, Dan O'Herlihy, Cyril Cusack, Richard Harris, Marianne Benet.

*This Is My Father* (1998), US/Canada, 120m, col.
W/D: Paul Quinn. Ph: Declan Quinn. C: Aidan Quinn, James Caan, Moya Farrelly, Françoise Grattan, Gina Moxley, Jacob Tierney, Maria McDermottroe, Donal Donnelly, Karl Hayden, Gavin O'Connor, Michael Devaney, Frank O'Dwyer, Marian Quinn, Eamon Morrissey, Kevin Meaney, John Cusack, Peadar Lamb.

*Time Lost and Time Remembered* (1965), UK, 91m, b/w, aka *I Was Happy Here.*
D: Desmond Davis. W: Edna O'Brien, Desmond Davis. Ph: Manny Wynn. M: John Addison. C: Sarah Miles, Cyril Cusack, Sean Caffrey, Julian Glover, Marie Kean, Eve Belton.

*Titanic Town* (1998) UK, 100m, col.
D: Roger Michell. W: Anne Devlin, adapting Mary Costello's novel of the same title. C: Julie Walters, Ciaran Hinds, Nuala O'Neill.

*To Live for Ireland* (1984) USA, 30m, docu.
W/D/Ph: Mary Pat Kelly. Prod: WTTW-TV [Chicago].

*Too Long a Sacrifice* (1984), UK, 85m, col, docu.
D: Michael Grigsby. Prod: Central TV.

*Top o' the Morning* (1949), USA, 100m, b/w.
D: David Miller. W: Edmund Beloin, Richard Breen. Ph: Lionel Lindon. M: James Van Heusen. C: Bing Crosby, Barry Fitzgerald, Ann Blyth, Hume Cronyn, John McIntyre, Eileen Crowe. (Distinguish from the silent feature of the same title [1922, USA], directed by Edward Laemmle.)

*Ulysses* (1967), UK, 132m, b/w.
D: Joseph Strick. W: Joseph Strick, Fred Haines, adapting the novel of the same title by James Joyce. Ph: Wolfgang Suschitsky. M: Stanley Myers. C: Milo O'Shea, Maurice Roeves, Barbara Jefford, T. P. McKenna, Anna Manahan, Maureen Potter, Martin Dempsey, Joe Lynch.

*Violent Enemy, The* (1968), 98m, col.
D: Don Sharp. W: Edmund Ward, adapting the novel by Hugh Marlowe. Ph: Alan Hume. M: John Scott. C: Tom Bell, Ed Begley, Owen Sullivan, Susan Hampshire, Noel Purcell, Michael Standing.

*War of Children, A* (1973) USA, 73m, col.
D: George Schaeffer. W: James Costigan. C: Jenny Agutter, Vivian Merchant, John Ronane, Anthony Andrews, Aideen O'Kelly. Prod: NBC-TV.

*War of the Buttons* (1994/5), UK/France, 94m, col.
D: John Roberts. W: Colin Welland, adapting the French novel and film, *La guerre des boutons* (1962). Ph: Bruno de Keyzer. C: Gregg Fitzgerald, Gerard Kearney, Daragh Naughton, Brendan McNamara, Kevin O'Malley, John Cleere.

*Widow's Peak* (1994), UK, 101m, col.
D: John Irvin. W: Hugh Leonard. Ph: Ashley Rowe. M: Carl Davis. C: Mia Farrow, Joan Plowright, Natasha Richardson, Adrian Dunbar, Jim Broadbent, Britta Smith, Gerard McSorley.

*Wings of the Morning* (1937), UK, 89m, b/w.
D: Harold Schuster. W: Tom Geraghty, adapting a short story by Donn Byrne. Ph: Ray Rennahan, Jack Cardiff. M: Arthur Benjamin; songs: John McCormack. C: Henry Fonda, Annabella, Stewart Rome, John McCormack, Leslie Banks, Irene Vanbrugh.

*Writing on the Wall, The* (1982), France/Belgium, 114m, col, docu, aka
    *Nous étions tous des noms d'arbres.*
W/D: Armand Gatti. Ph: Armand Marco. M: Philippe Hemon-Tamie, The Demons. C: John Deehan, Brendan "Archie" Deeney, Paddy Doherty, Nigel Haggan, John Keegan.

*Yeats Remembered* (1975), USA/UK, 35m, col, docu.
D: Brian and Sheila Szed. C: Anne Yeats, Michael Yeats. Prod: Guidance Associates, from BBC Archives.

*Young Cassidy* (1964), UK, 110m, col.
D: Jack Cardiff, John Ford (uncredited). W: John Whiting, adapting autobiographies of Sean O'Casey. Ph: Ted Scaife. M: Seán Ó Riada. C: Rod Taylor, Maggie Smith, Edith Evans, Flora Robson, Michael Redgrave, Julie Christie, Jack MacGowran, T. P. McKenna.

**Notes**

**Bibliography**

**Index**

# Notes

## 2. Poetic Documentary: The Films of John T. Davis

1. Marshall McLuhan, *Understanding Media: The Extensions of Man* (London: Ark, 1964), 286.

2. Arnold Hauser, *The Social History of Art: Naturalism, Impressionism, The Film Age* (London: Routledge, 1962), 214–46.

3. Charles Eidsvik, *Cineliteracy: Film among the Arts* (New York: Horizon Press, 1979), 152–53.

4. "Aspiring to the Condition of Language: Poetry and Irish Cinema, Part 1," *Circa*, no. 53 (Sept./Oct. 1990): 32–34; "Aspiring to the Condition of Language, Part 2," *Circa*, no. 54 (Nov./Dec. 1990): 34–37.

5. Pam Cook, ed. *The Cinema Book* (London: British Film Institute, 1985), 119.

6. Quoted in Cook, 132.

7. Cook, 132.

8. John T. Davis, "Looking Through John T. Davis' Eyes," interview by Tony Clayton-Lea, *Hot Press* (Christmas/New Year 1989), 19.

9. John McKenna, "Portrait of the City as a Rock 'n' Roll Town," *Hot Press* (July 1979): 17.

10. David Ballintine, "Ulster Gets Set for Film Premiere," *Newsletter* (June 1979).

11. John T. Davis, *Route 66* promotional brochure (Birmingham, Eng.: Central Independent Television, 1979), np.

12. John T. Davis, interview by Charlie and Maraid Whisker, *Rant* (Sept./Oct. 1985), 1.

13. Fintan O'Toole, Introduction, "Light Rain and Governments Falling: Ireland in the Eighties," *A New Tradition: Irish Art of the Eighties* (Dublin: The Douglas Hyde Gallery, 1990), 10.

14. *Rant*, 3.

15. Mike Catto, "Dust on the Bible: A Film by John T. Davis," Promotional Brochure (Belfast: DBA TV, 1990), n.p.

16. Ken Gorman, "Powerful Combination," *TV Production International* (April 1989): 56.

17. Brian McAvera, *Making the North: The Work of Victor Sloan* (Dublin: Open Air, 1990), 12.

## 3. History Without Borders: Neil Jordan's *Michael Collins*

1. Neil Jordan, *Michael Collins: Screenplay and Film Diary* (London: Vintage, 1996), 65.

2. Quoted by Philip Johnson, *International News Electronic Telegraph*, 2 Nov. 1996. Simon Partridge is a member of New Dialogue, a British-Irish Peace Group.

3. Robert A. Rosenstone, *Visions of the Past: The Challenge of Film to Our Idea of History* (Cambridge: Harvard Univ. Press, 1995); Robert A. Rosenstone, ed., *Revisioning*

*History: Film and the Construction of a New Past* (Princeton, New Jersey: Princeton Univ. Press, 1995). Other works of interest on the interaction of history and film are K.R.M. Short, *Feature Films as History*, ed. (London: Croom Helm, 1981); Vivian Sobchack, ed., *The Persistence of History: Cinema, Television, and the Modern Event* (New York: Routledge, 1996); Pierre Sorlin, *The Film in History: Restaging the Past* (Totowa, N.J.: Barnes and Noble, 1980); Marc Ferro, *Cinema and History* (Detroit: Wayne State Univ. Press, 1988).

4. The most heated critical debates were in local and national newspapers in Britain and Ireland. A summary of these, and some comments upon them, may be found in Elizabeth Cullingford's "The Reception of *Michael Collins*," *Irish Literary Supplement* (spring 1997): 17–18; and Luke Gibbons's "Demisting the Screen: Neil Jordan's *Michael Collins*" *Irish Literary Supplement* (spring 1997):16. Both writers take account of the objections by revisionist Irish historians, such as Paul Bew and Roy Foster. Various other articles and reviews are of interest: Thomas Flanagan, "Tales of Hope and Sorrow in Bloodied Ireland," *New York Times*, 13 Oct. 1996; Philip Dodd, Ronan Bennett, and Tom Paulin, "Ghosts from a Civil War," *Sight and Sound* (Dec. 1996): 31–32; Gary Crowdus, "The Screening of Irish History," *Cineaste* 22, no. 4 (1997): 14–19; Glen Newey, "Both Gangster and Gandhi. Agency Without Blame: The Significant Omissions of *Michael Collins*," *Times Literary Supplement*, 15 Nov. 1996, 20; Anthony Lane, "The Thrill of a Cause," *New Yorker*, 14 Oct. 1996, 101–3; Charles Townshend, *"Michael Collins," Sight and Sound* (Nov. 1996): 55–56. Jordan has offered many interviews, and his film diary is indispensable. See, for example, Seamus McSwiney, "Trying to Take the Gun out of Irish Politics: An Interview with Neil Jordan," *Cineaste* 22, no. 4 (1997): 20–23.

5. Strangely, Neil Jordan appeared to be confused on this very point. In an article in *The Irish Times* (23 Oct. 1996), he writes that film is not history, and that one can only compare films with films, but then he goes on to argue that his *Michael Collins* script is far more accurate to the historical record than a script written by Eoghan Harris for Kevin Costner, entitled *Mick* (unproduced).

6. See Guy Westwell's review of Rosenstone's two books in *Screen* 38, no. 1 (spring 1997): 99–105.

7. See David Bordwell, "Classical Hollywood Cinema: Narrational Principles and Procedures," in *Narrative, Apparatus, Ideology: A Film Theory Reader*, ed. Philip Rosen (New York: Columbia Univ. Press, 1986), 17–34.

8. Jordan's critique of Eoghan Harris's *Mick* script reveals that the latter utilized invented childhood experiences to explain Collins's political views. See Jordan's article "Tally Ho! Mr. Harris," *Irish Times*, 23 Oct. 1996. It is also worth reading Harris's response, "Tally Ho: Not So Funny, Mr Jordan," *Irish Times*, 26 Oct. 1996, which, among many other points, draws a distinction between basing a fiction upon an actual life (*Mick*) and claiming a film is true to the historical record (*Michael Collins*), as Harris sees Jordan doing.

9. Of course, arguments exist that the Easter Rising and the War of Independence were unnecessary, since Home Rule was on the statute book, delayed by the First World War, and the eventual treaty of 1921 still required an oath of allegiance to the British Crown. Furthermore, the setting up of Northern Ireland in December 1920 was a fait accompli by the time of the treaty negotiations, so acceptance of partition was already on the cards to most republican observers and was surprisingly not a sticking point at negotiations nor did it figure largely in the Dáil debates on the treaty provisions.

10. Jordan read all the biographies of Michael Collins for his script, and he talked to Tim Pat Coogan, who is credited in the film, author of *Michael Collins: The Man Who Made Ireland* (Boulder, Colo.: Roberts, Rinehart Publishers, 1996). Tim Pat Coogan quotes a source that indicates de Valera knew but did not approve of the ambush plans.

11. See Marilynn J. Richtarik, *Acting Between The Lines: The Field Day Theatre Company and Irish Cultural Politics 1980–1984* (Oxford: Oxford Univ. Press, 1994), 84. On a personal note, I could not help thinking as I watched Neil Jordan's hagiography of Michael Collins that Stephen Rea would be a perfect actor for a portrayal of Roger Casement, one of the executed rebels in 1916. The subject of an Irish Protestant who saw British Colonial Service in Africa and who was persuaded to run guns from the Germans to the Irish Volunteers, and whose homosexual status played no small part in the decision to have him hanged, would be a challenging and intriguing Irish political film.

12. At the screening I attended at the Vancouver International Film Festival in September 1996, audience members cheered at this scene. As a counterpoint to the narrative dynamics in operation here, the Disabled Police Officers Association in Northern Ireland called for the film to be boycotted, pointing to the scene of the car bomb. The association's chairman was both blind and deaf as the result of an IRA bomb, so could not judge the film for himself (reported by Toby Harnden, Ireland correspondent, *UK News Electronic Telegraph*, 22 Oct. 1996).

13. Clarke's short fiction film profiled eighteen murders. Each portrayed anonymous killers and victims.

14. The supposedly undramatic nature of the treaty negotiations did not stop Jonathan Lewis from directing for Thames Television and Radio Telefís Éireann *The Treaty* (1991), which focused on the period of negotiations in London.

15. Quoted by Jay Carr of the *Boston Globe*, reprinted in "Fighting Irish," *Vancouver Sun*, 24 Oct. 1996.

16. The phrase is Tom Nairn's. See his summary of the anti-imperialist myth in *The Break-Up of Britain: Crisis and Neo-Nationalism* (London: Verso, 1981), 231.

### 4. "The Past Is Always There in the Present": *Fools of Fortune* and the Heritage Film

1. Charles Barr, "Introduction: Amnesia and Schizophrenia," in Charles Barr, *All Our Yesterdays: 90 Years of British Cinema* (London: British Film Institute, 1986), 11.

2. Andrew Higson, *Waving the Flag: Constructing a National Cinema in Britain* (Oxford: Clarendon Press, 1995), 26.

3. David Wilson, "*Fools of Fortune* (Review)," *Monthly Film Bulletin* (June 1990): 196, and Anne Billson *Sunday Correspondent*, 24 (June 1990): 36.

4. Andrew Higson, "Re-presenting the National Past: Nostalgia and Pastiche in the Heritage Film," in *British Cinema and Thatcherism: Fires Were Started*, ed. Lester Friedman (London: UCL Press, 1993), 113.

5. Higson, "Re-presenting the National Past," 113.

6. Ronan Farren, "Fools of Fortune (Review)" *Sunday Independent* (24 June 1990): 30.

7. Jennifer Johnston, *The Old Jest* (1979; reprint, Glasgow: Fontana, 1980), 59.

8. Even the "factual" plot summary provided by the *Monthly Film Bulletin* (July 1990), 196, is wrong on this score.

9. Philip French, "*A Month in the Country* (Review)," *The Observer* (22 Nov. 1987), 26.

10. Andrew Higson, "Re-presenting the National Past," 118.

11. Peter Brook, *The Melodramatic Imagination: Balzac, Henry James, Melodrama and the Mode of Excess* (1976; reprint, New York: Columbia Univ. Press, 19 1984, 5.

12. See John Hill, "Images of Violence," in *Cinema and Ireland*, ed. Kevin Rockett, Luke Gibbons, and John Hill (Syracuse, N.Y.: Syracuse Univ. Press, 1988), 147–93. Although Brook (ibid., 15) links the "moral occult of melodrama to what he calls a "post-sacred era," it is also apparent that the workings of fatalism in *Fools of Fortune*, as in other Irish-theme films such as *The Informer, Odd Man Out*, and *Cal* are nonetheless connected to a religious sense of sin and possible redemption.

13. Celeste Loughman, "The Mercy of Silence: William Trevor's *Fools of Fortune*," *Éire-Ireland*, 28, no. 1 (spring 1993): 89.

14. See also Luke Gibbons, "The Politics of Silence: *Anne Devlin*, Women and Irish Cinema," *Framework* 30/31 (1986): 2–15.

15. Luke Gibbons, "Romanticism, Realism and Irish Cinema," *Cinema and Ireland*, eds. Kevin Rockett, Luke Gibbons, and John Hill, 203.

16. Jacqueline Stahl Aronson, "William Trevor: An Interview," *Irish Literary Supplement* (spring 1986), 8. This idea is also expressed in the original novel: see William Trevor, *Fools of Fortune* (Harmondsworth, Eng.: Penguin, 1983), 28.

17. Gregory A. Schirmer, *William Trevor: A Study of His Fiction* (London: Routledge, 1990), 1–2.

18. Ibid.

19. Christine St. Peter, "Jennifer Johnston's Irish Troubles: A Materialist-Feminist Reading," in *Gender in Irish Writing*, eds., T. Johnson and D. Cairns. (Milton Keynes: Open Univ. Press, 1992), 118.

20. Ibid.

21. Seamus Deane, 'Jennifer Johnston,' *Bulletin of the Department of Foreign Affairs* [Dublin] no. 1015 (Feb. 1985), 4.

**5. *December Bride:* A Landscape Peopled Differently**

1. Patricia Dobson, "Festival Britain—*December Bride*," *Screen International* no. 754 (28 Apr. 1990):8–9.

2. Thaddeus O'Sullivan, "Fragments in Pictures, An Interview with Thaddeus O'Sullivan," Interview by Luke Gibbons, *Film Base News* (Nov/Dec 1990):8–12.

3. O'Sullivan, interview, *Screen International*.

4. Luke Gibbons, "Romanticism, Realism and Irish Cinema," in *Cinema and Ireland*, ed. Kevin Rockett, Luke Gibbons and John Hill, (Syracuse, N.Y.: Syracuse Univ. Press, 1988), 194–257.

5. Eamonn Slater, "Contested Terrain: Differing Interpretations of Co. Wicklow's Landscape," *Irish Journal of Sociology* 3 (1993): 23–55.

6. Luke Gibbons, "Romanticism in Ruins: Developments in Recent Irish Cinema," *The Irish Review* 2 (1987): 59–63.

7. Slater, "Contested Terrain," 30–32.

8. Gibbons, "Romanticism, Realism and Irish Cinema," 198.

9. Mark Kermode, "December Bride," *Monthly Film Bulletin* 58, no. 685 (Feb. 1991): 43–44.

10. Gibbons, "Romanticism, Realism and Irish Cinema," 226.

11. Ibid., 197.

12. Slater, "Contested Terrain," 24.

13. O'Sullivan, "Fragments in Pictures," 12.

## 6. Revising Resistance: *In the Name of the Father* as Postcolonial Paternal Melodrama

1. Moore, *The Voyage*.

2. Declan Kiberd, "The War Against the Past," in *The Uses of the Past: Essays on Irish Culture* (Newark, Del.: Univ. of Delaware Press; London: Associated Univ. Presses, 1988), 47.

3. Ibid.

4. Frantz Fanon, *The Wretched of the Earth*, trans. Constance Farrington (New York: Grove Press, 1963), 38–52.

5. Frederic Jameson, "Nationalism, Colonialism and Literature: Modernism and Imperialism," in *Nationalism, Colonialism and Literature* (Minneapolis: Univ. of Minnesota Press, 1990), 50–1.

6. Ann Cvetkovich, *Mixed Feelings: Feminism, Mass Culture, and Victorian Sensationalism* (New Brunswick, N.J.: Rutgers Univ. Press, 1992), 112.

7. I wish to make it clear that I oppose and, wherever possible, actively resist the patriarchal, hegemonic forces that constitute the disempowerment of men as an *especially* poignant and/or unnatural condition. My aim in this essay is to describe the impact of disempowerment on men whose lives and expectations necessarily have been, like my own, profoundly conditioned by such forces, and to assess the complex vagaries of subject formation in a context in which the normative equation of masculinity to agency and authority constitutes a painful double bind.

8. In times of revolution, Fanon claims, this process occurs backwards—it is the son who reclaims a previously absent sense of agency on behalf of the father, who then may "inherit" a sense of masculine agency and authority from his son (Kiberd, "The War Against the Past, 48). Certainly the film *The Mountain of Fire*, a documentary on the children of the Palestinian Intifada, suggests that precisely such a process took place during the years of the Intifada for adults of both sexes, who felt the shame of their community to be redeemed through the resistance of their (male and female) children.

9. Indeed, for Conlon to have suggested that his period of wrongful incarceration and abuse in British prisons was in some way an important part of his maturation process would have represented a form of self-betrayal, as well as the artificial foreclosure of a psychological process of resolution that will undoubtedly be ongoing throughout the rest of his life. We respect the Gerry Conlon we meet in the autobiography because despite what they have done to him, they have not been able to stop him from laughing at them.

10. Fanon, *The Wretched of the Earth*, 41.

11. At the time of this essay's final revisions, work continues in Northern Ireland to elaborate a postmilitarist political praxis analogous to the postmilitarist postcolonial moment that transformations of masculine subjectivity in Sheridan's and Kureishi's films prefigure. Historically, the British state has, at such junctures, engineered new legal and extralegal dramas to resituate Irish men within binary victim/victimizer positions, thereby reinstating the circuit of masochistic denial or sadistic, defensive opposition I have delineated above. Whether the British state will succeed in disrupting the powerful and moving efflorescence of forces that have been steadily gathering strength within the Republican movement since the time of the No Wash protests and the Hunger Strikes— moments that, not coincidentally, I think, constituted a prison-based, communal confrontation with images of male abjection and a corresponding long-term shift from military to representational politics—will remain to be seen. Also consulted: (1) Feld-

man, Allen. *Formations of Violence: The Narrative Body and Political Terror in Northern Ireland*. Chicago: Univ. of Chicago Press, 1991; (2) Finnegan, Patricia, and Frank Harrington. "Factors in the Genesis of Stress and Mental Ill Health Amongs the Irish in Britain." [n.p.]: Irish Mental Health Forum, 1990; (3) Patterson, Orlando. *Slavery and Social Death: A Comparative Study*. Cambridge: Harvard Univ. Press, 1982.

### 7. "Different Countries, Different Worlds": The Representation of Northern Ireland in Stewart Parker's *Lost Belongings*

1. John Wilson Foster, ed., *The Idea of the Union: Statements and Critiques in Support of the Union of Great Britain and Northern Ireland* (Vancouver B.C.: Belcouver Press, 1995).

2. See Stewart Hall, "Encoding and Decoding in the Television Discourse," in *Occasional Papers No. 7*, Birmingham University Centre for Contemporary Cultural Studies, 1973; and Philip Schlesinger, Graham Murdock, and Philip Elliot, eds., *Televising Terrorism* (London: Comedia Publishing Group, 1983).

3. John Hill, "Images of Violence," in *Cinema and Ireland* ed. Kevin Rockett, Luke Gibbons, and John Hill, London: Routledge, 1988.

4. Department of Economic Development [Belfast], *Tourism in Northern Ireland: A View to the Future*. Belfast: HMSO, 1990. Recent figures indicate that the tourist trade is now on the rise, a trend that is predicted to continue if the ceasefires hold.

5. Margo Harkin, "Broadcasting in a Divided Community (Session III)," *Culture, Identity and Broadcasting in Ireland: Local Issues, Global Perspectives*, ed. Martin McLoone (Belfast: Institute for Irish Studies, 1991), 110–16.

### 8. "I Kinda Liked You as a Girl": Masculinity, Postcolonial Queens, and the "Nature" of Terrorism in Neil Jordan's *The Crying Game*

1. See Gloria Anzaldua's *Borderlands/La Frontera* (San Francisco: Spinsters/Aunt Lute, 1987).

2. Caryn James, "You Are What You Wear," *New York Times*, 19 Oct. 1993, H13.

3. Ibid., H23.

4. Judith Halberstam, "Crying at the Moon," *On Our Backs* 9, no. 5 (1993), 10–11, 44.

5. Ibid., 11.

6. David Lugowski, "Genre Conventions and Visual Style in *The Crying Game*," *Cineaste* 20, no. 1 (1993); 32.

7. Kristen Handler, "Sexing *The Crying Game*," *Film Quarterly* 47, no. 3 (1994): 32.

8. Robyn Wiegman, "Feminism, 'The Boyz,' and Other Matters Regarding the Male," in *Screening the Male: Exploring Masculinities in Hollywood Cinema*," ed. Ina Rae Hark and Steven Cohan (New York: Routledge, 1993), 176.

9. See Kevin Rockett's "From Atlanta to Dublin," *Sight and Sound* 2, no. 2 (June 1992): 26–28, 29.

10. Sigmund Freud, "Mourning and Melancholia," (1917), in *The Standard Edition of the Complete Psychological Works of Sigmund Freud*, trans. and ed. James Strachey (London: Hogarth Press, 1953–74), 14:237–58. See Diana Fuss's "Monsters of Perversion: Jeffrey Dahmer and *The Silence of the Lambs*," in *Media Spectacles*, ed. Marjorie Garber, Jann Matlock, and Rebecca Walkowitz (New York: Routledge, 1993), 181–205, for an excellent discussion of the violence implicit in Freudian metaphors of identification, including incorporation and cannibalism.

11. Vanessa Place, "The Politics of Denial," *Film Comment* 29 (May-June 1993), 86.

12. Homi Bhabha, "Of Mimicry and Men: The Ambivalence of Colonial Discourse," *October* 28 (1984), 129.

13. Steven Neale, "Masculinity as Spectacle," in *Screening the Male: Exploring Masculinities in Hollywood Cinema,* ed. Ina Rae Hark and Steven Cohan (New York: Routledge, 1994), 14.

14. Halberstam, "Crying at the Moon," 11.

15. Edward Pearce, "The Irish Question and the Only Solution," *Encounter* 58, No. 2 (Aug. 1981): 31.

16. Susan Jeffords, *The Remasculinization of America: Gender and the Viet-Nam War* (Bloomington: Indiana Univ. Press, 1989).

17. Wiegman, "Feminism, 'The Boyz,' and Other Matters," 179.

### 9. Neil Jordan's *Miracle:* From Fiction to Film

1. Neil Jordan, *A Neil Jordan Reader* (New York: Vintage, 1993), 20–21.

2. Ibid., 26.

3. Ibid., 75.

4. Ibid., 73.

5. Ibid., 83.

### 11. Huston and Joyce: Bringing "The Dead" to the Screen

1. John Simon, "Death and Soul-death," *National Review* 40 (22 Jan. 1988): 64.

2. Denis Donoghue, "Huston's Joyce," *New York Review of Books* 35 (3 Mar. 1988): 18.

3. Richard A. Blake, "The Living and the Dead," *America* 158 (20 Feb. 1988): 194.

4. Richard Schickel, "Huston's Serene Farewell," *Time* 131 (4 Jan. 1988): 64.

5. Information on the filming of the *The Dead* presented by Tony Huston at a public forum on 14 June 1989 in conjunction with the International James Joyce Conference held in Philadelphia. All subsequent comments by Tony Huston on the making of the film are from this forum.

6. David Denby, "The Living," *New York* 21 (18 Jan. 1988): 59.

7. Ibid., 59.

### 12. Cathal Black's *Pigs:* Ambivalence, Confinement, and the Search for an Irish Sense of Place

1. Patrick Sheeran, *"Genius Fabulae:* The Irish Sense of Place," *Irish University Review* 18, no. 2 (autumn 1988): 191. Sheeran examines a number of sources, from older Gaelic verse to modern English poetry, that focus formally on naming places and thematically on the disappearance or ruin of those places. This tendency for poets to "save" the Irish landscape through representation and discourse, Sheeran concludes, is not a result of colonialism or recent historical situations per se but is a product of the native tradition itself.

2. Ibid., 192.

3. Ibid., 194.

4. Ibid., 197.

5. For a discussion of the Western bias toward space as a stabilizing concept, see, for instance, Neil Smith and Cindi Katz, "Grounding Metaphor: Toward a Spatialized Politics," in *Place and the Politics of Identity,* ed. Michael Keith and Steve Pile (London: Routledge, 1993), 67–83. The authors trace a series of genealogies of geographic terms and

spatial metaphors in twentieth-century social, cultural, and literary discourses. Western traditions of capitalist logic, they argue, produced a conception of space as a neutral, un-problematic container—an "absolute space"—that occludes power struggles, instabili-ties, differences, and multiple perspectives. Smith and Katz conclude: "Newton, Descartes and Kant were the philosophical progenitors of spatial modernism, as much as Columbus, Napoleon and the Duchess of Sutherland were its practitioners. The depth of their collective influence, the taken-for-grantedness of the absolute space they estab-lished, is only beginning to be challenged" (80).

6. Martin Heidegger, "Building, Dwelling, Thinking," in *Poetry, Language, Thought,* trans. Albert Hofstader (New York: Harper Colophon Books, 1971), 152–53.

7. Ibid., 150–51.

8. Ibid., 153.

9. Sheeran, *"Genius Fabulae,"* 196.

10. Ibid., 197.

11. David Harvey, *The Condition of Postmodernity* (Cambridge, Eng.: Blackwell, 1989), 207.

12. Ibid., 240.

13. Ibid., 35.

14. Heidegger, "The Thing," *Poetry, Language, Thought,* 165.

15. Harvey, *The Condition of Postmodernity,* 35.

16. Ibid., 239.

17. Doreen Massey, "Power-Geometry and a Progressive Sense of Place," in *Mapping the Futures: Local Cultures, Global Change,* ed. Jon Bird, et al., (London: Routledge, 1993), 63.

18. Ibid., 61.

19. Ibid., 64.

20. Sheeran, *"Genius Fabulae,"* 197.

21. Ibid., 192–93.

22. Ibid., 198.

23. Michel Foucault, "Madness and Civilization [excerpts]," trans. Richard Howard, in *The Foucault Reader,* ed. Paul Rabinow (New York: Pantheon Books, 1984), 128.

24. Sheeran, *"Genius Fabulae,"* 191.

25. Seán Ó Tuama, "Stability and Ambivalence: Aspects of the Sense of Place and Reli-gion in Irish Literature," in *Ireland: Towards a Sense of Identity,* ed. Joseph Lee, (Cork: Cork Univ. Press, 1985), 23.

26. Ibid., 26.

27. Ibid., 30.

28. Massey, "Power-Geometry," 66.

29. Ibid., 67.

30. Ibid., 67.

31. Ibid., 67.

32. Ibid., 68.

33. Kevin Kearns, *Georgian Dublin* (North Pomfret, Vt.: David and Charles, 1983), 15.

34. Massey, "Power-Geometry," 68.

35. Ibid., 68.

36. Michel Foucault, "The Politics of Health in the Eighteenth Century," trans. Colin Gordon, in *Power/Knowledge: Selected Interviews and Other Writings, 1972–1977,* ed. Colin Gordon (New York: Pantheon, 1980), 276.

### 13. An Elephant at the Altar: Religion in Contemporary Irish Cinema

1. Janet Roach, "Ireland Finds the Green and Weaves a Spell," *New York Times*, 2 Jan. 1994, H1.

2. David Lloyd, "Conflict of the Borders: Filmic and Historical Representations of Northern Ireland" (Keynote address to the Eighth Annual Graduate Irish Studies Conference [*Remapping the Borders: Irish Cultural Studies in the 1990s*], Univ. of Texas at Austin, 25 Mar. 1994).

3. See also David Lloyd, *Anomalous States: Irish Writing and the Post-Colonial Moment* (Durham: Duke Univ. Press, 1993), 126.

4. Roach, "Ireland Finds the Green," H1.

5. John Shout, "Joyce at Twenty-Five, Huston at Eighty-One: *The Dead*," *Literature/Film Quarterly* 17, no. 2 (1989):93.

6. Ibid.

7. James M. Wall, "Universal Connections among Living and Dead," *Christian Century* 105 (20 Jan. 1988): 43.

8. In response to the questions about the legitimacy about this current crop of "Irish" films, given that so many of them received foreign funding, Jim Sheridan responded that "it's the raw materials—the history, the people—that give them their soul. And that soul is Irish. There's no mistaking that" (Roach, "Ireland Finds the Green," H6).

9. Mark Kermode, "The American Connection," *Sight and Sound* 2, no. 2 (1992): 29.

### 16. *The Quiet Man* Speaks

1. A neglect addressed by Steve Matheson's biography, *Maurice Walsh: Storyteller* (Dingle: Brandon, 1985).

2. Ibid., 16–17, 73.

3. Lindsay Anderson, *About John Ford* (New York: McGraw-Hill, 1981), 28–29.

4. Dan Ford, *Pappy: The Life of John Ford* (Englewood Cliffs, N.J.: Prentice-Hall, 1979), 240–41.

5. Anderson, *About John Ford*, 242; letter dated 3 May 1953.

6. Ford, *Pappy*, 243; Yates also preferred that the title be changed to *The Man Untamed* or *Uncharted Voyage*.

7. Molly Haskell, *From Reverence to Rape: The Treatment of Women in the Movies* (New York: Holt, Rinehart and Winston, 1974), 269–70.

8. Brandon French, *On the Verge of Revolt: Women in American Films of the Fifties* (New York: Ungar, 1978).

9. "Maurice Walsh," *Dictionary of Irish Literature*, ed. Robert Hogan (Westport, Conn.: Greenwood, 1979), 676–77.

10. Further homage to Boucicualt appears in the scene where the old man on his deathbed (Francis Ford) jumps up to see the Thornton-Danaher fisticuffs, a steal from *The Shaughraun* (1875). Also consulted: (1) Campbell, Marilyn. "*The Quiet Man*." *Wide Angle* 2, no. 4 (1977):44–51; (2) McNee, Gerry. *In the Footsteps of the Quiet Man*. Edinburgh: Mainstream Publishing, 1990.

# Bibliography

Anderson, Lindsay. *About John Ford.* New York: McGraw-Hill, 1981.

Anzaldua, Gloria. *Borderlands/La Frontera.* San Francisco: Spinsters/Aunt Lute, 1987.

Aronson, Jacqueline Stahl. "William Trevor: An Interview." *Irish Literary Supplement* (spring 1986): 8.

Astruc, Alexandre. "Naissance d'une nouvelle avant-garde: La caméra stylo." *L'écran français,* no. 144 (30 Mar. 1948): 5.

Ballintine, David. "Ulster Gets Set For Film Premiere." *Newsletter* (June 1979).

Barr, Charles. *All Our Yesterdays: 90 Years of British Cinema.* London: British Film Institute, 1986.

Bhabha, Homi. "Of Mimicry and Men: The Ambivalence of Colonial Discourse." *October* 28 (1984): 125–33.

Billson, Anne. "*Fools of Fortune* (Review)." *Sunday Correspondent* 24 (June 1990): 36.

Blake, Richard A. "The Living and the Dead." *America* 158 (20 Feb. 1988): 194.

Bordwell, David. "Classical Hollywood Cinema: Narrational Principles and Procedures." In *Narrative, Apparatus, Ideology: A Film Theory Reader,* edited by Philip Rosen, 17–34. New York: Columbia Univ. Press, 1986.

Brook, Peter. *The Melodramatic Imagination: Balzac, Henry James, Melodrama and the Mode of Excess.* 1976. Reprint. New York: Columbia Univ. Press, 1984.

Campbell, Marilyn. "The Quiet Man." *Wide Angle* 2, no. 4 (1977): 44–51.

Conlon, Gerry. *Proved Innocent.* London: Penguin, 1990.

Coogan, Tim Pat. *Michael Collins: The Man Who Made Ireland.* Boulder, Colo.: Roberts, Rinehart Publishers, 1996.

Cook, Pam, ed. *The Cinema Book.* London: British Film Institute, 1985.

Crowdus, Gary. "The Screening of Irish History." *Cineaste* 22, no. 4 (1997): 14–19.

Cullingford, Elizabeth Butler. "The Reception of *Michael Collins.*" *Irish Literary Supplement* (spring 1997): 17–18.

Cvetkovich, Ann. *Mixed Feelings: Feminism, Mass Culture, and Victorian Sensationalism.* New Brunswick, N.J.: Rutgers Univ. Press, 1992.

Davis, John T. Interview by Charlie and Marai Whisker. In *Rant* (Sept./Oct. 1985): 1–3.

———. "Looking Through John T. Davis' Eyes." Interview by Tony Clayton-Lea. *Hot Press* (Christmas/New Year 1989): 18–19.

————. *Route 66*. Birmingham, Eng.: Central Independent Television, 1979.

Deane, Seamus. "Jennifer Johnston." *Bulletin of the Department of Foreign Affairs* [Dublin], no. 1015 (Feb. 1985).

Denby, David. "The Living." *New York* 21 (18 Jan. 1988): 59.

Dobson, Patricia. "Festival Britain—*December Bride.*" *Screen International,* No. 754 (28 Apr.–4 May 1990): 8–9.

Dodd, Philip, Ronan Bennett, and Tom Paulin. "Ghosts from a Civil War." *Sight and Sound* 6 (Dec. 1996): 31–32.

Donoghue, Denis. "Huston's Joyce." *New York Review of Books* 35 (3 Mar. 1988): 18.

Eidsvik, Charles. *Cineliteracy: Film among the Arts.* New York: Horizon, 1979.

Fanon, Frantz. *The Wretched of the Earth.* Translated by Constance Farrington. New York: Grove Press, 1963.

Farren, Ronan. "*Fools of Fortune* (Review)." *Sunday Independent* (24 June 1990): 30.

Feldman, Allen. *Formations of Violence: The Narrative of Body and Political Terror in Northern Ireland.* Chicago: Univ. of Chicago Press, 1991.

Ferro, Marc. *Cinema and History.* Detroit: Wayne State Univ. Press, 1988.

Finnegan, Patricia, and Frank Harrington. "Factors in the Genesis of Stress and Mental Ill Health Amongst the Irish in Britain." [n.p.]: The Irish Mental Health Forum, 1990.

Flanagan, Thomas. "Tales of Hope and Sorrow in Bloodied Ireland." *New York Times,* 13 Oct. 1966.

Ford, Dan. *Pappy: The Life of John Ford.* Englewood Cliffs, N.J.: Prentice-Hall, 1979.

Foster, John Wilson, ed. *The Idea of the Union: Statements and Critiques in Support of the Union of Great Britain and Northern Ireland.* Vancouver, B.C.: Belcouver Press, 1995.

Foucault, Michel. "Madness and Civilization [excerpts]." In *The Foucault Reader,* translated by Richard Howard and edited by Paul Rabibnow, 123–67. New York: Pantheon, 1984.

————. "The Politics of Health in the Eighteenth Century." In *Power/Knowledge: Selected Interviews and Other Writings, 1972–1977,* translated and edited by Colin Gordon, 166–82. New York: Pantheon, 1980.

French, Brandon. *On the Verge of Revolt: Women in American Films of the Fifties.* New York: Ungar, 1978.

French, Philip. "*A Month in the Country* (Review)." *The Observer* (22 Nov. 1987): 26.

Freud, Sigmund. "Mourning and Melancholia" [1917]. In *The Standard Edition of the Complete Psychological Works of Sigmund Freud.* Translated and edited by James Strachey, 14:237–58. London: Hogarth Press, 1953–74.

Fuss, Diana. "Monsters of Perversion: Jeffrey Dahmer and *The Silence of the Lambs.*" In *Media Spectacles,* edited by Marjorie Garber, Jann Matlock, and Rebecca Walkowitz, 181–205. New York: Routledge, 1993.

Gibbons, Luke. "Demisting the Screen: Neil Jordan's *Michael Collins.*" *Irish Literary Supplement* (spring 1997): 16.

―――. "Fragments in Pictures: An Interview with Thaddeus O'Sullivan." *Film Base News* (Nov./Dec. 1990): 8–12.

―――. "The Politics of Silence: *Anne Devlin,* Women and Irish Cinema." *Framework* 30/31 (1986): 2–15.

―――. "Romanticism in Ruins: Developments in Recent Irish Cinema." *Irish Review* 2 (1987): 59–63.

―――. "Romanticism, Realism and Irish Cinema." In *Cinema and Ireland,* edited by Kevin Rockett, Luke Gibbons, and John Hall, 194–257. Syracuse, N.Y.: Syracuse Univ. Press, 1988.

Gorman, Ken. "Powerful Combination." *TV Production International* (Apr. 1989): 56.

Halberstam, Judith. "Crying at the Moon." *On Our Backs* 9, no. 5 (1993): 10–11, 44.

Hall, Stewart. "Encoding and Decoding in the Television Discourse," Occasional Papers No. 7, Birmingham University Centre for Contemporary Cultural Studies (1973).

Handler, Kristin. "Sexing *The Crying Game.*" *Film Quarterly* 47, no. 3 (1994): 32.

Harris, Eoghan. "Tally Ho: Not So Funny, Mr. Jordan." *Irish Times,* 26 Oct. 1996.

Harkin, Margo. "Broadcasting in a Divided Community. (Session III)." In *Culture, Identity and Broadcasting in Ireland: Local Issues, Global Perspectives,* edited by Martin McLoone, 110–16. Belfast: Institute of Irish Studies, 1991.

Harvey, David. *The Condition of Postmodernity.* Cambridge, Eng.: Blackwell, 1989.

Haskell, Molly. *From Reverence to Rape: The Treatment of Women in the Movies.* New York: Holt, Rinehart and Winston, 1974.

Hauser, Arnold. *The Social History of Art: Naturalism, Impressionism, The Film Age.* London: Routledge, 1962.

Heidegger, Martin. "Building, Dwelling, Thinking." In *Poetry, Language, Thought,* translated by Albert Hofstadter, 145–61. New York: Harper Colophon Books, 1971.

―――. "The Thing." In *Poetry, Language, Thought,* translated by Albert Hofstadter, 165–86. New York: Harper Colophon Books, 1971.

Higson, Andrew. "Re-presenting the National Past: Nostalgia and Pastiche in the Heritage Film." In *British Cinema and Thatcherism: Fires Were Started,* edited by Lester Friedman, 109–21. London: UCL Press, 1993.

―――. *Waving the Flag: Constructing a National Cinema in Britain.* Oxford: Clarendon Press, 1995.

Hill, John. "Images of Violence." In *Cinema and Ireland,* edited by Kevin Rockett, Luke Gibbons, and John Hill, 147–93. Syracuse, N.Y.: Syracuse Univ. Press, 1988.

Hogan, Robert, ed. *Dictionary of Irish Literature.* Westport, Conn.: Greenwood, 1979.

Huston, Tony. "Forum of John Huston's *The Dead.*" International James Joyce Conference, Philadelphia, Pennsylvania, 14 June 1989.

James, Caryn. "You Are What You Wear," *New York Times,* 19 Oct. 1993, H13.

Jameson, Fredric. "Nationalism, Colonialism and Literature: Modernism and Imperialism." In *Nationalism, Colonialism and Literature.* Minneapolis: Univ. of Minnesota Press, 1990.

Jeffords, Susan. *The Remasculinization of America: Gender and the Viet-Nam War.* Bloomington: Indiana Univ. Press, 1989.

Johnston, Jennifer. *The Old Jest.* London: Fontana, 1979.

Jordan, Neil. *Michael Collins: Screenplay and Film Diary.* London: Vintage, 1996.

———. *A Neil Jordan Reader.* New York: Vintage, 1993.

———. "Tally Ho! Mr. Harris." *Irish Times,* 23 Oct. 1996.

Kearns, Kevin. *Georgian Dublin.* North Pomfret, Vt.: David and Charles, 1983.

Kermode, Mark. "The American Connection." *Sight and Sound* 2, no. 2 (1992): 29.

———. "*December Bride.*" *Monthly Film Bulletin* 58, no. 685 (Feb. 1991): 43–44.

Kiberd, Declan. "The War Against the Past." In *The Uses of the Past: Essays on Irish Culture,* 24–54. Newark, Del.: Univ. of Delaware Press; London: Associated Univ. Presses, 1988.

Lane, Anthony. "The Thrill of a Cause." *New Yorker,* 14 Oct. 1996, 101–3.

Lloyd, David. *Anomalous States: Irish Writing and the Post-Colonial Movement.* Durham: Duke Univ. Press, 1993.

———. "Conflict of the Borders: Filmic and Historical Representations of Northern Ireland." Keynote address, Eighth Annual Graduate Irish Studies Conference, Univ. of Texas at Austin, 25 Mar. 1994.

Loughman, Celeste. "The Mercy of Silence: William Trevor's *Fools of Fortune.*" *Éire-Ireland* 28, no. 1 (spring 1993): 87–96.

Lugowski, David. "Genre Conventions and Visual Style in *The Crying Game.*" *Cineaste* 20, no. 1 (1993): 32.

McAvera, Brian. *Making of the North: The Work of Victor Sloan.* Dublin: Open Air, 1990.

McCracken, Kathleen. "Aspiring to the Condition of Language: Poetry and Irish Cinema, Part 1." *Circa,* no. 53 (Sept./Oct. 1990): 32–34; "Aspiring to the Condition of Language, Part 2." *Circa,* no. 54 (Nov./Dec. 1990): 34–37.

McKenna John. "Portrait of the City as a Rock 'n' Roll Town." *Hot Press* (July 1979): 17.

McLoone, Martin, ed. *Culture, Identity and Broadcasting in Ireland: Local Issues, Global Perspectives.* Belfast: Institute for Irish Studies, 1991.

McLuhan, Marshall. *Understanding Media: The Extensions of Man.* London: Ark, 1964.

McNee, Gerry. *In the Footsteps of the Quiet Man.* Edinburgh: Mainstream Publishing, 1990.

McSwiney, Seamus. "Trying to Take the Gun Out of Irish Politics: An Interview with Neil Jordan." *Cineaste* 22, no. 4 (1997): 20–23.

Massey, Doreen. "Power-Geometry and a Progressive Sense of Place." In *Mapping the Futures: Local Cultures, Global Change,* edited by Jon Bird, 59–67. London: Routledge, 1993.

Matheson, Steve. *Maurice Walsh: Storyteller.* Dingle: Brandon, 1985.

Moore, Christy. *The Voyage* [sound recording]. London: WEA Records, Atlantic Corporation, 82034–2, 1984.

Nairn, Tom. *The Break-Up of Britain: Crisis and Neo-Nationalism.* London: Verso, 1981.

Neale, Steven. "Masculinity as Spectacle." In *Screening the Male: Exploring Masculinities in Hollywood Cinema,* edited by Ina Rae Hark and Steven Cohan, 9–20. New York: Routledge, 1994.

Newey, Glen. "Both Gangster and Gandhi. Agency Without Blame: The Significant Omissions of *Michael Collins.*" *Times Literary Supplement,* 15 Nov. 1996, 20.

O'Sullivan, Thaddeus. "Frequents in Pictures: An Interview with Thaddeus O'Sullivan." Interview by Luke Gibbons. *Film Base News* (Nov./Dec. 1990) 8–12.

————. Interview by. *Screen International* (28 Apr. 1990).

O'Toole, Fintan. *A Mass for James Joyce.* Dublin: Raven Arts, 1990.

————. *A New Tradition: Irish Art of the Eighties.* Dublin: Douglas Hyde Gallery, 1990.

Ó Tuama, Seán. "Stability and Ambivalence: Aspects of the Sense of Place and Religion in Irish Literature." In *Ireland: Towards a Sense of Identity: The UCC-RTÉ Lectures,* edited by Joseph Lee, 22–30. Cork: Cork Univ. Press. 1985.

Patterson, Orlando. *Slavery and Social Death: A Comparative Study.* Cambridge: Harvard Univ. Press, 1982.

Pearce. Edward. "The Irish Question and the Only Solution." *Encounter* 58, no. 2 (Aug. 1981): 31.

Place, Vanessa. "The Politics of Denial: Race, Gender and Sexuality as Seen in *The Bodyguard* and *The Crying Game.*" *Film Comment* 29 (May–June 1993): 84–86.

Richtarik, Marilynn J. *Acting Between the Lines: The Field Day Theatre Company and Irish Cultural Politics 1980–1984.* Oxford: Oxford Univ. Press, 1994.

Roach, Janet. "Ireland Finds the Green and Weaves a Spell." *New York Times,* 2 Jan. 1994, H1.

Rockett, Kevin. "From Atlanta to Dublin." *Sight and Sound* 2, no. 2 (June 1992): 26–28, 29.

Rockett, Kevin, Luke Gibbons, and John Hill, eds. *Cinema and Ireland.* Syracuse: Syracuse Univ. Press, 1988.

Rosenstone, Robert A. *Visions of the Past: The Challenge of Film to Our Idea of History.* Cambridge: Harvard Univ. Press, 1995.

————, ed. *Revisioning History: Film and the Construction of a New Past.* Princeton: Princeton Univ. Press, 1995.

St. Peter, Christine, "Jennifer Johnston's Irish Troubles: A Materialist-Feminist Reading." In *Gender in Irish Writing*, edited by Toni O'Brien Johnson and David Cairns. Milton Keynes, U.K.; Philadelphia: Open University Press, 1991.

Schickel, Richard. "Huston's Serene Farewell." *Time* 131 (4 Jan. 1988): 64.

Schirmer, Gregory A. *William Trevor: A Study of His Fiction.* London: Routledge, 1990.

Schlesinger, Philip, Graham Murdock, and Philip Elliot, eds. *Televising Terrorism.* London: Comedia Publishing Group, 1983.

Sheeran, Patrick. *"Genius Fabulae:* The Irish Sense of Place." *Irish University Review* 18, no. 2 (autumn 1988): 191–206.

Short, K.R.M., ed. *Feature Films as History.* London: Croom Helm, 1981.

Shout, John. "Joyce at Twenty-Five, Huston at Eighty-One: *The Dead." Literature/Film Quarterly* 17, no. 2 (1989): 90–100.

Simon, John. "Death and Soul-death." *National Review* 40 (22 Jan. 1988): 64.

Slater, Eamonn. "Contested Terrain: Differing Interpretations of Co. Wicklow's Landscape." *Irish Journal of Sociology* 3 (1993): 23–55.

Smith, Neil, and Cindi Katz. "Grounding Metaphor: Toward a Spatialized Politics." In *Place and the Politics of Identity*, edited by Michael Keith and Steve Pile, 67–83. London: Routledge, 1993.

Sobchack, Vivian, ed. *The Persistence of History: Cinema, Television, and the Modern Event.* New York: Routledge, 1996.

Sorlin, Pierre. *The Film in History: Restaging the Past.* Totowa, N.J.: Barnes and Noble, 1980.

Townshend, Charles. *"Michael Collins." Sight and Sound* 6 (Nov. 1996): 55–56.

Trevor, William. *Fools of Fortune.* Harmondsworth, Eng.: Penguin, 1983.

United Kingdom. Department of Economic Development [Belfast]. *Tourism in Northern Ireland: A View to the Future.* London: HMSO, 1990.

Wall, James M. "Universal Connections among Living and Dead." *Christian Century* 105 (20 Jan. 1988): 43.

Walsh, Maurice. "The Quiet Man." *Saturday Evening Post,* 11 Feb. 1933, 10–11, ff.; revised, *Green Rushes.* New York: Stokes, 1935; Reprint, *Three Roads.* New York: Stokes, 1936; Reprint, *The Quiet Man and Other Stories.* Belfast: Appletree, 1992.

Westwell, Guy. "Review of Robert Rosenstone." *Screen* 38, no. 1 (spring 1997): 99–105.

Wiegman, Robyn. "Feminism, 'The Boyz,' and Other Matters Regarding the Male." In *Screening the Male: Exploring Masculinities in Hollywood Cinema*, edited by Ina Rae Hark and Steven Cohan, 173–193. New York: Routledge, 1993.

Wilson, David, *"Fools of Fortune* (Review)." *Monthly Film Bulletin* (June 1990): 195–96.

# Index